AN INTRODUCTION TO
THE STUDY OF
SOCIAL ADMINISTRATION

Contributors

JOAN L. M. EYDEN
RICHARD L. SILBURN
ARTHUR J. WILLCOCKS
DAVID C. MARSH

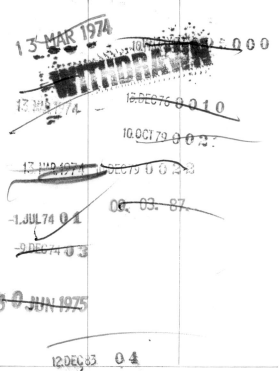

An Introduction to the Study of
SOCIAL
ADMINISTRATION

Edited by

PROFESSOR DAVID C. MARSH

Head of the Department of Social Science
University of Nottingham

LONDON

ROUTLEDGE & KEGAN PAUL

First published 1965
by Routledge & Kegan Paul Ltd
Broadway House, 68–74 Carter Lane
London, E.C.4

Printed in Great Britain
by Latimer Trend & Co Ltd, Plymouth

© *David C. Marsh 1965*

CONTENTS

v

Contents

PREFACE

SINCE the end of the Second World War there has been a remarkable increase in the numbers of students studying Social Administration at Universities, Technical Colleges, in Adult Education classes, and on *ad hoc* courses provided by a variety of statutory and voluntary organizations, and there is undoubtedly a continuing and growing interest in this field of study. From the comments which have been made to us on numerous occasions by full-time and part-time students, and indeed members of the general public attending courses at classes of departments of Adult Education, it would seem that there is a need for a general introductory textbook which will provide an outline of the subject matter of the discipline of Social Administration. In particular it has been suggested that what is needed is, firstly, a book which describes briefly the nature and scope of the study so that a potential student may see what is involved before embarking on such a course, and, secondly, for the student who has begun to study the subject a book which will act as a guide showing the framework of the discipline and point the way to specialized studies. It is these needs we have attempted to satisfy.

Social administration as a systematic discipline of study is concerned primarily with social policy and its implementation through the social services, and though (as is discussed in Chapter 1) it requires the support of and the knowledge derived from the other social sciences for its full understanding, we have concentrated on the core of the discipline—social policy and the social services. We have adopted a straightforward approach and begin by examining the way the discipline came into being, its nature and scope, and its inter-relatedness with the other social sciences. Then we trace the historical development of social policy as reflected in the growth of social action, and the main body of the book is concerned with an examination of the major social services, and even though we have of necessity had to be brief we would hope that this examination will be sufficiently comprehensive for introductory purposes. Finally we comment on the problems involved in translating social policy into social action by a brief reference to the complex methods of administration which have been developed and the vital roles of administrators and social workers in providing social services in a Welfare State.

Obviously we have not attempted to make definitive studies of each of the social services in the way in which Miss M. P. Hall has in her comprehensive book, *The Social Services of Modern England*, and there are complex issues of the determination of social need and the creation of social policies which cannot be discussed in an introductory text. Equally we have not attempted to introduce the reader to the important field of the study of comparative social administration, or the growing discipline of the analysis of formal organizations and administrative methods. We have, in essence, set up signposts on which there is more information than the usual place-names and to enable the reader to proceed further we recommend a variety of books for specialized study.

If this book achieves its limited purpose of satisfactorily introducing the reader to this complex field of study the authors will be satisfied, and they will be delighted if it encourages the student to proceed further by delving more deeply into the mysteries of the creation of social policies and their implementation through social action. All too often in the past social policies have been formulated, social services created and methods of administration devised without any clear expression of aims or tests of their effectiveness. It is hoped that as the study of social administration becomes more refined and mature that its students will contribute through research to more systematic analyses of the aims, purposes, methods and effectiveness of social policy and social action which in a Welfare State affects us all as citizens.

To my colleagues in the Department of Social Science at the University of Nottingham, Miss Joan L. M. Eyden, Mr. Richard L. Silburn and Dr. Arthur J. Willcocks, who have spent so much time, thought and energy in contributing to this book, my grateful thanks are due and are willingly given. Their co-operation and readiness to accept suggestions designed to make the book a uniform whole and not a series of disjointed contributions considerably lightened the task of the editor. They are, of course, individually responsible for their separate contributions, but any errors or omissions in the book as a whole are my responsibility.

DAVID C. MARSH

Nottingham, November, 1964

PART ONE
The Essential Background

1. THE NATURE AND GROWTH OF SOCIAL ADMINISTRATION AS A SYSTEMATIC FIELD OF STUDY

David C. Marsh

IN the twentieth century there has been such a remarkable increase in the rate of growth of knowledge in nearly all fields of study that it is becoming exceedingly difficult to define concisely the subject matter of even the long established academic disciplines. The frontiers of knowledge are continually being pushed farther forward, and as part of this process of advancement new fields of study are developed. The outstanding example of a rapid rate of growth of specialized fields of study in modern times is of course to be found in the natural sciences. The scientific revolution has resulted in the emergence of an array of specialisms within the core disciplines of mathematics, physics, chemistry and biology, and indeed in new fields of study based on knowledge derived from more than one of the core disciplines. We have become accustomed to accepting the dramatic nature of the scientific revolution, and those of us who are not natural scientists sometimes look with envy on the achievements in science and with despair on the rate of growth of knowledge in other disciplines. But need we despair or be envious? Certainly not, because real advances have been made in other fields especially those concerned with the study of human beings and the societies in which they live.

The study of man and society is by no means new, but the rate of growth of knowledge about human societies has not been as rapid or spectacular as has that about the forces of nature or the properties of matter. It may well be that we have been so intent on unravelling the secrets of nature that we have tended to ignore the necessity of knowing more about human beings and their relationships to each other. It is significant that when the Royal

Society was founded at the end of the seventeenth century its founder members were just as interested in the problems of man as they were in unravelling the secrets of nature, but by the twentieth century it is predominantly concerned with the physical and natural sciences. The only real attempt made to form an organization whose members were interested predominantly in the human sciences was in 1857 when the National Association for the Promotion of Social Science was founded. However, it ceased to exist in 1885, but during its life a number of interesting papers were published and serious discussions held on social problems. The extent to which it contributed to the development of systematic studies in social science is difficult to determine, but at the least it did show that 'problem centred' research could contribute to a clearer understanding of society and its problems.

Whilst societies were composed of relatively small numbers of people living in close proximity to each other and with traditionally defined roles of conduct and of authority, the task of analysing the social structure would have been relatively simple. In large societies where population has grown rapidly in a comparatively short span of time, and where agricultural, industrial and scientific revolutions have completely transformed the economic and social structures the tasks of analysing the networks of human relations and the factors which contribute to the smooth working of society become more difficult, but not impossible. Whose responsibility is it to undertake this interesting and necessary task, and through which disciplines can it be achieved?

For thousands of years philosophers have thought about man and society, and the discipline of philosophy has contributed to the development of, for example, theories about the systems by which men govern themselves and the codes of conduct which produce the good society; historians by systematically tracing the development of human societies and the institutions devised by men to regulate their relationships to each other and to the State have provided us with frames of reference over time; archaeologists have added to our knowledge about ancient man and the way he lived; anthropologists have analysed and described primitive societies and their systems of social relationships, and in recent years have examined contemporary societies; economists have attempted to establish the principles on which the systems of production, exchange and consumption operate in industrialized societies; psychologists are trying to explain the mysteries of human behaviour; and political scientists have attempted to explain how we govern ourselves and the operation of the political system. All these disciplines of study have contributed to our knowledge of man and society, but essentially from the point of view of particular facets of the social, economic or political structure. In the nineteenth century an attempt was made to introduce a comprehensive and unifying science which would deal with the whole social life of man through the discipline of sociology, but the high hopes of some of the founding fathers of sociology that there could be an encyclopaedic science which would reveal the nature and structure of society and the relationship of man to his society have not been fully realized. Nevertheless, sociology is a discipline devoted wholly to an analysis of society and its problems, and by now there are specialisms within the field of sociology which analyse in considerable depth particular features of social systems and the problems which arise within them.

A host of disciplines have therefore grown up each of which individually contributes to our knowledge of man in society, and collectively the social sciences provide a range of knowledge far greater than ever before. Their boundaries are by no means clear cut and often they overlap so that to be especially knowledgeable in one discipline it is essential to have at least a working knowledge of some of the others.[1] And indeed advances in one discipline have often been made by persons who were originally educated in quite a different field of study, for example, some of the leading sociologists of the mid-twentieth century were originally philosophers, or historians or economists. It is out of this cross fertilization of disciplines that the rate of growth of the social sciences has been accelerated in recent years, and that new specialisms like the study of social administration have been developed.

The systematic study of social administration is of comparatively recent origin, and even now there is no full consensus of opinion as to its exact nature and scope. Because of the diversity of views as to its precise content and methods there are those who doubt its claims to be called a discipline of study, but equally there are some of us who believe that in complex industrialized societies with conscious and ever growing governmental 'welfare' programmes there is a real need to study the aims and methods of social policy, its implementation through statutory and voluntary action, and its effects on the individual and society. The fact that the student of social administration has to make use of knowledge derived from, for example, history, economics, politics, demography, psychology and sociology does not mean that there can therefore be no single study called social administration. There is probably no discipline of study nowadays which can be said to consist entirely of knowledge derived solely from within its own confines, certainly one cannot, for example, study physics without a knowledge of mathematics, or theology without a knowledge of archaeology. All subjects now are essentially hybrid, and the newer the subject the greater its mixed origins. What then are the subjects out of which social administration has emerged, what is its particular focus of study, and how does it differ from those disciplines which contributed to its development?

Economics, politics, philosophy, history and sociology are the disciplines which have contributed most to the emergence of social administration, and of course they continue to provide essential frames of reference and additional new knowledge. But it was probably the social surveys carried out at the end of the nineteenth century and their revelations of the existence of 'poverty in the midst of plenty' which provide evidence of the need to study more systematically the facts of social life and the nature of social problems. Even though the nineteenth century was looked upon as the age of political reform and of economic revolutions the social surveys of Booth and Rowntree showed that despite the rise of a democratic system of government and an increase in the rate of production of wealth hitherto undreamed of, the existing political and economic systems were not capable of ensuring social justice for all.[2] Hence in the twentieth century we see an increasing emphasis placed on the need for action by the State to deal with such problems as those of poverty and disease, and gradually to the development of social policies which in turn were to be implemented through 'social services' of various kinds.[3] It was therefore the identification of 'problem groups' in society and the attempts to find solutions through deliberate policies on the part of the State to modify or nullify the effects of market forces which gave rise to a new field of study we now call social administration.

For most economists, sympathetic as they may have been personally, the problem of poverty was capable of solution through the normal processes of economic activity, and under the system of a laissez-faire the less the interference by the State with the operation of the market forces of supply and demand the greater the chance of solving problems of this kind. Economics as a discipline was (and to a great extent still is) concerned with analysis and descriptions of the economic system and not with human problems, therefore even if human problems arose out of imperfections in the economic system the economists' task was to identify the faults in the economic mechanisms and not to prescribe remedies for social problems. History and philosophy were predominantly concerned with the past, and much of the discipline of politics was concerned either with theories about the nature of government and the State or with descriptions of the machinery of government, so that historians, philosophers and political scientists could not justify claim to be concerned with the contemporary problems of man in society. Some of the early sociologists were interested in human problems, but all too often sociology was thought of in terms of the whole social life of man, and of being capable of producing general laws about the nature of society, so that the identification of social problems and the search for methods of solving them were not the prime interest of many sociologists. The main stimulus for the development of the study of social problems was therefore to come not from the established academic disciplines but from the natural curiosity of two practical business men, Seebohm Rowntree and Charles Booth, whose revealing social surveys provided essential data for the founding of 'social studies' and of course ammunition for social reformers like Sidney and Beatrice Webb.[4]

The ferment of interest at the end of the nineteenth century in the problems of poverty and in the need for social reform created a favourable climate of opinion in some universities for the introduction of courses of study designed specifically to train social workers who at this time were concerned solely with helping the poor. For example, in 1901 the London School of Sociology and Economics was established after experimental courses for voluntary social workers had been provided in the previous four years by a joint committee of representatives of the Women's University Settlement, the Charity Organization Society and the National Union of Women Workers, and in 1912 this school became the Social Science Department of the London School of Economics and Political Science which had been founded essentially by Sidney and Beatrice Webb; in 1904 arrangements were made by the University of Liverpool, the Victoria Settlement for Women, and the Liverpool Central Relief and Charity Organization Society to establish a School of Social Science, and in 1917 this was fully incorporated in the University of Liverpool; and in 1908 the University of Birmingham registered 'social study' students as internal students of the university and accepted full responsibility for their training. The acceptance by these universities of responsibility for social study courses was due, in the main, to a few enlighted professors who were interested in social reform and social action, for example, at Birmingham University Professor Muirhead, a philosopher, was keenly interested in 'social questions' and supported movements aimed at social reform, and Professor Ashley, an economist, believed that a system of laissez-faire could not solve social problems and that 'the State and Municipality could and should be used as instruments to enlarge freedom and promote social betterment'.[5] The extent of Professor Ashley's influence can be gauged from the fact that he was consulted privately by Sidney Webb about the Minority Report on the Poor Laws; he encouraged William Beveridge to write a book on unemployment; coined the term 'social study' because (according to Muirhead) 'sociology seemed to him to stand for nothing in particular but everything in general that had any connexion with society'; and in 1917, when there were seven other university social study departments, it was Ashley who was invited by the Home Office to be chairman of a conference which resulted in the creation of the Joint University Council for Social Studies (now called the Joint Universities Council for Social and Public Administration and which in 1964 had 25 'social studies' departments from the United Kingdom and Ireland in its membership). Within the first decade of the twentieth century, therefore, social study courses had been established in the universities and so acquired a degree of academic respectability, and it is out of this 'training movement for social workers' that the subject of social administration was gradually evolved.

These early courses were concerned primarily with economic problems and with teaching social workers how the economic system worked and the conditions of the poor. They were unashamedly 'problem centred' and students were given the tools derived from economics, social history, elementary statistics, central and local government, and philosophy to enable them to deal with the problems of the poor and the working classes. At this stage psychology and anthropology had little contribution to make to the understanding of human problems, and certainly a discipline of social administration had not yet been founded. However, legislative developments in the period 1905–11 such as, for example, the Old Age Pension Act, 1908, the Labour Exchanges Act, 1909, and the National Insurance Act, 1911, were to alter substantially the range of services made available by the State to meet the needs of the working classes and the aged poor, and indeed they constituted a remarkable transformation of the concept of poverty, its causes and methods of treatment. Henceforth, therefore, social studies students were required to know about and understand these and other kinds of social legislation, and of course the functions and methods of the Statutory and Voluntary organizations concerned with the provision of social services.

It is out of the growth of the social services[6] (as they have since come to be called) that the study of social administration has emerged, and with the remarkable extensions in the twentieth century in the role and functions of the State in relation to individual and social problems, it has become an exceedingly complex field of study. Before the Second World War it could hardly be called systematic, and the major contributions to knowledge in this field were, for example, detailed accounts of the growing variety of legislative measures whose implementation led to the establishment of social services;[7] an attempt to analyse the administrative processes involved in the implementation of social legislation;[8] and an attempt to define what the social services were, how they operated and how they should be reformed.[9] The real difficulty in this period for these pioneers who were attempting to systematize this field of study was that there was no consensus of opinion as to what the role of the State should be in relation to social policy, and of course the nature of social and economic problems was distorted by the overwhelming and seemingly insoluble problems of unemployment. Partly because of the unemployment problem in the 1930's attention had to be directed at the age-old problem of poverty, and therefore less thought could be given to the ways in which society could and should meet the needs of its members in normal circumstances. How to meet the material needs for food, clothing and shelter were the questions up-permost in the minds of those who thought about 'social questions' in those years, but there was a growing awareness that such needs could only be satisfied by radical changes in the role of the State in relation to deliberate social policies, and indeed the recognition that man's needs were not solely material. Unemployment was begin-ning to be seen not only as a situation in which a man could not provide materially for himself and his family, but also as a problem of social and psychological relationships. As a result the rights and duties of an individual were re-examined, and the impact of the Second World War on our economic and social systems was to lead to a radical transformation of our views on the nature of individual and social rights and duties.[10]

A revision of our attitudes towards the individual and society obviously necessitated a change in our approach to and methods of providing social services. In the past they were essentially directed at the needs of the few, usually grudgingly provided and administered restrictively on the basis that the recipient was a suppliant who had few rights as a citizen. The pre-Second World War student of social administration therefore thought of the social services as a means primarily of dealing with the poor, and with his (or more commonly her) concern for the problems of poverty was content to study their historical development and their methods of operation. The study was essentially descriptive and designed to answer the question how do the social services operate, when did they come into being and when and by whom can they be used? All too often 'the social services' were studied as a 'useful' subject which one had to know in order to be a social worker, and few attempts were made to analyse the eco-nomic and sociological relationships and implications of the social services as social institutions, or to question their aims, purposes and methods of administration. As none of the established dis-ciplines showed much interest in this growing field of govern-mental activity, for example, it would be difficult to find many references to the social services in the standard textbooks on economics and sociology written before the second war, it is understandable that the number of people prepared to devote their time to analytical studies of them was relatively few, and that this field should be looked upon as peripheral to the main streams of study concerned with man and society

The deliberate plans made by the Government during the second war for social reconstruction when peace came, and their implementation in the immediate post-war years through an array of social services on a scale vastly greater than ever before meant that they could no longer be considered peripheral. They became in fact a major activity of the State, and their social and economic implications could not be dismissed as peripheral when a significant proportion of the national income and of the labour force was to be used in ensuring education for all children according to their age, aptitude and ability; income security for everyone at all times; health services for everyone from the cradle to the grave; special services to meet the needs of deprived and neglected children, the physically and mentally handicapped, the aged and other groups with special needs; and the concept of the Welfare State was to become a vital issue of practical politics.[11] The social services henceforth were to be concerned not only with the poor but with society as a whole as a means of ensuring social justice for all, of raising living standards, and creating a new kind of society, and therefore they were to be deliberate instruments of social policy.

New kinds of social services required new kinds of social workers and social administrators to run them and the demand for more and better trained 'social servants' led to requests being made to the universities for an increase in the numbers of 'social studies' students.[12] Many of the British universities immediately after the war increased the number of places for students on 'Certificate in Social Studies' courses; new courses were established, and some universities planned degree courses in 'Social Studies' or 'Social Administration'. Academic recognition of social administration as a subject is evidenced by the appointment of a Professor of Social Administration at the University of Nottingham in 1948 and at the London School of Economics and Political Science in 1950. Since then a second chair has been created at the latter, and in 1959 the University of Birmingham appointed the first Professor of Social Policy and Administration. Clearly if a person is appointed to a University Chair he must believe that he has a subject to profess, and indeed Professors Titmuss and Donnison devoted their inaugural lectures to the subject of social administration and Professor Lafitte entitled his 'Social Policy in a Free Society'.[13]

The addition of the term 'social policy' extends the boundaries of social administration as a discipline of study, and by the 1950's most teachers of social administration would think of their subject as being wider than a descriptive study of the growth and development of the social services. Nevertheless, it is the study of the social services which forms the core around which this newer conception of the subject revolves, and one view at least of what social administration is in the middle of the twentieth century has been expressed by Professor R. M. Titmuss in his inaugural lecture. He holds the view that

> Social administration may broadly be defined as the study of the social services whose object, to adapt Simey's phrase, is the improvement of the conditions of life of the individual in the setting of family and group relations. It is concerned with the historical development of these services, both statutory and voluntary, with the moral values implicit in social action, with the roles and functions of the services, with their economic aspects, and with the part they play in meeting certain needs in the social process. On the one hand, then, we are interested in the machinery of administration, which organises and dispenses various forms of social assistance; on the other, in the lives, the needs, and the mutual relations of those members of the community for whom the services are provided by reason of their belonging to that community.[14]

If this view of social administration is accepted then it is not enough merely to ask the question, how do these services work, it is essential to ask the more fundamental, and indeed more interesting questions, why are they needed; why do they operate in the way they do; and what are their effects on the economic and social system? Inevitably, therefore, further questions must be asked about the aims and purposes of social policy, and though this phrase is far from explicit Professor Lafitte has suggested that

> in our kind of society, social policy is not essentially interested in economic relations but is very much concerned with the extent to which economic relations and aspirations should be allowed to dominate other aspects of life; more specifically that social policy addresses itself to a whole range of needs—material, cultural, emotional—outside the wide realm of satisfactions which can conveniently be left to the market. There is attraction too in Professor Mydrial's description of 'social policy in its broadest sense'

simply as a convenient way of referring to 'the continuous growth in the volume of public, quasi-public and private interventions in social life'—interventions which are 'no longer sporadic but more and more take the form of a continuing activity, steered to influence and control a social process in a certain direction'. Implied in all the foregoing accounts of social policy is the judgment that, if left alone by political authority, the state of society would rapidly become intolerable.[15]

Implicit in this view of social policy is the need to make value judgments, and if it is accepted then obviously the boundaries of social administration are very much wider than they would have been in the past because we have to look at the social services (as commonly understood though by no means clearly defined[16]) in relation to the standards and values of society. They must be seen in the perspective of the social, economic and political systems in which they operate, and if they are deliberate devices used to modify or offset the pull of market forces which are assumed to influence the economy then it is absolutely essential to recognize their social and economic implications. Hence the student of social administration must be familiar with, for example, the historical development, and the demographic and sociological factors which have moulded and may well change the pattern of his society; with the political attitudes which create the system of government; with the economic system and the changes which have occurred in economic policies especially as a result of the process of industrialization; and of course with the basic principles of administration.

For too long the social services have been looked upon as an accidental growth and the organizations responsible for their administration as equally accidental, and requiring little examination from the point of view of administrative processes. In part this was due to the belief that since they were essentially personal services therefore it was more important to study the services provided than it was to study how and why they were provided, and that especially for social workers problems of administration were of little concern to them. However, now that the statutory social services are organized on a vast scale and require systems of administration as complex as those required to run big business enterprises it has become recognized that it is not enough to know that, for example, the National Assistance scheme is administered by an *ad hoc* board; the National Health Service by the Ministry of Health, Executive Councils, a variety of appointed boards and local authorities; National Insurance through a ministry and regional offices, and so on. Questions must be asked about why there are these different methods, and what are the consequences of using different kinds of organizations and methods of administration? The study of administration *per se* is by no means common in this country, but there is a growing body of knowledge dealing with administration in industry, governmental agencies, and even voluntary organizations, and sociologists are now devoting far more attention to this important field of study.[17] It is to be hoped that as the study of social administration develops so will as much attention be given to the principles and problems of administration as used to be given to the 'social' aspects.

Whether the emphasis is to be on 'social' or on 'administration' there is clearly a consensus of opinion that social administration as a whole has been, and probably will be for some time to come, 'problem centred'. That is to say the student of social administration is concerned, as Professor D. V. Donnison suggests, 'with an ill-defined but recognisable territory: the development of collective action for the advancement of social welfare. Our job is to identify and clarify problems within this territory, to throw light upon them—drawing light from any discipline that appears to be relevant—and to contribute when we can to the solution of these problems'.[18] Which means, of course, being concerned not only with social policy and the social services as they are, but also with social research and its endless quest into the human problems which arise in society, and with the efficacy of existing social institutions to prevent or deal with the problems which have arisen or may arise. All too often too little attention has been paid to the measurement of the success which existing social services have achieved in preventing or dealing with the problems they were designed to solve. How effective, for example, have our educational services been in ensuring equality of educational opportunity; how effective has our system of National Insurance been in preventing unemployment or sickness, or in ameliorating the sufferings of the unemployed and the sick; how have our housing policies been planned and programmes designed, and what effect have they had on slum areas and on the housing situation; what contribution has been made to the solution of the problems of crime by the development of our penal and probation services; and overall what has been the effect on us as individuals and on our society of the growth of the Welfare State? Social administration must direct attention to answering questions of this kind if it is to be a 'know-why' and not merely a 'know-how' discipline of study, and there are encouraging signs that as the study grows so does the degree of curiosity in its students.

It is no longer followed only in the universities, because in recent years technical colleges have begun to provide 'Younghusband' courses,[19] which though designed essentially as vocational courses for social workers, nevertheless require a considerable degree of knowledge about the problems of man and society, and as the numbers of students increase so will the boundaries of social administration be pushed further forward. The directions in which they will be extended are not easily foreseeable, but there are indications of a tendency to move away from an over-emphasis on the social services (though they must remain a basic interest) towards the wider issues of social policy, the analysis of social institutions of various kinds, and of social change. A list of the research projects which have been undertaken in Departments of Social Administration, Social Studies, and Social Science in many universities in recent years would show a variety of topics, many of which would not in the past have been considered as falling within the field of social administration, for example, studies of income distribution; of housing policy and housing needs; of mental health and social policy; of the changing social structure; of the concept of poverty; of family planning; of crime and delinquency; of recruitment to various professions; and of the assimilation of immigrants. All of which of course have a bearing or are affected by the social services which in the words of Professor D. V. Donnison

> are not an unproductive frill tacked on to the economy as a charitable afterthought. They are an integral and (in some form or other) a necessary part of our economic and social structure—a form of collective provision required to meet the needs of an expanding industrial society. They are developed, differentiated, and developed again, in accordance with the changing aspirations of those who work in them and those whom they serve.[20]

The scale of operation of the social services in this and other countries in the second half of the twentieth century would itself be sufficient justification for specialist studies to be devoted to them, but they cannot be studied in isolation, they must be looked at as one feature of the economic, social and political systems of the society in which they operate, and therefore contributions to the advancement of knowledge in this field will depend not only on those who are primarily interested in social administration, but also on the growth of knowledge in, for example, sociology, economics and politics. And, furthermore, with the coming together of nations and the establishments of international organizations, there is an increasing need to make comparative studies. Some have already been carried out, for example, by the International Labour Organization, the Division of Social Affairs of the United Nations Organization, and U.N.E.S.C.O., and from these comparative studies we can learn about other systems and methods of organization which will enable us to see our own in the perspective of other societies. This may well contribute to changes in the future based not only on our own experience but also that of other peoples.

The kinds of changes which will be made in social policies and their implementation through the social services in the future cannot easily be foreseen, but it is certain that there will be changes because they must be responsive and contribute to the dynamic processes of social change which are ever present in any society. Social administration, therefore, is concerned with a dynamic and not a static field of study, and if the rate of change of recent years is to continue, then specialisms within the broad field will inevitably emerge as they have in the natural sciences. Indeed the stage has already been reached when no person can lay claim to a complete knowledge of all the complex issues of social policy, the intricate details of every measure of social legislation, the extraordinary varieties of methods of organization and administration of all the social services in this country, but it is essential to have a basic knowledge of the whole field before specializing in one particular sector, and in the remaining chapters of this book an attempt is made to provide an introduction to the main principles and practices on which the social services operate in Britain.

NOTES

[1] For a valuable introduction to the nature and scope of sociology, see T. B. Bottomore, *Sociology: a Guide to Problems and Literature*. Anyone who is unfamiliar with the main social sciences might be interested in *The Social Sciences: An Outline for the Intending Student,* edited by David C. Marsh. This book aims simply to provide an outline of the scope and methods of the main social sciences.

[2] For the growth and scope of social surveys see D. Caradoc Jones, *Social Surveys*; and Mark Abrams, *Social Surveys and Social Action*.

[3] For a good account of nineteenth- and twentieth-century attempts at social reform see Maurice Bruce, *The Coming of the Welfare State*. And for a discussion of the nature, growth and development of the social services see Chapter 2.

[4] See T. S. and M. Simey, *Charles Booth*, and Asa Briggs, *Social Thought and Social Action: a Study of the Work of Seebohm Rowntree*. For a brief study of the early social surveys see Note 2.

[5] The quotations attributed to Ashley and Muirhead have been taken from the inaugural lecture of Professor Francois Lafitte on *Social Policy in a Free Society*; delivered at Birmingham University in 1962.

[6] See Chapter 2 for an account of the nature, growth and development of the social services; *The Social Services of Modern England* by M. P. Hall; and *The Welfare State* by D. C. Marsh.

[7] See, e.g. *Social Administration* by J. J. Clarke, published in 1934.

[8] See T. S. Simey, *Principles of Social Administration*; first published in 1937.

[9] See P.E.P. Report on *The British Social Services*, 1937

[10] See R. M. Titmuss, *Problems of Social Policy*, and D. C. Marsh, *The Welfare State* for a discussion on the change in attitudes during and after the war.

[11] On the growth and development of the concept of the welfare state see D. C. Marsh, op. cit.

[12] For an interesting account of the changes in the methods of training social workers up to 1945 see Elizabeth Macadam, *The Social Servant in the Making*; and the first report by Eileen Younghusband on *The Employment and Training of Social Workers,* published in 1947.

[13] R. M. Titmuss, 'Social Administration in a Changing Society', in *Essays on the Welfare State*, Chapter 1; D. V. Donnison, *The Development of Social Administration,* published by the London School of Economics and Political Science in 1962; and Francois Lafitte's inaugural lecture published by the University of Birmingham in 1962. For a survey of the teaching of social administration in universities in 1960 see D. V. Donnison, 'The Teaching of Social Administration,' *British Journal of Sociology*, Vol. XII, No. 3, September 1961.

[14] R. M. Titmuss, inaugural lecture, op. cit.

[15] F. Lafitte, inaugural lecture, op. cit.

[16] For a discussion of the problems of defining the social services see R. M. Titmuss, *Essays on the Welfare State*, chapter 2, and D. C. Marsh, *The Welfare State*.

[17] See, for example, Blau and Scott, *Formal Organisations*.

[18] D. V. Donnison, inaugural lecture, op. cit.

[19] See *The Report of the Working Party on Social Workers in the Local Authority Health and Welfare Services*, H.M.S.O., 1959.

[20] D. V. Donnison, inaugural lecture, op. cit.

2. THE GROWTH AND DEVELOPMENT OF THE SOCIAL SERVICES AND THE WELFARE STATE

Joan L. M. Eyden

INTRODUCTION

THE previous chapter has sought to show how the study of social administration has developed as an academic discipline and that central to this study has been a concern with social problems. Many of the problems which have become matters of public interest have been the result of thousands of individual, apparently unrelated, choices; some arise from attempts to meet basic human needs for food, for clothing, for shelter; some problems have developed as the unintended and unforeseen results of attempts to meet other problems. Thus, for example, the attempt to promote healthy living and working conditions in the last hundred years coupled with rising standards of living through the increase in industrial production has led to a dramatic drop in death-rates, many more people survive into old age, and as a result western societies consider that they have a social problem concerned with the care and maintenance of the elderly.

Common human needs are met in any society in a variety of ways—through the family, through neighbours, through associations of one kind or another, and through the economic and political systems. Increasingly it has been found that as societies have become larger, more complex and more industrialized, so it has been necessary to make special provision as, for instance, through the social services to ensure that these are met. Social services therefore have developed as organized responses to individual and social needs which under modern conditions and with today's level of expectation of living standards, can no longer be adequately met by the individual, the family or the unorganized neighbourhood group. It must be recognized that the establishment of statutory social services is but one way in which action is taken to meet social problems and needs. The problem of long-term unemployment such as dominated life in this country in the 1920's and 1930's, was primarily an economic problem and as such required to be met chiefly by economic measures. But it was a personal disaster for those who were unemployed and for their families, a disaster calling for a system of financial aid, of supporting health and educational services and for some means whereby the unemployed might be occupied. The provision of unemployment assistance, the extension of medical facilities through, for example, the development of local health authority general hospitals, the establishment of clubs and community centres for the out-of-work not only did something to meet the personal needs of those families affected; these measures also had economic and political consequences. Expenditure on assistance and welfare services in the 1930's helped to stimulate demand, to maintain an unused labour force in some degree of health and working efficiency, and to provide a fighting force when war broke out in 1939.

Just as social administration as an academic study has its roots in many different branches of study—economic, philosophical, political, legal—so social policy and its implementation have been affected by many factors and the social services have been shaped by divers influences and in their turn have widespread effect. There is considerable disagreement among scholars as to the determinants of social policy and to the relative importance of the various factors which have led to the emergence of the modern complex of social services and the concept of the Welfare State.

In this introduction to social administration, it is only possible to comment on some of the major differences of definition, interpretation and opinion. One of the earliest uses of the term 'public social service' was in connection with the first return of expenditure under certain Acts of Parliament which provided 'direct beneficiary assistance'—a return made at the request of Mr. Drage in 1913. This return included money spent on unemployment and health insurance, education and public health, poor relief, etc. Lord Eustace Percy, in *Government in Transition*, suggested that what people usually thought of as social services were those 'which are designed more directly to benefit the citizen as an individual'.

The P.E.P. Report of 1937 on the British Social Services, defined them as those 'which have as their object the enhancement of the personal welfare of individual citizens'. These descriptions would appear to contain two points on which all are agreed; that social services are benevolent in intention and that they are designed to benefit people directly or individually. There is unlikely to be much dispute over the first of these points: no one is likely to argue that a social service is meant for the disadvantage rather than the welfare of the recipient. But is there an individual personal element in all social services? Sir George Newman in the *English Social Services* includes libraries, museums, and even communications and transport. The latter seem clearly to be public utilities provided as a matter of convenience and usually paid for directly by the recipient of the service. However, the recent controversy over the reorganization of British Railways has brought even this into dispute! In The P.E.P. Broadsheet *Planning*, No. 354, 1953, it was argued that 'public water and sewage services, although socially provided, are normally regarded as environmental or physical services and not services personal to the family or individual. Public parks, libraries and museums are seen primarily as local amenities rather than personal welfare services, although the distinction is not sharp'. The environmental services instanced here can be clearly distinguished from personal, individual services and a line can be drawn between public and social services. A definition which seems to cover the points under discussion is 'a social service is a social institution which has been developed to meet personal needs of individual members of society not adequately or effectively met by either the individual from his own or his family's resources or by commercial or industrial concerns'.[1]

A distinction must also be drawn between the statutory (or public) social services and the voluntary social services. The former are based on legislation which gives permissive or mandatory powers to the Government to create and develop certain kinds of provision either for all citizens or for particular categories of those in need. A voluntary social service is one provided by an organization or group of organizations which is initiated and governed by its own members: the distinctively 'voluntary' character of such bodies is the product not of the kind of workers they employ (as volunteer or unpaid workers may be used in connection with both statutory and voluntary services), but of their mode of birth and method of government.[2]

The scope of modern social services is very wide and many of them are used extensively by most citizens. However, the problem of poverty has been traditionally the basic social problem, with which the social services were originally concerned to meet, for 'the condition of having little or no wealth or material possessions; of indigence, destitution, want' (*Shorter O.E.D.*), entails that none of one's material needs are adequately met and probably few of one's non-material needs either. According to G. D. H. Cole,

> the problem of poverty . . . has presented itself to a sequence of generations animated by widely different social philosophies. One essential spirit, that of philanthropy pure and simple, has been always present; but with it have mingled from time to time motives and impulses which have changed greatly from age to age. It has made, for example, a vast difference whether the philanthropists have believed that there were too many people, or too few; whether they have been readier to attribute the sufferings of the poor to vice, or to misfortune; whether they have been in the main 'other-worldly' or 'this worldly' in their attitude to the problems of mankind; and whether they have, or have not believed in the 'invisible hand' or in the sovereign virtues of an economic system of laissez-faire.[3]

The relief of poverty has always been a Christian duty and the virtue of charity has been extolled. W. K. Jordan agrees with the view that there have been three broadly held historical attitudes towards poverty in the Christian world.[4] In the first poverty was idealized possibly because its amelioration lay wholly beyond the resources of society. In the second historical stage, poverty came to be regarded as a social cancer which, while it could not be eradicated, must be treated with all means available. In the third, extending to this century, society has increasingly undertaken a variety of constructive measures to provide opportunity or care according to need.

CHARITY AND THE POOR LAW IN THE SIXTEENTH CENTURY

The social aspects of poverty were perhaps first emphasized in the sixteenth century. The transition from an age of status to one of

21

contract was gathering pace; the agricultural, commercial, social and religious changes all tended to greater insecurity for the many and to unemployment and destitution for a growing 'few'. W. K. Jordan comments that 'poverty, wide scale and endemic poverty did not burst unannounced on the early modern world. To a degree the nature of poverty was to change, but more importantly man's sensitivity to the fact and social threat of poverty was to be enormously sharpened'.[5] It should perhaps be added that unemployment and destitution were also a political threat to which successive Tudor statesmen and their more modern counterparts were increasingly sensitive. Thus it is in the sixteenth century that poverty was first systematically attacked. Not until a national economy began to supersede town and local economies did the central government begin to interfere effectively in economic matters. The Statute of Artificers, 1563, by the enforcement of apprenticeship and wage-fixing was primarily an economic measure to reduce unemployment, although it had important social and educational aims as well. At the same time the central government found itself compelled to take step after step to provide for the destitute not only or mainly by traditional repressive measures against the vagrant, but by developing a comprehensive system of relief. The 1531 Act Concerning Punishment of Beggars and Vagabonds attempted to distinguish between the deserving and undeserving poor and gave Justices of the Peace the power of granting licences to beg to 'all aged poor and impotent persons'. Today with the modern concept of the Welfare State this may seem little enough, yet for the first time there was statutory recognition that some people were unable to support themselves and in the absence of relatives able to care, society had a responsibility for their support. A series of acts made each parish responsible for its own destitute (1536); introduced a compulsory poor rate (1572); authorized J.P.s to put the genuinely unemployed to work on raw materials supplied at the expense of the parish, and to erect bridewells or houses of correction for the 'idle rogue or vagabond' (1576) and defined those relatives who could be legally made to support a destitute person if they were able. These provisions were re-enacted with some admendments in the famous Act for the Relief of the Poor of 1601. Famous because it firmly established a nation-wide system of relief for the destitute, children, the disabled and infirm, the unemployed and the workshy, based on the parish as the responsible unit of administration; famous also because it remained the basis for the statutory provision for destitution until the National Assistance Act, 1948.

The year 1601 was important however for another reason as well. The personal and religious charities typical of the Middle Ages had tended to be replaced by more secular concerns. The same century which saw the development of the Poor Law also saw a great number of charitable bequests and endowments designed to eradicate the causes of poverty by a variety of undertakings including the extension of educational opportunities. According to W. K. Jordan, 'the momentous shift from man's primarily religious preoccupation to the secular concerns that have moulded the thought and institutions of the past three centuries . . . is quite perfectly mirrored in their benefactions'.[6] The Statute of Charitable Uses enacted in 1601 was a recognition of the importance of these massive endowments and endeavoured to protect them. It secured the enforcement of charitable uses by instructing the Chancellor to appoint commissioners to inquire into abuses, to take evidence, to impanel juries and to hand down decisions subject only to his own review. Although by the eighteenth century it had largely fallen into disuse, and the nineteenth century witnessed a new attack on the maladministration of charitable trusts, it remained unrepealed until 1888, but the famous preamble to the Act listing those uses properly considered as charitable was retained as a working definition until the Charities Act, 1960.

PHILANTHROPY, POVERTY AND THE POOR LAW ON THE EVE OF THE INDUSTRIAL REVOLUTION

Philanthropy and the Poor Law continued their two-pronged attack on poverty for the next three centuries, but the objects of the former and the way the latter was administered both reflected changing attitudes towards the problem of poverty. The factors at work in effecting these changes are the subject of some controversy. Tawney, in his *Religion and the Rise of Capitalism*, suggests that the effect of Puritanism in the seventeenth century was to usher in a period in which the poor were condemned as idle and irresponsible. By a fortunate dispensation, the virtues enjoined on Christians, diligence, moderation, sobriety, thrift, were the very qualities most conducive to commercial success. The Puritan 'convinced that character is all and circumstances nothing, sees in the poverty of those who fall by the way, not a misfortune to be pitied and relieved, but a moral failing to be condemned, and in riches, not an object of suspicion—though like other gifts they may be abused—but the blessing which rewards the triumph of energy and will'.[7] The wage-earners of the seventeenth and eighteenth centuries were considered to be self-indulgent and idle, 'everyone but an idiot knows that the lower classes must be kept poor or they will never be industrious'.[8] Tawney comments

> The most curious feature in the whole discussion and that which is most sharply in contrast with the long debate on pauperism carried on in the 16th century was the resolute refusal to admit that society had any responsibility for the causes of distress. Tudor divines and statemen had little mercy for idle-rogues. But the former always and the latter ultimately regarded pauperism primarily as a social phenomenon produced by economic dislocation.[9]

The political upheavals of the seventeenth century meant that central control of the Poor Law through the Privy Council was considerably relaxed and until the beginning of the nineteenth century there was much local variation in the way it was administered. The notion that the poor could be turned into a source of profit appealed to the growing commercialism of the age; the workhouse movement of the eighteenth century was an attempt to be both deterrent and economic. Bristol led the way, securing an Act of Parliament for the building of a single workhouse for all the poor of the town and this was followed by a general Act in 1722. 'There were two motives behind it: the business motive of assembling the poor under one roof and coping with them as a single problem, replacing as it were domestic by factory relief, and the ethical motive of punishing idleness by compulsory work.'[10] Maurice Bruce has pointed out 'it was the blurring in practice of the distinction between the genuinely unemployed and the merely idle, between the workhouse, the poor house and the house of correction, that was largely to characterise poor relief during the next two centuries and a half'.[11]

At the same time in both the seventeenth and eighteenth centuries philanthropic activities continued to flourish. But in the Age of Reason, and the Age of Enlightenment, the spread of toleration took a great deal of the fire out of religion and charitable concern alike. Nevertheless, the growing spirit of inquiry and interest in things scientific which was to help in the transformation of the economic organization of the country within a very few years, also had a profound effect upon the development of medicine. Throughout the eighteenth century the medical profession was moving out of the dark ages of traditional superstition and the physician, the surgeon, the apothecary and the unlicensed practitioner were all going forward apace in the knowledge and in devoted service, especially to the poor who had hitherto been horribly neglected in times of sickness and infirmity. It is interesting to note that some of the most popular objects of philanthropy at this time were hospitals and dispensaries.

Indeed the middle of the century saw the beginnings of a new humanitarianism that was to affect the later years of the century and to inspire reform in the nineteenth century. Fielding's novels, Hogarth's engravings, Captain Coram's Foundling Hospital, Jonas Hanway's concern for pauper children, John Howard's inquiries into the conditions of prisons, the foundation of the Retreat at York, all reflect a growing interest in the living and working conditions of the eighteenth century. And these conditions were beginning to change with ever-increasing rapidity so that within the next hundred years England was to develop from a predominantly rural society based on ancient village communities into a bustling industrial urban society.

NINETEENTH-CENTURY ANSWERS TO THE SOCIAL PROBLEMS
OF A DEVELOPING INDUSTRIAL SOCIETY

The eighteenth century witnessed a major agrarian revolution based on better farming methods, scientific animal breeding and a new enclosure movement which resulted in a great increase in productivity and a native agricultural industry which for many years was able to support a rapidly growing population. The steady growth of commerce in the seventeenth and eighteenth centuries, the opening up of new markets in all parts of the world led to the extension of demand for simple, easily standardized goods suitable for manufacture by machinery and produced what was the most striking external feature of the Industrial Revolution, the rapid expansion of machine methods of production. Economic and social change began to gather momentum after 1750. Thereafter developments in technology, in application of different forms of power, in transport, in banking and insurance, in agricultural methods and organization, in foreign trade all acted and reacted on one another to transform completely life in this country.

The social effects of the industrial revolution, coupled as it was with a rapid increase in the population, have been described and analysed and debated by many writers. Suffice it to say here that the development of large urban areas, the spread of the factory system, the much greater division of labour and the mass production of many goods led to an unprecedented rise in the standard of living, a bewildering choice of occupations, much greater mobility (both physical and social) and ease of communication. But they also led to slum areas, to the 'discipline of the factory whistle', to greater social and economic insecurity even for the prosperous working classes, and to a degree of mass squalor and poverty which was unprecedented. The two traditional methods of meeting social problems, philanthropy and the Poor Law fought a losing battle against these social problems thrown up by the economic and social dislocation resulting from all these changes.

Towards the end of the eighteenth century reform was in the air, reform of the law, reform of Parliament, reform of prisons, the freeing of trade and industry from outworn restrictions, but the French Revolution although at first welcomed in this country, soon aroused so much concern and insecurity that reform was postponed until the third decade of the nineteenth century. Instead a combination of economic and political cirumstances led on the one hand to repressive measures such as the Combination Act of 1800, born of the fear of rebellion and subversion, and on the other to attempts to stem the rising tide of rural destitution through the Poor Law by such devices as the Speenhamland system of allowances in support of wages, the Labour Rate, the roundsman system, etc. The cost of the Poor Rate rose from £619,000 in 1750 to £2,567,000 in 1790, and £7,329,000 in 1820, and the need for reform became painfully obvious. Philanthropy became more than ever tangled up with preaching to the poor the virtues of submission to Church and State, and 'of demeaning themselves in all humility towards their betters'.[12] Even Hannah

More, with a genuine concern for the education of the poor and who was instrumental in starting charity schools and women's clubs in the villages, was fearful lest the poor should be contaminated by revolutionary ideas. Writing in 1801, she says, 'My plan of instruction is extremely simple and limited. They learn, on week-days, such coarse works as may fit them for servants. I allow of no writing for the poor. My object is not to make fanatics, but to train up the lower classes in habits of industry and piety.'[13] Yet many of her contemporaries vilified poor Hannah More for her temerity and accused her of fanaticism and sedition! By the 1820's and 1830's there was growing interest in the teaching of such philosophers and political economists as, e.g. Bentham who advocated the testing of all social institutions by the criterion of utility and whose essay, *A Fragment on Government*, 1770, was to have such an effect on that single-minded advocate of sanitary reform, Edwin Chadwick; Adam Smith whose *Wealth of Nations*, 1776, was to dominate economic thought for a century and who stressed the beneficent working of the economic laws; and Malthus who was concerned with the pressure of the rising population on the food supply and whose essay on the *Principle of Population*, 1798, helped to earn for economics the soubriquet of 'the gloomy science'. Not until the Poor Law encouragement of marriage was brought to an end and the poor learnt through 'education that they are themselves the cause of their own poverty' . . . would everyone realize that his duty was 'not to bring beings into the world for whom he cannot find the means of support'.[14] Thus reform when it came gradually transformed the organization of government, freed industry and trade from outgrown restrictions, and liberalized the legal system, but was accompanied by a doctrinaire opposition to State intervention in economic affairs, an acceptance of the principles of 'deterrence' and 'less eligibility' enshrined in the Poor Law Amendment Act of 1834 and an attitude towards poverty fully as harsh as that which had characterized the earlier part of the eighteenth century.

The part which religious thought played in moulding economic and social developments in the nineteenth century is difficult to estimate. The religious toleration of the eighteenth century was ruffled by a religious revival which affected both the established Church and Nonconformity, but as Asa Briggs has recently pointed out, it is difficult to determine the role of organized religion in the industrial growth of the nineteenth century, or to evaluate the interaction between religion and capitalism in the heyday of the latter.[15] The international debate about their relationship has usually stopped short at the point where many social and economic historians begin—the industrial revolution. He suggests that Nonconformity, which according to Tawney and Weber had moulded capitalism; became in part an agency for its destruction.

> Nineteenth century Christian socialism, of which the Christian Social Union was only one expression, certainly not the most radical expression, was in frontal opposition to the values both of economic individualism and of narrow religious evangelicalism, as shared by most Nonconformists and many Anglicans. In its first manifestations in the 1840's and 50's it protested against the new industrial system in the name of co-operation against competition and in the name of the association of working men against the unbridled economic power of the capitalist. . . . In its later manifestations in the 1880's and 90's most Christian socialists looked more and more to the State and less to the association or group to control the working of the economic system[16]

Yet in spite of many Christian rebels, the most general impression of the nineteenth century is of a commonly held belief in a divinely appointed, harmonious order producing a sense of tranquility and of firm confidence in the future which tended to bring a feeling of optimism and complacency only occasionally punctured by the distress of the 'other nation'.

Throughout the nineteenth century the Poor Law remained the only statutory provision for the relief of poverty and the principles of the 1834 Poor Law Amendment Act ensured that such poverty had to amount to destitution before it could be relieved. This Act of 1834 was the direct result of the recommendations of the Royal Commission on the Poor Law set up in 1832 and whose members were concerned with the rising cost of the rates, with the diversity of administration and with the development of a pauper class which though able-bodied, was dependent upon relief. Its report issued in 1834, which Tawney described as 'brilliant, influential and wildly unhistorical', advocated a new *ad hoc* administrative system; locally, relief was to be administered by an elected Board of Guardians with paid full-time officials based on a union of parishes; a uniform policy of deterrence based on a workhouse test was to be enforced by a Central Board of three commissioners with assistant commissioners to serve as inspectors. Although the scheme was never as fully implemented as its creators hoped, it did remedy the worst of the abuses associated with the lax administration of the pre-1834 era, and eventually helped to force up wages to a more realistic level, particularly in agricultural districts. Nevertheless, the mixed workhouse, the hated 'Bastilles' of the poor, continued to be a symbol of social failure and degradation for a century; even the receipt of outdoor relief carried with it a social and political stigma which has still not been wholly eradicated in many people's minds and colours the attitude of the older generations even today towards the acceptance of national assistance.

It is not perhaps surprising that in an era when economic freedom and opportunity were so greatly stressed it seemed most natural that private enterprise in welfare should be considered the essential means of meeting the needs of those who fell by the wayside in the economic race. As the middle classes became richer and more politically powerful so they recognized a responsibility towards their less fortunate brethren. 'They firmly believed that it was theirs to heal the hurts of the people and they came only by degrees to doubt their ability to do so. . . . Private individuals were confident of their power to discharge a public function, and the government was willing to have it so.'[17] Thus there developed a great outpouring of private charity, much of it ephemeral and arbitrary in character, some providing constructively for the needs of the day. Soup kitchens, hospitals, reformatories, ragged schools, cripples' guilds, orphanages and many other institutions all witnessed to a growing concern for the victims of the violent social and economic upheaval of the nineteenth century. Contributing to charitable causes might be to some an insurance against revolution, a sop to an uneasy conscience, or an opportunity of participating at a small cost to praiseworthy and increasingly fashionable institutions; yet there were many who were genuinely concerned for the needs of others and were activated by humanitarian and religious motives. Their concern tended to find its expression in ways which were acceptable to the prevailing philosophies of the time. Yet the organizations set up by these charitably minded pioneers were the forerunners of the great voluntary organizations for social service which have been such a feature of life in this country during the past 100 years. Because these associations grew up spontaneously and were shaped by the interests and indeed the whims of their founders, they were infinitely varied in purpose and method, yet all in some way or other were designed 'to compensate for inequalities and to supplement the needs of the underprivileged'.[18] They were primarily concerned with those living in the slums of the great industrial areas, those who were apathetic and destitute to such a degree that they were unable to help themselves. Hit by sickness or unemployment these families soon exhausted their own and their neighbours' resources, particularly when they were first-generation migrants from the rural areas. A shifting and growing population tended to strain the organized resources of the civil and the ecclesiastical parish and poor relief or parish charity was either non-existent or shunned because of the deterrent nature of its administration. The voluntary philanthropic organizations did great service but by the end of the century some were beginning to accept the fact that they were only able to touch the edges of this mass of need.

Yet there were other voluntary organizations of a quite different character which also developed in the nineteenth century as one of the answers to the social problems thrown up by the industrial revolution. The mutual-aid or self-help movements, the trades unions, the friendly societies, the co-operative movement, were attempts at meeting the social and economic insecurity which was felt even by the more prosperous of the working classes. Indeed it was only those who had a margin of time, money and energy as a result of rising standards of living who could afford to make their weekly contributions to these associations and thus contribute through mutual aid to the fashioning of some defence for themselves and their families against the uncertainties of an expanding industrial economy. The attitude of the governing classes to the development of these movements was mixed. They welcomed the evidence of hard work, thrift and self-reliance among the labouring classes, but were concerned at some of the political and economic implications. The experience which members of the working classes gained through these movements was to have profound effects on the political situation, especially after the Acts of 1867 and 1884 which enfranchised the average workman.

Moreover these movements were the pioneers in social insurance which was later taken over and generalized by the State. In addition the Co-operative Movement besides providing for the investment of small savings was a means of protecting the working-class consumer against over-priced and adulterated goods and thus contributed to the subsequent development of legislation designed to safeguard health by the Food and Drugs Acts of a later period. Similarly, early Building Societies often of a democratic nature paved the way not only for the Small Dwellings Acquisition Act of 1899, but also for municipal action in the housing field.

But Philanthropy, Mutual Aid and the Poor Law proved totally inadequate to meet the problems of the nineteenth century. Even at the period when the doctrine of laissez-faire and individualism was apparently at its most influential the Government was forced by events to take an ever-increasing part in social and economic affairs. Indeed, ideas of individualism did not necessarily imply opposition to all forms of state interference. On the contrary as J. D. Chambers has pointed out, Bentham might be described as a precursor to the Fabians in his advocacy of state action to promote the greatest happiness of the greatest number, the principle of utility. 'For this supreme end he proposed, in effect, a revolution in the machinery of administration in order to achieve a universal minimum of justice, health and education; and when he found that the existing ruling class were primarily interested in promoting the happiness, not of the greatest number but of themselves, he became an advocate of a radical widening of the franchise.'[19]

One of the most notable legislative achievements of the nineteenth century was the control of environmental conditions developed to safeguard the health of the public. But the battle for sanitary reform associated with the names of Edwin Chadwick, Dr. James Kay, Dr. Southwood Smith and others, was a hard one. A long series of investigations and reports from the Moral and Physical Condition of the Working Class, 1832, and the Sanitary Condition of the Labouring Population, 1842, to the Royal Commission on the Housing of the Working Classes, 1885, revealed the connection between impure water supplies, inadequate sanitation, bad housing, disease and destitution. Perhaps for the first time, poverty began to be seen not as a simple problem of the individual lacking adequate resources, but as a complex one which necessitated action on a wide front.

Cholera, typhus and other infectious diseases were no respecters of persons and the comfortably-off classes were shocked into action both by the danger to their own health and by the drain on their pockets through the claims on the poor rate of the ill and infirm, as well as by a genuine concern for the welfare of others. The fear of government interference and of bureaucratic control delayed much effective legislation for nearly half a century, and although the first Public Health Act was passed in 1848, yet it was not until the Act of 1875 that the battle for government responsibility for promoting environmental health was really won.

The movement to ensure a more healthy working environment primarily originated with a concern to protect women and young people by regulating the hours they could work and the conditions under which they could be employed and by a ban on the employment of young children in factories. This protective and regulatory type of legislation was not thought to conflict with individualism or laissez-faire for it did not interfere with the personal liberty or freedom to bargain of the adult male. In practice, however, owing to the dependence of mills and other factories on the work of women and young people the limitation of their hours of work and the regulation of their working conditions meant indirectly that all workers benefited from the Factory Acts. Regulation was gradually extended to include not only the textile trades but other industries, and was concerned not only with hours of work, etc., but with the adequate fencing of machinery and with the special hazards to which those working in dangerous trades were exposed.

The same desire to protect those who were unable to care for their own interests manifested itself in the long fight for the abolition of the use of 'climbing boys', for the reform of lunatic asylums and even of prisons. Side by side with this reforming legislation was a growing demand on humanitarian, social and economic grounds, for a more positive and constructive government policy for better educational facilities. First by subsidies to the national religious societies for the training of teachers and later for the actual provisions of schools, then by the setting up by the legislation of 1870 of School Boards to fill the gaps in the provision of elementary schools by voluntary organizations, the State gradually assumed responsibility for ensuring that every child in the country had access to at least a minimum of educational facilities. It was not, however, until 1880 that education became compulsory up to the age of 10 (raised to 11 in 1893 and 12 in 1899), and not until 1891 that it was free. The progress of the industrial revolution inevitably demanded the development of technical education, but although state subsidies were given to encourage local initiative for the establishment of technical schools, it was not until the Act of 1889 that County Councils, created in the previous year, were given permissive powers to provide technical and other secondary schools, and to take part in the provision of evening and other advanced classes.

Thus from the early years of the nineteenth century there developed a movement of social reform and public provision, which was to have unforeseen results. This 'adaptation of social policy in Britain to the economic changes of machine, industry and the free market,' says J. D. Chambers, 'was largely achieved by an alliance of forces between Benthamite interventionists under the leadership of Edwin Chadwick and the forces of traditional paternalism under the leadership of Lord Shaftesbury.'[20]

To sum up, the Victorians primarily put their faith in industrial development through the expansion of capitalism and overseas trade in a free society, to solve ultimately the social problems caused by rapid change. To ease the burden on the weakest they were prepared to pour large sums of money into private charity and to countenance legislative reforms designed to protect the weak and to transform environmental living and working conditions as well as to look with favour on any movement which promoted thrift and self-reliance among the poor. Yet by the end of the century, thinking members of the public were becoming uneasily aware that economic growth was not curing all ills; that the thrift of the working classes could not provide adequately for their economic security and that philanthropy could mitigate the poverty of only a few of those who were the victims of industrial change. Some were even beginning to ask whether poverty was really necessary in an age of apparent progress and affluence.

TOWARDS THE WELFARE STATE

In *The State and the Standard of Living*, Gertrude Williams pointed out that 'in 1890 the ordinary working man was expected to provide for the maintenance of himself and his family and to make arrangements for their welfare in all contingencies'.[21] Forty years later there was hardly any province of a worker's life and affairs which was not substantially affected by legislation and the part played by the State in the day-to-day affairs of the ordinary man had increased unprecedentedly.

By 1950 this development had proceeded even further and the comprehensiveness of collective provision to meet the needs of citizens had led to the general acceptance of the title of the Welfare State as a fitting term to designate the role of government in this country. How did this transformation come about?

As indicated earlier there is considerable difference of opinion about the concept of the Welfare State and the factors which have been responsible for its development. David Roberts sees the Victorian origins of the Welfare State in the administrative revolution brought about by Bentham and his followers; 'there can no longer be doubt that the origins of British collectivism run back to the Victorian era, alive with social reforms and bureaucratic growth'.[22] The reform of central and local government, the gradual emergence of a strong efficient and uncorruptible Civil Service and the advent of the inspector—in factories, in mines, in public health, in education, in the administration of the lunacy acts—contained within themselves a dynamic which led inevitably to the extension of State intervention.

As B. Kirkman Gray put it at the beginning of the century, 'inspection without advice is idle; advice without prescription is incomplete; prescription without treatment is a mockery'.[23] And in discussing the work of the new public health inspectors he says graphically:

> but just as inspection of places was incomplete without inspection of persons, so also mere inspection of persons is of little worth. We would add that if the inspector be a woman such a restriction is almost impossible. When the Female Sanitary Inspector goes to a house she gives such advice as 'may appear to be necessary'. This giving of advice represents a new function the importance of which may easily be overlooked but can hardly be exaggerated. At first there is only an inspector of things empowered to demand the observance of certain rules. Action in regard to things is limited in extent, and it might be possible for the legislator to foresee all that should need be done. But action in regard to persons is illimitable in range and infinitely delicate. It would be absurd to

limit the function of the inspectors of infants to any statutory schedule. Two women and a baby are beyond the philosophy of the Parliamentary draftsman. The real business is not so much to tell the mother what she must do as to advise her as to what she can and should do.[24]

Thus legislation of a regulatory kind developed imperceptibly into legislation providing constructive services; concern for environmental health led on to concern for personal health. Legislation to protect children from exploitation and from cruelty and ill-treatment by taking action against those responsible resulted in the necessity of making alternative provision for their victims. The hesitant experiments of pioneer philanthropist and working-class group were used as prototypes for increasing government action.

Many factors hastened this development. O. R. McGregor considers that 'Beneath the garish surface of political events there can be discerned the cumulative adjustment of an advanced industrial society to the inescapable imperatives, coincident in point of time, of a mass franchise, of restless technological change in an economically aggressive world, and of the menace of mechanized belligerance. The welfare state has that derivation.'[25] The working-class vote was certainly something with which successive governments after 1884 had to reckon with and inevitably had its effect on policy. The development of periodic booms and slumps, of increasing economic insecurity and unemployment led to the attempt to organize the labour market through the Unemployed Workmen Act, 1905, and the Labour Exchange Act, 1909, and to provide a cushion against destitution by means of unemployment insurance (1911) and unemployment assistance (1934), as well as to the designation of depressed areas and to the concept of economic as well as town and country planning.

Anxiety concerning the large percentage of recruits rejected for the Boer War on physical grounds led to the setting up of an Inter-departmental Committee on Physical Deterioration. Its report pointed the connection between the possibility of national military weakness and the physical condition of the young. Partly as a result of its recommendations the school health service, school meals, care committees and the maternal and child welfare service became securely established. Two world wars hastened this development of specialized personal services. R. R. Titmuss, in *Problems of Social Policy*, one of the volumes of the official war history, shows how many services, started as experimental, make-shift methods of meeting the needs of citizens exposed to conditions of total war, profoundly influenced the pattern of post-war provision when subsequent legislation gave these temporary expedients a permanent place in peace time.

Added to these factors in the genesis of the Welfare State has been an increasing knowledge of the facts of poverty, ill health, overcrowding, unemployment, delinquency, etc. The regular censuses, social surveys such as those pioneer inquiries of Booth and Rowntree in London and York respectively, the statistical returns of the Registrar-General, the information gained through the working of the new statutory services themselves has gradually led to the massing of more and more statistical material which has helped to delineate the size and shape of many social problems.

The ferment of thought and opinion in the last decades of the nineteenth and the early years of the twentieth century on the proper division of responsibility between the individual, the family, the neighbourhood and the State was entangled with debate about the nature and end of man himself. This debate was given a new twist by the bitter controversy over Darwin's *Origin of Species* which led to a torment of doubt as to the value of any of the convictions which had formed the foundations of individual and social life of many Victorians. The influence of Marx, of the Christian Socialists, of the Fabians was increasingly felt but resulted in no clear-cut concept of the future role of State intervention. Kirkman Gray, writing at the beginning of the twentieth century, says:

> It is now generally recognised that in addition to such want as results to the ill-doer from his own ill-doing there is a vast amount of suffering which comes from general social causes; and for which the sufferer is responsible either remotely or not at all. For such distress society is responsible, and it is bound to alleviate or remove it. The work which was left to philanthropy is coming to be accepted as an integral part of social politics. . . . The movement which I describe as a transition from philanthropy to social politics, rests on the breaking down of the simple old doctrine of individualism. What social faith is to be substituted is yet undetermined, and that hesitation explains the confusion which still exists as to the proper spheres of philanthropy and social politics respectively.[26]

Sixty years later this confusion still exists—perhaps inevitably as the debate concerning the role and function of the State appears to be one in which each generation must engage afresh.

Nevertheless the first half of the twentieth century has witnessed the development of a complex of State provision increasingly designed not only to alleviate or remove suffering which comes from 'general social causes', but to ensure for every citizen as a citizen an optimum standard of health and well-being. Una Cormack considers that the formative years of the Welfare State were coincident in time with the deliberations of the famous Royal Commission on the Poor Laws, 1905–9, whose Majority and Minority reports caused much controversy but both of which profoundly influenced public opinion in the ensuing decades. She holds that the Welfare State developed unsystematically, almost haphazardly because of the confusion and cleavage of opinion concerning the two essential principles of the provision of a basic minimum for those members of the community who cannot do so for themselves, and a basic optimum for all citizens without distinction. 'Between them', she says, 'the Majority and Minority Reports, with differing emphases, acknowledged both responsibilities, for good and all.'[27]

To many people the concept of the Welfare State is associated with the legislation of 1944–8, which reorganized the educational system, provided family allowances, set up a comprehensive and integrated scheme of social insurance underpinned by national assistance, brought into being a national health service and assumed greater responsibility for deprived children, the handicapped, the homeless and for providing better housing, industrial training and more employment opportunities. Yet if each of the measures which brought about these developments is examined it is not always easy to see precisely where the changes lay or what was new in them. Successive Education Acts made it possible to make comprehensive and varied provision for the education of children, adolescents and adults including handicapped children before 1939. Since the Act of 1911 some measure of security in sickness, unemployment, and later in old age, widowhood and orphanhood had been provided on an insurance basis. Financial assistance for old people, the blind, the chronically unemployed and their families, and for pensioners had been given outside the Poor Law, while the Poor Law itself, reformed and liberalized had developed into a residual service underpinning the other specialist provisions which had been growing in such profusion since the beginning of the century. Medical services were available for the poorer members of the community, through voluntary and local authority hospitals, through dispensaries and doctors' clubs, through the medical benefit of the national health insurance scheme as well as for the treatment of those suffering from such conditions as tuberculosis and other infectious disease, mental illness and mental deficiency. The maternal and child welfare services, the school health service as well as public health legislation all aimed at the prevention of ill health and disease.

What, then, were the great changes brought about by the spate of social legislation of the late 1940's? From one point of view, this legislation was part of an attempt at 'tidying-up', at administrative simplification and integration. But perhaps the greatest difference discernable in the legislation of the period is its comprehensive nature and its explicit recognition of the responsibility of the State for the provision of certain services for all members of the community and the corresponding right of the individual citizens to use them. Lord Beveridge, whose famous report on Social Insurance and Allied Services in 1942 did so much to shape public thinking about the scope and purpose of social provision, used an illustration appropriate to the time in the middle of the Second World War, when he wrote:

> We should regard Want, Disease, Ignorance, and Squalor as common enemies of all of us, not as enemies with whom each individual may seek a separate peace, escaping himself to personal prosperity, while leaving his fellows in their clutches. That is the meaning of social conscience; that one should refuse to make a separate peace with a social evil. Social conscience should drive us to take up arms in a new war against Want, Disease, Ignorance and Squalor at home.[28]

This sentiment was in line with the great philanthropic tradition whose concern for others in distress infused the social legislation of the pre-1939 period and was reinforced by war-time revelations of slums, of neglected children, of undernourished wives and mothers. But perhaps the immediate post-war period cannot be fully understood without remembering the contribution of that other tradition of mutual aid and fraternal solidarity which inspired the working-class movements of the nineteenth century and early twentieth century and lead at least one writer to describe the Welfare State as one vast friendly society. This is in line with the idea that the development of mid-twentieth-century social services are one manifestation of a process which has been going on for several centuries to re-establish citizen rights. T. H. Marshall has developed this theme in his essay, 'Citizenship and Social Class'.[29] Evidence for this concept can be found in much of the legislation of the late 1940's which sought to embody at least some degree of social rights, based not on financial need but on citizenship.

THE FUTURE OF THE WELFARE STATE

In the preceding pages an attempt has been made to outline some of the historical factors which led to the establishment of what has been called a Welfare State in this country. But what of the second half of the twentieth century? Has the Welfare State come to stay? Indeed has it ever really existed? Criticism of the present situation comes from many different sources. References to the 'Casualties of the Welfare State', 'Gaps in the Welfare State', 'The unfinished business of the Welfare State', indicate that there are many citizens whose needs are still not being adequately met. There is some evidence to suggest that large families where the father is unskilled, unemployed, or missing, are often undernourished; that the economic circumstances of many elderly people are straitened and have not been included in the growing affluence of the population as a whole; that many children are socially and educationally handicapped by a poor home environment; that there is need for massive modernization programmes for hospitals, homes and prisons beyond anything yet planned.[30] Thus one school of thought considers that State provision must go much further in the next decades while existing services are improved. Others though agreeing that in an age of automation, of nuclear power and rapid social change, the Government must continue to take an active part in economic and social planning and in making provision for those things which the citizen cannot do for himself, suggest that in an age of affluence, there are many more things which the citizen *can* do for himself and the State should withdraw. So the age-old debate concerning the role of the State and the balance between the claims of freedom of choice and equality of opportunity goes on.

The Essential Background: The Growth and Development of

In order to understand more clearly the issues involved and the range and limitations of present provision for social welfare in this country, the following chapters seek to outline the organization and scope of the social services and to indicate other aspects of social policy which are particularly relevant.

From the brief account of the development of social policy already given it has perhaps been realized that the student of social administration has considerable difficulty in undertaking any logical analysis of present-day social provisions or of tracing a coherent pattern. Services have tended to develop in a haphazard way and still bear traces of their voluntary ancestry. It is in the nature of action, which arises from the interest and initiative of individuals, to be arbitrary, biased, spasmodic and limited as well as creative, concerned, experimental and heroic. The development of statutory provisions from the pioneer work of voluntary organizations has meant that services are more adequate, open to those in need on like terms, more securely financed and reliably staffed. But social policy is affected by many pressures and Government action at any one time is a compromise between competing priorities, vested interests, and pressure groups. It is not surprising, therefore, if statutory and voluntary services in the field of welfare appear to be confused, overlapping and ill-co-ordinated.

The following chapters will reflect this. There will be considerable repetition and cross-reference. It is impossible to categorize or tabulate contemporary provision for the social and personal needs of citizens in any orderly way under neat chapter headings. To give but one example—is the school health service to be thought of primarily as part of the educational or health service? As one of the services for children, or for the assistance of the normal family? Or is it primarily a prudent investment for the future economic, political and military strength of this country?

SUGGESTED READING IN ADDITION TO THOSE BOOKS
MENTIONED IN THE NOTES

H. MESS, *Voluntary Social Services since* 1918.
G. D. H. COLE and RAYMOND POSTGATE, *The Common People* 1746–1946.
K. DE SCHWIENITZ, *England's Road to Social Security.*
C. BOOTH, *Life and Labour in London.*

the Social Services and the Welfare State

B. SEEBOHM ROWNTREE, *Poverty; a Study of Town Life.*
Poverty and Progress.
B. SEEBOHM ROWNTREE and G. R. LAVERS, *Poverty and the Welfare State.*
G. M. TREVELYAN, *English Social History.*
BETSY RODGERS, *The Cloak of Charity.*
WOMEN'S GROUP ON PUBLIC WELFARE, *Our Towns.*
There are innumerable textbooks on the Industrial Revolution. The following are some which may be useful.
J. H. PLUMB, *England in the Eighteenth Century.*
DAVID THOMSON, *England in the Nineteenth Century.*
J. H. CLAPHAM, *An Economic History of Britain.*
T. S. ASHTON, *The Industrial Revolution, 1760–1830.*
L. S. PRESSWELL, *Studies in the Industrial Revolution.*
Relevant biographies and autobiographies.
S. FINER, *The Life and Times of Edwin Chadwick.*
T. and M. B. SIMEY, *Charles Booth.*
J. L. B. HAMMOND, *Lord Shaftesbury.*
E. MOBERLY BELL, *The Life of Octavia Hill.*
M. STOCKS, *Eleanor Rathbone.*
BEATRICE WEBB, *My Apprenticeship.*
C. WOODHAM SMITH, *Florence Nightingale.*
A. BRIGGS, *Seebohm Rowntree.*

NOTES

[1] J. L. M. Eyden, 'Social Services in the Modern State,' *Case Conference*, February 1955.
[2] F. C. Bourdillon (ed.), *Voluntary Social Services*, Chapter 1.
[3] Bourdillon, op. cit. (G. D. H. Cole, 'A Restrospect of the History').
[4] W. K. Jordan, *Philanthrophy in England*, p. 54.
[5] Ibid., p. 54.
[6] Ibid., p. 16.
[7] R. H. Tawney, *Religion and the Rise of Capitalism.*
[8] Arthur Young, *Tours.*
[9] R. H. Tawney, op. cit.
[10] C. R. Fay, *Great Britain from Adam Smith to the Present Day*, p. 338.
[11] Maurice Bruce, *The Coming of the Welfare State,* p. 32.
[12] Bourdillon, op. cit. (G. D. H. Cole, 'A Retrospect of the History').
[13] Hannah More, *Letters.*
[14] Thomas Malthus, *Essay on the Principles of Population.*
[15] Asa Briggs, *The Listener*, 27th February 1964.
[16] Ibid.
[17] B. Kirkman Gray, *Philanthrophy and the State,* p. 4
[18] Bourdillon, op. cit , p. 2
[19] J. D. Chambers, *The Workhop of the World*, p. 195.
[20] Ibid., p. 198.
[21] Gertrude Williams, *The State and the Standard of Living*, p. 1.
[22] David Roberts, *Victorian Origins of the British Welfare State* (Preface).
[23] B. Kirkman Gray, op. cit., p. 271.

Notes

[24] Ibid., p. 268.
[25] O. R. McGregor, 'Sociology and Welfare', *Sociological Review Monograph*, No 4.
[26] B. Kirkman Gray, *Philanthropy and the State*, p. 13.
[27] Una Cormack, *The Welfare State* (Loch Memorial Lecture, 1953).
[28] William Beveridge, *Full Employment in a Free Society*, para. 378.
[29] T. H. Marshall, *Sociology at the Crossroads*, Chapter IV.
[30] D. Cole and J. E. G. Utting, *The Economic Circumstances of Old People*; Royston Lambert, *Nutrition in Britain* 1950–60; J. W. B. Douglas, *The Home and the School: a Study of Ability and Attainment in the Primary School.*

PART TWO

Social Provision Organized
on a Functional Basis

INTRODUCTION

IT is extremely difficult to divide into convenient categories the wide range of social services which now operate in this country. We have made a division, partly for convenience, but, also on what appears to us to be a logical basis. In this section we are concerned with those services which are intended to apply to the population 'at large' and are essentially designed on a functional rather than on a personal basis. Thus the services for the maintenance of income, even though they in fact meet the needs of an individual, are in essence functional in that they provide income for specified periods when there has been an interruption from specified causes, irrespective of the particular individual. Equally education, housing and industrial services are primarily serving a function and not the needs of a particular individual. This distinction is, of course, arbitrary because an individual receiving, say, unemployment benefit, education, medical care, or living in a council house is in fact having his 'need' satisfied. But, having his need satisfied in this way is different from the need which arises because he is a particular individual who is, for example, blind or mentally disordered. Hence we consider that particular persons with special needs, such as the blind or the mentally ill, are among the special groups with special needs for whom particular kinds of services are provided and so they are discussed in another section.

There are a variety of ways in which these different kinds of services may be studied. In the main we have adopted an historical approach, which involves tracing the origins of the services from the past to the present. We could equally well have started from the present and suggested ways of looking into the origins, but for most (though not all) of the existing services we believe that looking at the origins and then examining the present is the simplest way to introduce the reader to the existing situation. Inevitably this approach reduces the possibility of more fundamental analysis of the contemporary scene, but if the reader has a foundation in the past and an understanding of the present then deeper analysis of the existing and future patterns can be made.

3. SOCIAL SERVICES FOR THE MAINTENANCE OF INCOME

David C. Marsh

IN a complex industrial society where the majority of citizens rely on the money they earn from employment to give them their standard of living, any interruption or cessation of earnings is clearly of vital personal and social significance. In Britain the problem of ensuring income at all times has been recognized for centuries past, but until the twentieth century the State was reluctant to take positive action through systematic social policies which would ensure a basic standard of living for everyone at all times. There was, of course, in the past a partial recognition of the State's responsibilities through the provision of Poor Relief and up to the nineteenth century the problems of poverty were to a limited extent the concern of the Poor Law Authorities and of voluntary charitable organizations. Whilst a large proportion of the population depended on agriculture for their livelihood it was at least possible for farm labourers to grow a little food and so ensure at least that they and their families survived, but once agriculture ceased to be the main source of employment and the greater proportion of the working population had to depend on money earned in manufacturing, commercial and other activities for their means of subsistence then the maintenance of money incomes became of paramount importance for physical survival.

The acceleration of the process of industrialization in Britain in the nineteenth century; the rapid rate of growth of population, especially of the working classes; and the increasing complexity of the economic system were accompanied by problems of poverty on a scale which could not be ignored by the ruling classes. As population increased in the newly industrialized areas so did more and more people have to rely on money from employment as their sole means of earning a living standard with little or no possibility of supplementing their need for food by growing a few vegetables.

Money wages became all important and obviously they were determined by employment opportunities. Employment opportunities did not necessarily increase at the same rate as population, hence a plentiful supply of labour often resulted in the payment of low wages for long hours of work and of course in unemployment. The causes of poverty therefore became far more varied in the nineteenth century than they were in the past and different measures had of necessity to be adopted if these problems were to be eased or solved.

There are a variety of methods of ensuring income maintenance. Thus if one's personal income regularly exceeds one's personal expenditure then personal saving is one method of providing against interruption or cessation of earnings. Savings may be 'pooled', as, for example, through Friendly Societies, or Commercial Insurance Companies will offer, in return for regular premiums, specified benefits to meet specified contingencies. All these methods, however, depend partly on a regular surplus of personal income and certainly in the nineteenth and the early years of the twentieth century most working men would have found great difficulty in being able to set aside sufficient savings to meet the contingencies of unemployment, sickness and old age.

It is, however, with the statutory services which have grown up since the nineteenth century to deal with the problems of poverty in an industrialized society that this chapter is concerned, but in view of their complexity and of their varying stages of development the only practicable method of briefly examining them systematically is to treat each kind of service separately despite the fact that they all have the same objective, namely, ensuring the maintence of income. We shall therefore examine briefly the Poor Law Relief system from the nineteenth century onwards; the Non-Contributory Pensions system; and finally the system of Social Insurance and Assistance.

The Poor Law system had been maintained relatively unchanged for three centuries when the processes of industrialization began to be accelerated in the nineteenth century, and in 1834 the first real attempt was made to reorganize the system and methods of poor relief. The 'New Poor Law', as it came to be known, was to remain for the rest of the century the main statutory social service for helping the poor. Under the 'New Poor Law' of 1834 an attempt was made to provide a national system. Three Poor Law

Commissioners were appointed by the Crown to supervise Poor Relief through local-elected Boards of Guardians, and an attempt was made to discourage 'outdoor relief' and through the principle of 'less eligibility' to make even relief in institutions as distasteful as possible. Much has been written about the nineteenth-century Poor Law modifications and all that need be said here is that it provided some means of survival, introduced an interesting method of administration, and was the only statutory means of assistance to the poor, by giving 'relief' out of taxation to poor persons.[1]

By the beginning of the twentieth century this system of poor relief was subjected to considerable criticism, and of course the whole subject of poverty and its causes had become transformed by the surveys of Booth and Rowntree. In 1905 a Royal Commission on 'the Poor Laws and Relief' was appointed by the Government, and it examined in remarkable detail the problems of poverty and the existing methods of providing poor relief. Its reports, published in 1909, recommended radical changes many of which were adopted in later years, and at the same time new social policies were being designed which were to alter substantially the functions of Government in relation to the problems of maintenance of income. The first major change in the system of organization and administration of Poor Relief itself came in 1929 when County and County Borough Councils were charged with administering the system as a function of Local Government, and 'poor relief' was renamed 'public assistance'. From the point of view of social policy this new name was significant because it implied that a person was being socially assisted and not relieved. The problems of mass unemployment in the 1930's were, however, to prove more than local authorities could bear and so, in 1934, the responsibility for the long term (i.e. over 26 weeks) unemployed became a National responsibility and the Unemployment Assistance Board was created. At this stage poor relief was becoming a national service and moving away from being a local to a national responsibility, which was carried a stage further in 1940 when the Unemployment Assistance Board took over the additional responsibility for assisting primarily old people and was renamed the Assistance Board; finally the whole question of giving assistance to the poor was examined in 1941 by the Beveridge Committee and in 1948 the system of National Assistance to persons in 'need' was established. Hence we had moved away from local responsibility for the relief of poverty to the acceptance of national responsibility and so to a new kind of social policy.[2]

Poor Relief was intended (and still is under its new name) to prevent destitution, and basically it was a method of compulsorily transferring income from the taxpayers and ratepayers to the destitute irrespective of the cause of their poverty. That is not to say that it was made available freely and of right; indeed some of the procedures for determining eligibility in the past were far from humane and there was a tendency to discriminate between the deserving and the undeserving poor, and there was no real attempt to relate the relief given to the different causes of poverty. Consequently the basis for determining the amount and kind of relief was by no means systematic, and there was no certainty that a person genuinely in need would receive relief appropriate to his or her need. It was not until the National Assistance Act, 1948, that an attempt was made to provide relief according to need. The basis of granting assistance since then is simply proof of 'need', and the determination of need is made on a monetary scale which relates the income deemed essential to provide subsistence and the resources of the applicant.[3]

The methods of organizing and administering the National Assistance service established in 1948 are, as compared with the past, relatively simple. The National Assistance Board is composed of a chairman and independent members appointed by the Crown, and it is therefore an *ad hoc* administrative body theoretically independent of the Government, but answerable to Parliament through the Minister of Pensions and National Insurance. The administrative system is quite straightforward, there is a headquarters (which is equivalent to a ministry), a central office for Wales and for Scotland, and eight regional offices in England, which in turn control area offices throughout Britain. The number of area offices has varied but normally there are about 430, and it is of course the area offices which are in direct contact with applicants for assistance. For the membership of the Board, its functions and a full report of its activities, see the Annual Reports of the National Assistance Board published by H.M.S.O. The Board's organization is founded on the principle that administration must be decentralized and indeed it is applied even to the granting of discretionary powers at area office level.

No longer, therefore, is there a confused and complicated pattern of organization and administration as there was in the past. There is now a truly national service of financial assistance to anyone in need in every part of Britain. Equally simple is the method of financing the service. It is paid for by monies provided by Parliament and not as in the past by a mixture of local authority contributions and some support from Central Government. The inequitable burdens borne by some areas in the past have therefore been removed, but there are of course still variations in the quality and kinds of 'welfare' services provided under the National Assistance Act because these are made available by local authorities (see Part 3). The overall cost of providing National Assistance has grown substantially in recent years; for example, the total net expenditure for the years ended 31st December 1950 and 1960 was as follows:

	1950 £	1960 £
National Assistance Grants	56,430,000	166,200,000
Non-Contributory Old Age Pensions	25,230,000	10,900,000
Reception Centres and Re-establishment Centres	485,000	470,000
Polish Hostels	—	51,000
Administrative Expenses	4,230,000	9,900,000
Total	86,375,000	187,521,000

Whether financial assistance will continue to be provided nationally through the National Assistance Board is an open question. The original intention was that it should be provided during the transitional period whilst National Insurance Benefits were gradually being raised to a satisfactory level and applicable to the whole population. However, since 1948, the value of money has fallen, National Insurance rates of benefit have not kept pace with changes in the cost of living, the number of retirement pensioners has grown substantially, and consequently 'supplementation' of benefits, particularly retirement pensions, has been necessary. Thus, in the early 1960's, over 70 per cent of the weekly allowances paid out by the Board were in respect of supplementation of National Insurance benefits, and obviously if there were a real increase in the rates of these benefits, then national assistance would no longer be necessary except for the relatively few cases of persons in need who for some reason were not covered by National Insurance, or to meet a temporary emergency.

National Assistance is obviously a residual service, a safety net which ensures that no one should fall below a minimum level of subsistence and therefore it is presumably the last resort of anyone in need. However, even in the supposedly affluent Britain of the 1950's and early 1960's there were usually between 1,600,000 and 1,900,000 persons in receipt of weekly allowances, despite the fact that we have developed a vast and complicated system of social insurance and that occupational pension schemes have grown rapidly in recent years.

The first attempt to provide an income maintenance service outside the Poor Law was made in 1908 with the introduction of a non-contributory old age pension. Under the Old Age Pensions Act, 1908, persons of British nationality aged 70 and over of limited means became entitled to a weekly pension of between 1s. and 5s. per week for the remainder of their lives. The funds out of which the pensions were paid were made available by Parliament out of taxation, and the main problem from the point of view of social administration was which department of State could accept the responsibility for organizing and administering the scheme. There was no obviously suitable department, other than perhaps the Treasury, and in the event a mixed system was adopted consisting of the Commissioners of Customs and Excise having general responsibility and working through pensions officers appointed by the Treasury, and local Pensions Committees. The paying agency was, however, the Post Office. We need not be unduly concerned with this system of administration except to note the problems involved in creating a suitable statutory organization for a new social service and that for the next forty years after 1908 we continued to devise a variety of forms of administration as new services were created.

Non-contributory old age pensions were undoubtedly a boon to the aged and perhaps most important of all they constituted a real break-away from the Poor Law tradition. They were, in effect, granted as a right of citizenship and there was no stigma attached to drawing an old age pension. A number of amending Acts in later years made no substantial alterations in principle and the only extension of the non-contributory pension principle was in 1920 when blind people qualified for an old age pension at the age of 50, and in 1938 the qualifying age was lowered to 40. The non-contributory system, useful as it proved to be, was soon overshadowed by the introduction of a contributory system of national insurance.

Voluntary insurance against the interruption or cessation of earnings as a result of sickness, unemployment and old age, and even to meet the expense of burial, had been provided especially from the mid-nineteenth century onwards by friendly societies, trade unions and, of course, commercial insurance companies. In Germany a State system of compulsory insurance against sickness, invalidity (i.e. incapacity for work from any cause), and old age, had been introduced as early as 1881, and therefore by the beginning of the twentieth century a considerable body of experience had been built up concerning the practicability of insuring against the main causes of poverty among the working classes. Furthermore, during the first decade of this century new attitudes were being developed concerning the causes of poverty, the rights of the working man and the duties of the State. It was undoubtedly a period conducive to social reform, and despite grave misgivings and violent opposition, the Government was able in 1911 to introduce, what seemed to be at the time, revolutionary plans for the establishment of a system of national insurance against loss of earnings due to sickness and unemployment.[4]

The object of the National Insurace Act, 1911, was 'to provide for insurance against loss of health and for the prevention and cure of sickness and for insurance against unemployment and for purposes incidental thereto'. We cannot be concerned with the intricate details of the Act (see, e.g. D. C. Marsh, *National Insurance*; J. J. Clark, *Social Administration*), but broadly all manual workers, and all other employed persons earning less than £160 a year (with some exceptions and exemptions) had to become contributors to the Health Insurance Scheme and were thefore to become entitled to a weekly payment for themselves (though not for any dependents) when out of work because of illness, and to the services of a 'panel' doctor; and manual workers employed in certain trades which were particularly susceptible to variations in employment had to become contributors to the Unemployment Insurance Scheme, and were therefore to become entitled to a weekly payment for themselves (and later for any dependents) when thrown out of work through no fault of their own.

The number who became compulsorily insured against sickness was about 14 million, whereas only about 2,250,000 became compulsorily insured against unemployment. However, in succeeding years the coverage of both schemes was to be considerably widened and our main interest now is to see the essential principles underlying these schemes and the methods of administration. The basic principle was quite simple, namely that an insured person should make regular contributions into a State fund and in return for a specified number of contributions he (or she) would be entitled to a sickness or unemployment benefit for specified periods. This is the celebrated 'contributory principle' which has become enshrined as the fundamental principle of social insurance in this country, and allied to it is the 'tripartite system' of contributions in which an employed insured person is supported by additional contributions from his employer and from the State. Furthermore, it was assumed that the contributory principle would be synonymous with an insurance principle, that is to say that the contribution (from the three parties) would be calculated so as to ensure that sufficient funds would be available at any time to cover benefits, hence actuarial calculations were made in relation to the incidence of sickness and unemployment over time. However, mass unemployment in the 1920's and 1930's showed that a contributory principle was not synonymous with an insurance principle; nevertheless we have continued to believe that benefits in return for contributions means the strict application of the principles of insurance despite the fact that in the depression years the Unemployment Insurance Fund was heavily overdrawn.

The application of the contributory principle meant that accurate contribution records had to be maintained for each contributor and the method used was for the insured person and his employer to purchase a stamp representing the amount of his contribution and this was placed on his insurance card, and of course regulations had to be made of the number of contributions required in order to qualify for benefit, hence from the beginning an elaborate administrative system was necessary to run the schemes. Due to violent opposition from a number of vested interests to the introduction of health insurance the administrative structure for this scheme differed substantially from that for the Unemployment

Insurance Scheme. In 1911 there was no Government department which could be said to be appropriate for either scheme. Even though labour exchanges had been established in 1909 there was no Ministry of Labour until 1917, and for Health Insurance there was no immediately suitable department since the Ministry of Health was not established until 1919. Mixed, cumbersome and complicated administrative systems were therefore created. For health insurance central Government organization was handed over to Insurance Commissioners appointed by the Treasury, local Insurance Committees were established to administer medical benefits, and Approved Societies were specially created to administer (for most insured persons) the financial benefits. In 1919 the Ministry of Health became the responsible Government department, but the mixed system of Local Committees and Approved Societies was retained. For Unemployment Insurance the Board of Trade became the responsible Government department and it appointed Insurance Officers who were usually attached to Labour Exchanges, until 1917 when the Ministry of Labour took over complete responsibility.

There were no consistent administrative principles applied in these first years of the operation of these two schemes, and even after the creation of the Ministries of Labour and Health the administrative system was extremely complex and cumbersome. The addition of a new contributory pensions scheme in 1925 to cover Old Age, Widows and Orphans (through The Widows', Orphans' and Old Age Contributory Pensions Act of 1925) added further complications despite the fact that this scheme was linked to Health Insurance and administered by the Ministry of Health. All persons insured under The Health Insurance Acts became contributors for Widows', Orphans' and Old Age pensions, but in addition certain classes of voluntary contributors and some of the exempted and excepted persons were also made eligible to join. The main principles of benefits in return for contributions were continued, but the varieties of contribution conditions were by now extremely complex, and as the years went by so new classes of contributors became eligible, for example, in 1937 the benefits of national insurance pensions were extended to independent workers with limited incomes like ministers of religion and small shopkeepers. By 1937, therefore, a very large proportion of the adult population was covered by national insurance and the complexities of the schemes were so great as to defy understanding by ordinary persons.

In 1937 an attempt was made to examine these and other statutory social services by the independent research organization—Political and Economic Planning—and its report showed clearly how complicated and irrational the original schemes had become.[5] However, it was not until June 1941 that an official full-scale investigation was carried out by a committee appointed by the Government, under the chairmanship of Sir William Beveridge.

The terms of reference given to this committee were 'to undertake, with special reference to the interrelation of the schemes, a survey of the existing national schemes of social insurance, and allied services, including workmen's compensation, and to make recommendations'. The Government intended that the committee as a whole should examine the schemes and make recommendations, but in January 1942 it was decided that since most of the members were permanent officials of various Government departments it would be preferable for Sir William to write the report and use the other members of the committee as his advisers. In November 1942 the now famous Beveridge Report on Social Insurance and Allied Services was published.[6]

It was, of course, quite remarkable that an investigation of this nature should be made at a time when we were engaged in a major war, and when the prospects of victory were by no means bright. However, it was a part of the process of planning for reconstruction when the war ended, and the dramatic proposals made by Sir William contributed substantially to the determination to win the war and build a new kind of society in the future.

In his analysis of the existing schemes Sir William showed only too clearly how they had grown sectionally and how they had given rise to improvised bits of administrative machinery which were not appropriate for solving the basic problems of maintenance of income. Every student of social administration should read his report because it contains a brilliant summary of the way the separate schemes had grown and reveals in glaring detail the complexities of the administrative system. Indeed 'The Summary and Analysis of Existing Schemes of Social Insurance and Assistance Administration' given in the Report is one of the most succinct and lucid accounts yet written about the tangled maze of legislation and administration in the period 1911 to 1941. Having analysed their defects and their virtues he proceeded to plan a more systematic method of abolishing 'want' which he saw as one of the five 'giants' which barred the way to social progress, the others being 'ignorance, squalor, disease and idleness'. One of the ways of preventing 'interruption or destruction of earning power from leading to want' was, he believed, through a unified, comprehensive and universal system of Social Insurance, but this would be a 'part only of a comprehensive policy of social progress'. In other words even the best system of Social Insurance could only work effectively if other social policies were devised to ensure the well-being of individuals and in particular he suggested that there must be a systematic policy for maintaining employment, a national policy for the maintenances of health, and a system of 'adjustment of income, in periods of earning as well as interruption of earning, to family needs, that is to say in one form or another it requires allowances for children'.

Underlying his proposals for a system of Social Insurance there was, therefore, the assumption that the State would have a policy for full employment, a national health service and a system of family allowances. His proposed scheme for social insurance cannot in this book be summarized in detail (see the Report, and a summary in D. C. Marsh, *National Insurance and Assistance in Great Britain*), but essentially the basic principles on which it is based are that 'social security must be achieved by co-operation between the State and the individual' through a contributory system of national insurance which is comprehensive in respect of persons and their needs. In return for regular contributions from the insured person, the State and employers, a fund would be built up out of which benefits would be paid to meet interruption or cessation of earnings arising out of unemployment, sickness, widowhood and old age. In addition, assistance would be given to insured persons to meet the costs of child-bearing and the costs of burial. The funeral grant was, in fact, the only new kind of benefit proposed though radical and sensible modifications were made in some of the standard benefits especially in removing some of the anomalies which existed in the past. On the benefit side, therefore, Beveridge carried out a rationalizing operation, on the contribution side however he was much more radical.

In his plan he classified the population into six main groups of (1) employees, (2) others gainfully occupied, (3) housewives,

(4) others of working age not gainfully occupied, (5) persons below working age, and (6) the retired above working age. Groups 1, 2 and 4 were to become compulsory contributors irrespective of their occupations or incomes together with the State and for group 1 their employers; group 3 would be covered by the contributions of their husbands' or if themselves employed could be given the option of contributing themselves; group 5 would be covered by Family Allowances; and for group 6, a scheme of retirement pensions was to be developed over a transitional period of 20 years in which pensions would gradually be raised to the full rate. All the irritating and administratively cumbersome restrictions in respect of occupation, income, exceptions, exemptions and the like of the past were therefore to be removed so that henceforth all citizens of working age would become contributors in one unified scheme of social insurance against the main causes of interruption or cessation of earnings. However, he proposed in addition a separate scheme of insurance for accidents or illness arising out of and in the course of employment to replace the old and not very satisfactory scheme of Workmen's Compensation for group 1 contributors, but again it was to be part of the unified system of administration. For any person whose needs could not be covered by any form of insurance there was to be a scheme of National Assistance based on proof of need and examination of means, but combined administratively with social insurance.

His plan for unification of all the sectional methods of administration developed in the previous thirty years was straightforward, all social insurance and assistance should become the responsibility of a Ministry of Social Security which could also take over the employment services of the Ministry of Labour, and be controlled politically by a minister of Cabinet rank who would appoint an Advisory Committee to give him advice on a wide range of questions.

This brief summary cannot do full justice to such a detailed, comprehensive and radical report which led to wholesale and almost revolutionary changes in our system of national insurance and its administration, but the extent to which it was acclaimed can be gauged from the fact that it became a 'best seller' and earned for its author a reputation achieved by few men in this century. Obviously it could not be implemented immediately, but the essential principles were accepted by the Government, and in 1944 three White Papers were published which contained the Government's views on how a social security system would be organized. The first (Cmd. 6502, 1944) dealt with the establishment of a National Health Service; the second (Cmd. 6527, 1944) outlined the Government's employment policy; and the third, which was published in two parts (Cmd. 6550, 1944 and Cmd. 6551, 1944), set out the proposals for the scheme of social insurance including family allowances, and for industrial injuries insurance.

Legislative action was soon taken. In November 1944 a Bill was read for the third time which dealt with the proposed establishment of a Ministry of Social Insurance, but an amendment to alter the title to the Ministry of National Insurance was accepted and the Ministry of National Insurance Act, 1944, was therefore placed on the statute book. This was the first of a number of departures in detail though not in vital principles from the Beveridge proposals. For a discussion of how Sir William Beveridge reacted to the differences between his proposals and those of the Government, see *Pillars of Security* and *Full Employment in a Free Society* by Sir William Beveridge. The new ministry took over the functions previously exercised in relation to National Insurance and Workmen's Compensation by the Ministries of Health, Labour and the Home Office, and in 1953 it took over responsibility for war pensions previously accepted by the Ministry of Pensions, and hence was renamed the Ministry of Pensions and National Insurance.

In 1945 the Family Allowances Act was passed which made provision for the new Ministry to pay 'out of moneys provided by Parliament, for every family which includes two or more children and for the benefit of the family as a whole, an allowance in respect of each child in the family other than the elder or eldest at the rate of 5s. per week' (later raised in 1952 to 8s. for every child other than the first and in 1956 to 10s. for the third and each younger child). This was a straightforward measure providing broadly for the payment out of Government funds and with no contribution conditions for the payment of a family allowance for every child (normally under 16 years of age) other than the first in a family of two or more children. Administratively it is equally simple, the Ministry of Pensions and National Insurance is responsible and payment is made through the Post Office.

Social Provision Organized on a Functional Basis

In 1946 the National Insurance Act, and the National Insurance (Industrial Injuries) Act, reached the statute book, and finally in 1948 the National Assistance Act was passed. So that within six years of the Beveridge Report the new system of Social Security had been established.

The object of the National Insurance Act, 1946, is to provide for 'a unified and comprehensive scheme of National Insurance which will eventually cover practically everyone in Great Britain' in respect of all the normal financial hazards of everyday life through 'an extended system of national insurance providing pecuniary payments by way of unemployment benefit, sickness benefit, maternity benefit, retirement pensions, widows' benefit, guardians' allowance and death grant'. All persons of working age that is from 15 to 60 for women and 65 for men became compulsorily insured as from the 5th July 1948 in one of three classes either as employed persons, self-employed persons or non-employed persons, except for those who were in full-time education and for married women in employment who could choose whether or not to be insured in their own right or rely on their husbands' contributions.

The basic principles of the scheme were not so very different from those established in earlier years. The contributory principle was firmly retained and hence there was and still is a variety of contribution conditions which have to be fulfilled before a benefit can be granted; the tripartite system of contributions from the employer, the insured person and the State was retained for employed persons; the method of contributing by means of a weekly stamp on an insurance card was maintained; the insurance principle was theoretically applied even though retirement pensions were granted at the outset to persons who could not possibly have qualified through contributions; and the flat-rate system of contributions and benefits was continued. However, the new scheme was at least unified and comprehensive in the coverage of persons and of needs, hence fulfilling one of the essential principles laid down by Beveridge.

Simple though the scheme appears at first glance it is in fact quite complicated and from the point of view of insured persons by no means easy to understand. We cannot be concerned with the variety of contribution and benefit conditions laid down in the Acts and regulations, but the Ministry has from time to time published *Guides to the National Insurance Scheme* which are reasonably informative and should be consulted by the student of social administration. Our main interest is in the system of finance and administration. The financial side is relatively straightforward. Contributions (which have been increased on a number of occasions since 1948) from insured persons, employers and the State are paid into a National Insurance Fund and out of this the costs of administration and of benefits are met. In addition, there is a National Insurance Reserve Fund which was established out of balances transferred from the previous schemes and which is maintained by the transfer of any surpluses arising out of the operation of the new schemes. Within a few years of coming into being financial difficulties arose primarily because of the burden of providing an increasing number of retirement pensions, but by numerous adjustments of the rates of contributions and benefits it has at least been possible to avoid the crisis situations which arose under the original unemployment insurance scheme.[7] Nevertheless, if unemployment on the scale of the 1930's were to reappear the financial structure of the new scheme would be seriously threatened. Indeed the magnitude of the funds now required to operate national insurance are a vital factor in influencing the economy, a fact recognized in the original Act by the requirement that the Government actuary must make at least a quinquennial review of the financing of the scheme.

The magnitude of the funds absorbed by the National Insurance scheme may be gauged from the following table:

APPROXIMATE RECEIPTS AND PAYMENTS OF THE NATIONAL INSURANCE FUND FOR THE YEAR ENDED 31ST MARCH 1950 AND 1960

	£ thousands	
Receipts	1950	1960
Flat rate contributions from Employers and Insured persons	400,647	708,440
Other Receipts e.g. Exchequer supplement, Interest from Investments	167,685	222,340
Total	568,332	930,780

Payments

Benefits	365,775	916,672
Administration expenses	23,865	38,987
Other payments	40,455	7,682
Total	430,095	963,341

Administratively the new system shows a great improvement on the past. The Minister of Pensions and National Insurance is answerable to Parliament, he is advised by an independent National Insurance Advisory Committee whose members give advice and assistance to the Minister in connection with the discharge of his functions under this Act and to perform any other duties allotted to them, and policy is implemented through the Ministry which, in turn, works through regional offices and local offices. The Insurance Officers at local level are responsible in general for determining claims to benefit, but there is, of course, a system of appeal from their decisions to a Local Appeal Tribunal composed of representatives of insured persons and employers, and beyond to the National Insurance Commissioner. The main administrative problems are those of maintaining accurate records of the contributions made and the benefits obtained by the millions of insured persons, and of course of dealing promptly, efficiently and accurately with claims, a gigantic task which the Ministry has attempted to solve by maintaining one enormous central records office and using modern office machines.

Obviously a scheme of this size requires an administrative structure larger than that of most large firms and the number employed in the Ministry of Pensions and National Insurance, about 38,000 in 1964, is much larger than that employed by most commercial concerns in the country. National Insurance is now a mammoth operation made more complicated of course by the acceptance of the contributory principle, and more recently by the addition of a system of graduated pensions.

Between 1948 and 1957 there were not many modifications made to the scheme as laid down in the 1946 Act. There were changes in rates of contributions and benefits, and some of the types of benefit, especially maternity benefits, were remodelled. In 1957, however, a new financial principle was introduced in respect of that part of the contribution originally diverted to meet some of the costs of the National Health Service. Under the 1946 Act the Minister was given power to make payments out of the National Insurance Fund towards the cost of the National Health Service, such payments being deducted from the total contributions received from all insured persons and employers. For example, for an adult male aged 18 or over a sum of 8½d. per week was included in the original total contribution of 4s. 11d. per week as the amount to be paid for the National Health Service, though of course these contributions represented only a small proportion of the total cost and even more important the services provided under the National Health Service were not in any way restricted to insured persons. In 1957 this contribution was abolished, under the National Health Service Contributions Act, 1957, and replaced by a separate National Health Service contribution which is collected in conjunction with the National Insurance contribution, so that as far as the insured person is concerned there is no real difference in practice except that he has to pay more than in the past (for example, for an adult male over 18 years of age the National Health contribution in 1961 was 2s. 8½d.).

Much more fundamental was the introduction of a Graduated Pensions scheme in 1959, because this constituted a partial breach in the almost sacred principle of flat rate of benefits and contributions. Under the Graduated Pensions Act, 1959 (which came into force in 1961), an attempt is made to provide to a limited extent a wage-related retirement pension. Insured persons earning between £9 and £15 per week (as from 1963 the upper limit has been raised to £18) are required (unless they contract out of the scheme which they may do under certain conditions) to pay an additional contribution of approximately 4½ per cent of that part of their weekly pay which lies between £9 and £15 (£18 from 1963), which will entitle them to a higher rate of retirement pension related to the additional contributions they have paid. Those earning over £18 are treated as though they earn £18 and those earning less than £9 must rely on the basic rate of retirement pension. This scheme is administered as an integral part of the system of National Insurance, except for the creation of the office of Registrar of Non-Participating Employments which is mainly concerned with determining who is entitled to contract out of the scheme, and on the financial side the graduated contribution of an employed person is calculated on the same basis as for P.A.Y.E.

Income Tax, and collected along with the income tax deducted by the employer. It does not, of course, achieve the aim of 'half-pay on retirement' which was publicly expressed by the Labour Party in their proposals for a national system of superannuation in 1957, and it remains to be seen how far this break away from the flat-rate principle of benefits and contributions will be extended in the future.

From this brief outline of the system of National Insurance it will be seen that it constitutes a vast and complicated field of study for the student of social administration, and that in some important ways it differs from the Beveridge proposals. In particular, we did not get a Ministry of Social Security; National Assistance did not become the responsibility of the Ministry of National Insurance; and that now we have moved slightly away from the flat-rate principle. The other major Beveridge proposal for a system of industrial injuries insurance was, however, implemented without substantial deviation.

Prior to 1948 a workman injured in an accident arising out of and in the course of his employment and therefore unable to earn because of his injuries could only obtain compensation through a complicated system of legal process under the Workmen's Compensation Acts the first of which was passed in 1897. In only a few industries were employers compelled to insure against their liabilities to pay workmen's compensation, but for most workpeople there was often the problem of obtaining compensation even after a successful court case because the employer was not insured. It was a chancy and troublesome method not always ensuring justice for the injured workmen and when Beveridge examined the scheme in 1941 he criticized it in strong terms and recommended that it should be replaced by a statutory system of Industrial Injuries Insurance.

The National Insurance (Industrial Injuries) Act, 1946, was designed to provide 'a system of insurance against personal injury caused by accident arising out of and in the course of a person's employment and against prescribed diseases and injuries due to the nature of a person's employment' (Preamble to the Act). In effect the liability for the payment of compensation is transferred from the employer to the State which in turn obtains its funds from the insured person, employers and taxpayer. However, only insured persons in Class 1 of the National Insurance scheme (i.e.

employed persons) are compelled to contribute to the Industrial Injuries scheme and, of course, their employers.

Unlike the complicated National Insurance scheme there are no contribution conditions. Once an insured person has made his (or her, because married women in employment cannot contract out of Industrial Injuries Insurance) first contribution he (or she) is then eligible for benefit. The contributory principle is therefore applied only in the very limited sense of having to be a contributor in order to qualify for benefit, and not in the accepted sense of a benefit having to be earned by a specified number of contributions. The flat-rate principle is applied, thus in 1948 an insured male over the age of 18 contributed 4d. a week (a female over 18 paid 3d. per week) and the employer the same amounts. Rates of contribution have not varied as often as those of National Insurance and in 1961 they were 7d. for males over 18 (plus 8d. from the employer) and 4d. for females over 18 (plus 5d. from the employer). The contribution is of course combined with that for National Insurance on the insured person's national insurance card.

There are three main kinds of benefit: (1) injury benefit which is a weekly payment for a maximum of 26 weeks; (2) disablement benefit which may be claimed after 26 weeks and may take the form of a weekly payment or gratuity depending on the degree of disablement and may be increased by a special hardship allowance, an unemployability supplement, a constant attendance allowance and a hospital treatment allowance; and (3) a death benefit for widows and dependents. (For details of the current types and rates of benefit see the latest issue of *Everybody's Guide to National Insurance*, published by H.M.S.O. for the Ministry of Pensions and National Insurance.)

The scheme is administered by the Ministry of Pensions and National Insurance, there is an Industrial Insurance Advisory Committee, an Industrial Injuries Commissioner and of course Local Insurance Officers. In addition, there are Medical Boards and Medical Appeal Tribunals and Local Appeal Tribunals. Obviously as this scheme is concerned primarily with medical questions and with determining whether the injury or disease arose out of and in the course of the employment there is bound to be a strong specialized appeal system within the administrative structure. But from the point of view of the insured person his point of contact is with the Local Insurance Officer and only in the event of his being dissatisfied with the result of his claim is he likely to become involved with the appeal procedure.

The grant of a benefit under this scheme does not prevent an insured person from making a claim for damages under common law if it can be proved that his injury was due to negligence on the part of the employer. What this scheme does is to provide income maintenance either wholly or in part for a personal disability arising out of an industrial accident, and it is of course vastly superior to the earlier workmen's compensation scheme.

The scheme has been financially sound from the start and the Industrial Injuries Fund (authorized by the original Act) has usually shown a healthy surplus annually, despite the fact that rates of benefit are higher than those for sickness benefit under National Insurance. For example, total receipts in 1950 were approximately £37 million and in 1960 £87 million, whereas payments of benefits and other expenses in 1950 were approximately £14 million and in 1960 approximately £55 million. Obviously the demands for benefits under this scheme are not, fortunately, as high as those for ordinary sickness, but there is an issue of principle as to the justification for paying benefits under Industrial Injuries Insurance at rates higher than those for sickness. Sir William Beveridge argued in his Report that higher rates of benefit were justifiable for industrial injuries in order to compensate persons working in dangerous occupations, but in fact the Act by making all Class 1 contributors insurable makes no distinction between different kinds of occupation. It could in any case be argued that the time to compensate a worker for engaging in a dangerous occupation is when he is employed and that for interruption or cessation of earnings through illness or accident the cause is irrelevant. However, it is by no means unusual in our system of social security to have conflicting and seemingly irrational principles.[8]

One other income maintenance service requires mention and that, of course, is the payment of War Pensions. Whether the payment of a pension for an injury sustained in war is a social service or whether it is simply a payment for services rendered on behalf of one's country is an open question. Whatever the answer the fact is that after two world wars pensions have been paid for disability and bereavement, and that since 1953 they have been the administrative responsibility of the Ministry of Pensions and

National Insurance. Previously, of course, they were under the control of the Ministry of Pensions, which under our irrational system of allocating administrative responsibilities, was concerned solely with War Pensions.

In this vast and complicated field of social policy which is concerned with income maintenance it is by no means easy to identify clearly defined principles of policy or of administration. Obviously we have by now reached the stage where it is seen that society has a responsibility to provide at all times a minimum level of subsistence to any person in need irrespective of the cause of that need, but what that minimum level should be, how much above the minimum should be made available in respect of particular identifiable causes over which the individual has no control, and what the relation should be between the amount of earnings lost and the social benefit provided as a substitute are by no means clear. Equally we have not reached a firm decision as to the appropriate kinds of administrative systems which will provide an efficient and personal service to individuals in situations of great personal distress. In part these uncertainties may be due to a lingering belief that 'social benefits' in the form of financial payments are demanded only by the shiftless, the feckless, the workshy and other irresponsible elements in our society, and that therefore we must have methods of administration which will ensure that discrimination is made between the deserving and the undeserving applicants. And, of course, so many of our present policies and practices are based on deep-rooted traditions which inhibit the development of new methods of ensuring income maintenance.

There are signs that at last we are prepared to consider new ways of solving these problems; some people have suggested that 'private' insurance should be more extensively used. In an affluent society with growing money incomes it is argued that each of us can more easily afford to insure ourselves against the risks of unemployment, sickness, widowhood and old age, in which case we should have to study not social but commercial administration. Others have suggested that what is needed is a radical revision of the existing schemes and the Labour Party in 1963 produced a new policy statement in 'New Frontiers for Social Security' which aims at providing wage-related benefits, paid for by wage-related contributions, yielding half-pay on retirement, in sickness and on redundancy, using of course the principles of social insurance. If these proposals are in fact ever implemented then clearly social security will continue to be a field of study of considerable significance to the student of social policy and social administration.

SUGGESTED READING

Books written about Social Security tend to become out of date within a short time of being published, and on some aspects, for example, the Poor Law they are now mainly of historical interest. Nevertheless, there is still a great deal of benefit to be derived from books and official reports written in the past.

On the Poor Law the classic study was that of Sidney and Beatrice Webb, *English Local Government: English Poor Law History*; and, of course, the official report of the Royal Commission on the Poor Laws and Relief of Distress (published in 1909). John J. Clarke, *Public Assistance*, published in 1937, contains a wealth of legal and administrative detail. So far there has been no comprehensive study of National Assistance, but the Annual Reports of the National Assistance Board should be examined.

On National Insurance (including Family Allowances) the Beveridge Report is of course essential reading. Books, other than those mentioned in the notes, which are well worth reading are:

W. A. ROBSON (ed.), *Social Security*.
KARL DE SCHWEINITZ, *England's Road to Social Security*.
SIR GEOFFREY KING, *The Ministry of Pensions and National Insurance*.
ELEANOR RATHBONE, *Family Allowances*.
A. T. PEACOCK, *The Economics of National Insurance*.
FREDA YOUNG, *Industrial Injuries Insurance*.

As an introduction to comparative studies:

RONALD MENDELSOHN, *Social Secuity in the British Commonwealth*.
INTERNATIONAL LABOUR OFFICE, *International Survey of Social Security*.

Anyone interested in the statistical aspects of Social Security should look at the report of the Inter-Departmental Committee on Social and Economic Research, Guides to Official Sources, No. 5, *Social Security Statistics*, H.M.S.O., 1961.

NOTES

[1] For a brief account of the growth of the system of Poor Relief and the aims and methods of the 'New Poor Law', see D. C. Marsh, *National Insurance and Assistance in Great Britain*.

[2] For a brief account of the growth of the system of the Poor Law up to 1948, see D. C. Marsh, op. cit.

[3] On the adequacy of this basis and the vagueness of the concept of poverty, see D. C. Marsh, *The Welfare State*, Penguin Books.

[4] For the controversies surrounding the introduction of National Insurance, see

Notes

Maurice Bruce, *The Coming of the Welfare State.*

[5] See P.E.P. report on *The British Social Services,* 1937.

[6] *Report on Social Insurance and Allied Services,* by Sir William Beveridge, H.M.S.O., Cmd. 6404.

[7] See the Report of the *Committee on the Economic and Financial Problems of the Provision for Old Age* (Cmd. 9333, 1954).

[8] See D. C. Marsh, *The Welfare State.*

4. SOCIAL POLICY IN RELATION TO INDUSTRIAL CONDITIONS

Richard L. Silburn

NEARLY all of us are obliged, at some time or another, to earn our living; for most men, and for an increasing number of women, their work is a quite crucial aspect of their life. It occupies about one-third of a person's waking hours for the greater part of his life; it provides him with the wages or salary that he needs to support himself and his family; sometimes it helps to give a sense of purpose and achievement to a person's life; sometimes it is the source of great dissatisfaction and frustration. Therefore the trade or profession that is followed, the skills that are learned, and the opportunities that exist for pursuing one's trade, and exploiting one's skills, are a matter of considerable significance, and legitimate concern to everyone. Therefore we need not be surprised to discover that there exists a wide range of organized services concerned with some of the outstanding difficulties and problems in this important aspect of life.

Some of the problems that are dealt with by the industrial services are by no means new problems arising out of the fact of industrialization as such, but are age-old problems caused by, for example, temporary or permanent inability to earn one's living because of illness or disablement. There are, however, other problems of relatively recent origin, which arise directly out of the peculiar nature of the industrialized society. Before examining in any detail the industrial services we ought to examine some of the characteristic features of an industrial society, features which may, by their very presence, generate problems. We may then see to what extent the industrial services are concerning themselves with fundamental social problems.

The two most obvious features of industrialization as we have known it in Britain have been (*a*) urbanization, that is the concentration of an ever-increasing proportion of the population into the large towns, so that today Britain is predominantly an urban society; and (*b*) the organization of production through a system of factories and workshops, and within the factories of the methods of mass-production. All of these are highly significant changes, but it is upon the second of them that we must concentrate, because the implications of a factory system of mass-production are of fundamental importance if we are to gain a proper understanding of the industrial problems of modern society.

A system of mass-production is based upon the breaking up of any job, or manufacturing operation into its component parts, and the giving of one such part to each worker. Thus, for example, the assembly of a motor car may be reduced to a series of basic operations, let us say, a hundred of them; and so a hundred workers will be required, each one to do one particular operation and no more. This system has the advantage of greatly increasing productivity—the manufacturing process becomes standardized, operational details are simplified as much as possible, and the entire process is so streamlined that the inefficient use of manpower or materials is minimized. Mass-production has made possible the vast increase in the availability of consumer-goods, and has permitted, indeed necessitated, the payment of relatively high wages and salaries. But techniques of mass-production have had a number of side-effects not quite so happy. First there is little place in a system of mass-production for individual attention to the quality of the product, there is no time for traditional craftsmanship, or the exercise of sophisticated individual skill—on the contrary, as we have seen, the constant aim is the simplification and standardization of the manufacturing process. This makes it very much harder for the individual to feel any sense of pride in his work; he completes only a fragment of the total task, and even that fragment he completes mechanically; he could be switched from one job to another at a moment's notice because all jobs require the same minimal skill.

This tendency affects the white-collar or clerical workers as well as manual or production workers. Office workers are finding that their function is changing under the impact of developments in the office-machinery field: every year more sophisticated machinery is being developed, machinery which can cope with administrative routines, and computors which can calculate accounts, machinery which is faster and more efficient than an army of clerks. This process is known as 'de-skilling' and presents a serious problem, because we are reducing the function of labour to that of machine minding, and we cannot expect people to accept this new role impassively; it is bound to have important effects on their attitude to their work, their morale and their self-respect.

But this is not the only aspect of factory-production that merits attention. Another important aspect of industrialization is that the vast majority of people in an industrial society are employees, that is to say, they do not work for themselves (as, for example, most farmers work for themselves, on their own land) but they sell their labour to an employer who pays them wages in return for the hours of work they give him. This applies to manual workers, clerical workers and even to managers and executives; even the managing director of a factory or business, although he will hold shares and to that extent can be said to be working for himself, will also earn a salary as an employed executive of the enterprise. The numbers of people who are truly self-employed are small, and mainly confined to agriculture and retail distribution, and even these fields of activity are being increasingly invaded by the techniques of mass-production and marketing, so that even here the self-employed person's position is vulnerable and threatened.

There is a further comment which can be made at this point. Mass-production methods imply industrial organization on a very large scale, and on a scale moreover which seems likely to become ever larger. In large-scale organizations, however, the critical process of decision making is itself subject to division of labour, so that decision-making becomes a specialized function, and the right and power to make decisions is (generally speaking) confined to a specific executive group. The implications of this concentration of decision-making powers have occasionally been examined and there have been (and are) one or two experiments with alternative forms of industrial organization,[1] but generally speaking the organization and structure of British industry is taken very much for granted, and is assumed to be in some way a 'natural' development, not to be subject to fundamental examination. But the concentration of controlling and decisive powers does require serious critical examination, particularly from those who believe that in a democracy powers of control should be extended into all areas of a person's life, and that decision-making in the economic and industrial sphere is as fundamental a human right as is decision-making in the political sphere. A study of the distribution of power within industry becomes even more pressing, if it is suggested that much industrial unrest, much of the individual frustration and resentment that constitutes a dangerous malaise of British industry can be attributed to a power-structure which deprives individuals of a sense of control and responsibility over their own lives.

The question of decision-making does not, of course, give rise to social problems of material distress, and perhaps for this reason it has not been the subject of widespread discussion or of social action. It may be, however, that many of the discontents and tensions in our society can be traced to some such factor as this, and that our social policy for industry, as it becomes less concerned with questions of survival and more preoccupied with questions of adjustment, should take some active interest in questions of this kind.

In the light of these remarks, let us first review very briefly the fairly limited range of problems with which the industrial services attempt to deal. The most basic task, one would have thought, of any system of industrial services would have been to ensure that there were enough jobs to go round, so that everyone has the opportunity to work, and is thus spared the demoralizing and humiliating consequences of unemployment. In fact, however, the numbers and type of new openings is left as a function of the free economy; the Distribution of Industry Acts[2] are the only factor which might influence the situation in some areas; under these Acts, inducements are offered to industrialists to build new factories or expand existing ones, in a certain number of so-called Development Areas; these are areas which are usually characterized by old and declining industries, and where the development of new forms of employment is a matter of urgency. Most of the industrial services do not take any initiative in this way, they simplify procedures so that the *status quo* works more smoothly. Thus, individuals who need work can benefit from an Exchange system which acts as a clearing-house, where they can obtain information about the numbers and types of jobs currently available; young people who are about to leave school and embark upon their working lives must receive expert advice about the openings that exist for young people—they must be helped to find a job that will interest them, that will at the same time offer a satisfactory career prospect. It may be necessary to encourage them to undergo special training, and appropriate training schemes and apprenticeships must be available to them. Older people, too, and particularly those in the areas of declining industries where continued employment in the traditional industries is uncertain, may need special training to develop new skills to equip them for employment in the expanding industries. Then there are the special needs of the invalid and disabled: someone who has been ill, and off work for a period of time might require some help in readjusting to the conditions and the pace of normal industrial jobs. Disabled persons might require special help to find a job which they can satisfactorily perform despite their disablement; the community has always recognized in this connection, a special responsibility for those whose disablement is a result of war-service.

Finally, and more generally, the conditions in which people work must be protected; minimum standards of health and safety provision and other amenities, must be laid down and if need be, enforced. In the event of some industrial dispute arising, then it may be necessary to urge the disputing parties to submit to impartial arbitration, so that production is not affected by a strike or a lock-out.

The industrial services are concerned with all of these problems and needs. But in what sense can these services be called social services? True, some of them have a welfare-content and interest, and in some instances offer a personal service to those in need of them. But is an Employment Exchange anything more than a convenient administrative device, which saves a lot of time and bother for all parties, an administrative convenience in rather the same way that a public library is a convenient way of bringing those who want to read books into contact with a supply of books? Or again, a Factory Act lays down certain minimum standards of amenity in a factory, and regulates the way in which an employer can treat those he employs; can such an Act be thought of as a social service? Is it fundamentally different from, say, the Highway Code, which regulates the way a driver should treat his fellow road-user, and which is never thought of as a social service? In short, are not the bulk of these services more properly considered as administrative conveniences or elementary regulatory devices rather than social services in any distinctive sense.

However, the industrial services merit our attention, if only because they affect a very large proportion of our population, and they represent a substantial area of State intervention in the practical workings of the economy and are a clear expression of social policy.

SOME BACKGROUND DEVELOPMENTS

When we examine the history and development of the State social services, we constantly see how any proposal for an extension of a service or the creation of a new service is greeted with opposition and resentment. And in no field is this observation more clearly demonstrated than in the field of the industrial services. Ever since the first factory legislation was introduced at the beginning of the nineteenth century,[3] any attempt to safeguard or control the health and security conditions of the employee, or to mitigate the worst consequences of a laissez-faire economic system, has been condemned as an unwarranted interference with individual freedom, and the probable consequences have invariably been foreseen to be disastrous, catastrophic and certain to produce immediate economic or moral collapse—predictions which, equally invariably, have proved to be groundless.

This form of opposition was, of course, very much in line with the dominant Victorian philosophy of laissez-faire.[4] According to this doctrine, happiness and prosperity were only to be won, if each individual were quite free to pursue his own economic interest; any interference or control of this freedom was bound to be destructive of both happiness and prosperity. We must all be familiar with some of the worst evils that this philosophy encouraged; nineteenth-century history and literature is full of graphic accounts of the bad working conditions in many factories and workshops, the long hours worked for low wages, the cruel exploitation of child labour and so on. Most of the energies of the nineteenth-century reformers were devoted to correcting the worst of these abuses; a series of Factories Acts[5] were passed which restricted the hours of work of children and women, and began to establish minimum standards of amenities within the factories.

Around the turn of the century, the doctrine of laissez-faire was being questioned most vigorously, more and more people came to query some of the assumptions of the theory as more and more came to be known about the working and living conditions of the population. It was in this atmosphere of questioning that William Beveridge made his first major contribution to the history of the Welfare State; in 1909 he published a book called *Unemployment; a Problem of Industry*. The very title of this book is significant, because it implies that unemployment is not a question of character or moral standards but of industrial organization; reducing the level of unemployment involved modifying the organization of industry rather than exhorting the redeeming virtues of hard work. The outstanding and permanent result of Beveridge's work at this time was the establishment of a national system of Labour Exchanges. In essence this was a very simple and straightforward idea—'the purpose of Labour Exchanges is to substitute a market for unguided hawking from door to door as the means of bringing the would-be buyer of labour and would-be seller together'. Looking back to this period it seems curious that the establishment of a simple clearing-house where the unemployed worker and the prospective employer could be brought face-to-face should arouse controversy, but in fact Beveridge and his supporters had been arguing this point of view for several years before they achieved their ambition, and Beveridge's book was only another step in the struggle.

One of the administrative problems that the Government had to face was which department of State was to be responsible for the organization of the new Exchanges; Beveridge felt that the established Civil Servant was not the right sort of person for this job. The organizer of an Employment Exchange, in his opinion, should be a man of very special character and ability. When the Act creating Employment Exchanges was passed in 1909, the Board of Trade was made the responsible department, and the task of implementing the Act was given to Beveridge who joined the Board of Trade while the final Act was still being discussed and debated.

In the following year, 1910, the Education (Choice of Employment) Act was passed; this gave education authorities the power to establish vocational guidance schemes for school-leavers. If an education authority did not establish such a scheme, then the

Board of Trade could organize one through the new Employment Exchanges. Thus from the outset, the scope of the Employment Exchanges work was extended from being merely a clearing-house to having a definite advisory function, at any rate in respect of the young.

The value of these new services became quite apparent during the First World War, when efficient use of man-power became a matter of urgent national priority. As the war progressed it became clear that to have all the legislative responsibility for man-power divided between a number of Government departments was an unsatisfactory and inefficient system; how much more satisfactory would be a single Government authority under the charge of a minister of Cabinet rank. So, in 1917, was founded the Ministry of Labour, which took over the labour responsibilities of all the other Government departments.

Between the First and Second World Wars, the Ministry of Labour was naturally preoccupied with the problem of mass-unemployment that characterized the period; to the job-placement function of the Employment Exchange was added the task of administering the unemployment insurance scheme, and the Exchanges became popularly associated with the dole-queue, and the relief of distress. However, even during these inter-war years the work of the Ministry in connection with industrial relations expanded considerably. This was a period of considerable unrest, and disputes between employers and the trade unions were often bitter and protracted. The policy of the Ministry always was, and still is, to encourage both sides of industry to establish their own voluntary arbitration systems, but in the last resort the Ministry became increasingly acceptable to both sides as a conciliating body itself.

With the outbreak of the Second World War, the efficient control of man-power became again a matter of national priority; from the outset the Ministry was directly involved in formulating and applying a man-power policy. Towards the end, and after the war, the Ministry was responsible for the enormously complex task of military demobilization, industrial resettlement and of organizing the change from production for war-time needs to production for peace.

Just as the blueprints for the post-war Welfare State were drawn up and publicized during the war, so a post-war industrial and employment policy was drawn up and publicized, and[6] the period at the end of, and immediately after the War, saw the passing of a series of Acts[7] which created or modernized a wide range of industrial services, most of which are still operative today.

YOUTH EMPLOYMENT SERVICE

The transition from school to work is one of the most important steps in a person's life, and it would be cruel and irresponsible to leave each child to fend for himself as best he may. The choice of a first job is far too important a decision to leave to chance. Therefore it is not surprising that since the early years of this century there has existed an advisory service aiming to provide just the information and help each child needs. This service, in its modern form, is known as the Youth Employment Service.

We have already seen above that the Education (Choice of Employment) Act, 1910, gave local education authorities powers to establish vocational guidance schemes for school-leavers, and if an education authority chose not to use these powers, the Board of Trade could organize such a scheme instead. Thus, from very early on, the Youth Employment Service has been divided for the purposes of administration between two different authorities at central and local level.

In many respects this division of responsibility between the Board of Education and the Board of Trade (and then the new Ministry of Labour) reflects a very real difficulty of distinction; is the task of teaching children about the sorts of job open to them, and of advising and guiding them into the jobs best suited to them, an educational or industrial responsibility? Is the difficulty and the challenge of the move from a school-life to a working-life a problem to be approached by the schools or the factories? Obviously it is a task which affects both of them, and in which both of them play a central role, and so the historical division of responsibility is a very natural one, even if it is illogical and (if it results in confusion or duplication and overlap of services) inconvenient.

Even after many years of practical experience, however, it has not become any easier to resolve the difficulty presented by this particular problem of delegation. In 1945, the Ince Committee[8] appointed by the Minister to examine the whole service and to 'consider measures necessary to establish a comprehensive Juvenile Employment Service', acknowledged that it would be logical and convenient if one department only were to be administratively responsible for the Service, but the Committee was quite unable to decide whether it should be the Ministry of Education or of Labour. Consequently they recommended an unusual compromise plan which was enacted in the Employment and Training Act, 1948. Central responsibility for the Service became the Ministry of Labour's; the Ministry delegates its authority to the Central Youth Employment Executive, which is staffed by officials of both Education and Labour Ministries. This ensures that the Service is unified at central level, while at the same time all interested parties are properly represented. At local level, however, the traditional administrative division of authority remains. Each Local Education Authority, after the passing of the Act, decided once and for all whether or not it chose to organize the Service in its area; the majority of authorities decided to do so. In the other areas the Service is organized directly by the Ministry of Labour. This may still seem to be an untidy arrangement, but in practice it seems to work. Relations between the departments are good, and there is little to suggest that the Service is made less effective by this administrative division.

Whatever form the administration takes, the aims of the Service remain the same; 'they are to assist the adolescent first to choose, and then to find the type of employment best suited to his aptitudes and abilities, and see him happily settled in it'.[9] These aims are usually fulfilled in the following ways; as the child's school career draws towards its close, so he learns about some of the different sorts of job available to him in a series of careers talks or conventions. He may meet people working in many different walks of life, or perhaps will see careers films, and may go on visits to factories and offices. In this and other ways the school-leaver gets to know something about the available openings. During this period the Youth Employment Officer in his turn learns as much as he can about the abilities and the interests of the child; he is helped by a confidential report from the school. The crucial contact is when the school-leaver and the Youth Employment Officer meet at a face-to-face interview. The officer by then should know enough about the young person to be able to offer some positive recommendations, and the young person should know enough about possible jobs to have some idea about what he wants to do. Ideally, the outcome of this interview (which parents can attend if they want to), is a suitable placement. Even after a job has been found the Youth Employment Officer still attempts to maintain some contact with the young people he has assisted. This contact is, of course, like every part of this service, quite voluntary, and usually takes the form of an Open Evening when the young worker can come and talk over any difficulties he is having in his new job; if he is dissatisfied with his job he can use the Service to find him another.

This necessarily brief description of the work typically done by the Youth Employment Service should be sufficient to show that it should be a skilled and personal service, and so the success with which it operates must to a large extent depend upon the skill and sensitivity of each individual Youth Employment Officer. It is therefore surprising that so little concern is shown over the training of officers. As long ago as 1951, the Piercy Committee on the recruitment and training of Youth Employment Officers[10] recommended that there should be a one-year full-time training course. This recommendation was accepted in principle but for reasons of economy, has never been properly implemented. For several years Kent Education Authority has organized a one-year course and there are a few other courses of differing length and character, run by a few other authorities and organizations, but the number who can benefit from them are of necessity small.

The Ministry of Labour organizes a four-week course for newly appointed officers but it is probable that many, if not most, officers learn their skills while they are actually doing the job.

The Youth Employment Officer meets very special difficulties if he works in an area which is dominated by one kind of employment, such as farming or mining. It may be very difficult or impossible for him to be able to offer any variety of jobs, and there may be insufficient variety of openings to allow for individual abilities and special talents to be exploited properly. If the dominant industry happens (as it all too frequently does) to be a declining industry, which may require only a very small annual intake of young workers, and that offering only limited prospects, then it may be impossible for the Youth Employment Service to prevent the development of a high level of unemployment among young people, a tragic situation with incalculable long-term consequences. Facilities are available for young people in this situation to move to some other part of the country where training and employment prospects are brighter; experience shows, however, that only a small number of young people are prepared to leave their families and friends to take advantage of these facilities.

One suggested long-term solution to difficulties of this sort would be to attract new industries into the declining areas, and the Minister of Labour has certain powers under the Distribution of Industry Acts,[2] to encourage and offer inducements to industrialists to develop factories and generate employment prospects in a number of designated Development Areas; so far these powers do not seem to have been over-successful.

Another, somewhat less intractable, problem lies in the fact that the Youth Employment Service is entirely voluntary; that is to say, the employer is under no obligation to recruit youthful labour through the Service, nor is any young person obliged to take advantage of the Service. Thus the Youth Employment Officer may not always be aware of all the vacancies in his area, nor will he always know all the young people who are in need of jobs. The Ince Committee examined this weakness in the system, but rejected any suggestion either that employers should be obliged to recruit through the Service or that young people should be obliged to report to the Youth Employment Officer. This reluctance to impose the Service upon any unwilling party is understandable and reasonable; it does however mean that any Youth Employment Officer who wishes to develop his service to the full must spend much time and energy familiarizing himself with local conditions, and must somehow get the sympathy and the support of all those employers, teachers and pupils who stand to benefit from his efforts. This is sometimes very difficult: there are many employers who invariably recruit their young staff without any reference to the Youth Employment Service, and who think that the Service is provided for the least able school-leaver. There are some teachers who resent the school-activities of the Youth Employment Service and who are not as co-operative or helpful as they might be, and there are pupils who are uninterested in the Service offered. Any and all of these factors will severely hinder the efficiency of the Service, and it would be very unusual if at least one of them was not operative in most situations.

It is difficult to evaluate the Youth Employment Service; little work has been done in assessing its efficiency and value. What little has been done is, regrettably, far from reassuring.[11]

THE EMPLOYMENT SERVICE

We have already seen that the major part of the work of the Employment Exchanges is basically simple; all relevant details about a person who is seeking employment are taken down and an effort is made to match these details to the recorded requirements of a vacancy reported to the Exchange by a prospective employer. If a vacancy cannot be filled locally the details of the job will be circulated among other Exchanges in the region or, if necessary, throughout the country; similarly, details of any applicant who cannot be placed locally, may be circulated among other Exchanges.

Traditionally the Exchanges have concerned themselves mainly with the employment of manual workers. Since the last war, however, the employment function of the Exchange has been expanded in two important ways. First of all a Nursing Appointments Service has been set up at a number of major Exchanges, to encourage the recruitment of young girls into the nursing profession. This provides a highly specialized recruitment service, in an attempt to overcome the serious shortage of suitable recruits into nursing. The second development has been the establishment of the Professional and Executive Register in forty-eight major Exchanges. This register is concerned with the appointment of men and women with professional qualifications, or with considerable managerial and executive experience. It has proved itself most valuable in the reappointment of ex-officers from the regular forces, whose military service often finishes while they are still comparatively young men, with many years of working life before them.

Another significant function of the Employment Exchanges is the payment of benefits under the National Insurance Acts on behalf of the Ministry of National Insurance; all those eligible to draw unemployment allowances must sign on at the Employment Exchange as in search of work, and it is from the Employment Exchanges that they collect their benefits. This helps to ensure that those drawing benefit are in weekly contact with the Exchange, and so will be notified of possible jobs as soon as they become available.

Rather more complex are the employment problems of the disabled or otherwise incapacitated person, who may clearly require some special assistance if he is to be able to lead a relatively normal working-life. Generally speaking, the policy adopted assumes that, after a certain amount of initial help, most disabled persons will not only be able to support themselves, but will be able to hold their own in competition with their able-bodied colleagues, under normal industrial conditions. For an examination of the provisions specifically made for disabled persons under the Disabled Persons (Employment) Act, 1944, see pages 165–170.

The use of the Industrial Rehabilitation Units set up under this Act is not confined to the disabled; anyone who has been ill, or has had an accident, or has been unemployed for a long time, and may therefore require a period of preparation for the pace and the discipline of the industrial life, can take advantage of the service provided by the I.R.U.s to restore his physical capacity. Similarly, people who find themselves, perhaps in the middle of their working lives, in need of training or retraining, can apply for entrance to one of the courses at a Government Training Centre. For example, many men who leave the armed services after a long period as a regular soldier take advantage of a Government Training Scheme to provide them with training for civilian employment. The value of these training courses will, one imagines, be particularly recognized in those areas of the country which are characterized by declining industry, and where the need for retraining for new and developing industries is most marked.

LEGISLATION AFFECTING WORKING CONDITIONS

Students of social history will know that throughout the nineteenth and twentieth centuries there has been a series of Acts passed which control the minimum standards of conditions in which people can be expected to work. Each successive Act has extended the scope of legislation to cover more and more types of factory and workshop, and to extend the range of circumstances and conditions which are under control. The most recent and comprehensive Act is the Factories Act, 1961; this consolidated and systematized the various regulations and controls established in three previous Acts. The Act covered such topics as: (*a*) the cleanliness, temperature, lighting and ventilation of any factory; (*b*) the safety precautions that must be taken in a factory, particularly when dangerous and moving machinery is involved; (*c*) the supply of certain welfare facilities such as washing places, drinking water supplies, rest rooms, and first aid facilities; (*d*) the hours of work of women and young people, and the amount of overtime which can reasonably be requested.

The task of ensuring that the requirements of the Factory Acts are effectively carried out is entrusted to the Factory Inspectorate. Originally created in 1833, Factory Inspectors were until 1940 employed by the Home Office. In that year they were transferred to the newly-formed Safety, Health and Welfare Department of the Ministry of Labour. Inspectors have the right to enter any factory premises by day or by night, without necessarily giving any prior warning of their arrival; they may inspect any part of the works, alone, or accompanied by managerial staff as they prefer, they may question anyone working on the premises, and examine any relevant documents. They aim not only to see that the law is respected, but also to encourage employers to take any initiatives in addition to the minimum requirements of the law which improve working conditions and safety precautions.

But the provisions of the Factories Acts do not cover all employees; a substantial proportion of the employed population work in shops, in offices, on the land and in many other situations not covered by the Factory Acts. For a long time it has been known that many of these employees were working in very unsatisfactory conditions. The Gowers Committee[12] reported in 1949 on conditions in places of non-industrial employment, which included the sorts of work situation mentioned above. Although the recommendations of this Committee were by no means startling, but were on the contrary extremely moderate, and although both the Labour and Conservative Parties accepted the recommendations, successive Governments have been slow to implement them. In 1960 eleven years after the publication of the original Report, an Offices Act was introduced into the House of Commons as a Private Member's Bill, and after some amendments, it passed on to the statute-book. The scope of this Act was widened and extended to cover a substantially larger number of people, including workers in shops, catering establishments, warehouses and railway premises, in the 1963 Offices, Shops and Railway Premises Act. Broadly speaking, this Act implemented many of the Gowers Committee recommendations.

Another important piece of legislation passed very recently, which came into force on 6th July 1964, is the Contracts of Employment Act, 1963. This Act introduces a new and important measure of security because it obliges employers to give to their employees a written statement of the main terms of their employment, that is to say written information about their pay, hours of work, holidays, sick pay, pension rights, and notice. The Act also gives employers and employees rights to minimum periods of notice of termination of employment; an employer is required to give a period of notice which increases with length of service up to a minimum of four weeks' notice if the employee has served the employer for five years or more. Thus, for the first time, every employee has some legally enforceable security against redundancy, a valuable and much-needed safeguard.

It is now claimed that about 80 per cent of the employed population are protected by some legislation; the remaining 20 per cent are notoriously difficult to protect in the same way. Family employees, for example, are felt to be in a special position, and the Government is reluctant to intervene on their behalf. Others work either in such small groups or are so scattered over the country, and work in such a variety of conditions and circumstances, that it is difficult to devise legislation which is precise enough to be effective, and is at the same time sensitive to the differing circumstances. At the same time, as was pointed out in the Parliamentary Debate, there are still some groups of employees who could be safeguarded by legislation without overmuch difficulty, who are at present not covered at all. The years to come may therefore witness further legislation of the kind described.

CONCLUSION

In the introduction to this chapter it was pointed out that most of the industrial services were more properly to be regarded as convenient protective and regulatory devices. Now that the major industrial services have been examined this point of view can be reiterated. With very few exceptions these services are uniformly and centrally organized and offer an impersonal service; true, at some point they all have some consideration for the interests and the happiness of individuals, but this is demonstrated more by ensuring that there is a satisfactory working environment in the first place rather than by providing a highly personalized service to make good the damage done by a faulty environment. This impersonality is reflected in the major administrative unit responsible for these services, the Ministry of Labour. Apart from the Youth Employment Service (in those areas where the Local Education Authority accepts responsibility for the Service) all the industrial services are directly and nationally organized through the regional offices of the Ministry of Labour. This form of systematic and bureaucratic administration is suitable for a system of services which is substantially impersonal and aims at providing as coherent and systematic coverage as possible of a population who share only one characteristic—that of being employed persons.

SUGGESTED READING

HOSELITZ and MOORE, *Industrialization and Society.*
R. M. TITMUSS, *Essays on the Welfare State* (esp. Chapter 6).
SIR GODFREY INCE, *Ministry of Labour and National Service.*
E. M. CARR, *The New Society.*
M. P. CARTER, *Home, School and Work.*
J. A. C. BROWN, *Social Psychology of Industry.*

NOTES

[1] See, for example, W. B. D. Brown's *Exploration in Management* for an account of the celebrated experiment at the Glacier Metal Works. For an examination of a fundamentally different form of industrial organization, with useful comments on its implications for our own system, see the Fabian pamphlet, *Worker's Control in Yugoslavia* by Frederick Singleton and Anthony Topham.

[2] Distribution of Industry Acts, 1945, 1950, 1958.

[3] The first Factory Act is usually considered to be an Act of 1802 concerning the employment of pauper children in cotton mills. The first effective Act was passed in 1833.

[4] A discussion of laissez-faire doctrines, and their curious history can be found in E. H. Carr, *The New Society*, especially Chapters II and III.

[5] Throughout the nineteenth century Acts were passed which concerned factory employment: among the more important are the Acts of 1833, 1847, 1867, 1878, 1901.

Notes

[6] Many reports contributed to the discussion on reconstruction plans—particular mention may be made of the 'Barlow Report', on the *Distribution of the Industrial Population,* Cmd. 6153, the 'Beveridge Report' on *Social Insurance and Allied Services,* Cmd. 6404 (particularly pp. 163–5); the Ince Committee on the *Juvenile Employment Service,* the Tomlinson Committee on the *Rehabilitation and Resettlement of Disabled Persons,* Cmd. 6415.

[7] Among the many Acts passed at this time, may be mentioned the Acts which authorized the Nationalization of key industries, the Disabled Persons (Employment) Act, 1944, and the Employment and Training Act, 1948.

[8] Report of the Committee on the Juvenile Employment Service, H.M.S.O., 1945.

[9] M. P. Hall, *Social Services of Modern England,* p. 239.

[10] *Report of the Committee on Recruitment and Training for the Youth Employment Service,* H.M.S.O., 1951.

[11] See, for example, *Home, School and Work* by M. P. Carter.

[12] *Health, Welfare and Safety in Non-Industrial Employments, House of Employment of Juveniles,* Report by a Committee of Inquiry, H.M.S.O., 1949, Cmd. 7664.

5. SERVICES FOR THE MAINTENANCE AND PROMOTION OF HEALTH

Arthur J. Willcocks

SO far in this book we have been discussing services of a somewhat impersonal nature, but in this chapter we turn to more personal services. Income maintenance and industrial services are very important in their turn, but they probably do not rank in importance for most people with the services for the prevention and cure of illness.

Few people welcome illness; most want to be healthy, to avoid illness and should it occur, to have it speedily and efficiently cured. It is, therefore, no surprise to find the National Health Service among the most popular of our social services.[1] Obviously anything the State does to protect our health, prevent and cure illness is of deep personal concern.

The factors which cause illness are likely to be found either in the environment around the sick person, or within his own physical and psychological framework. The persons and organizations, therefore, who provide us with clean streets, clean water, clean air and all the other important elements of our environment are helping to promote and protect our health. So, too, are those who advise and guide us on our own physical development from birth onwards. But health, or at least the avoidance of illness, implies a certain willingness on the part of everyone to take care and to avoid 'illness-producing' situations. The individual must, for example, go easy on smoking, take regular exercise, eat a proper diet, drive with care, use dangerous machines with circumspection and so on, if he is to avoid many of the illnesses and accidents that bring him in contact with the health services. No democratic country can compel us to take these steps—it is, surely an important right of the individual to take less than proper care and be ill if he so wants. As a community we, in this country, have decided that although we cannot compel people to take care in these ways, we should, nevertheless, provide all proper and efficient curative services for those who fall ill. We therefore offer free (or partially free) health services to all without censure or inquiry—this is the essence of the National Health Service.

In the provision of medical services, as of education and housing to take two other examples, the State is not alone, nor usually is it the pioneer. Most of the services we shall be discussing were provided either by voluntary and charitable bodies or in return for some sort of payment, before the State took on these duties. Hospitals, for example, did not begin with an Act of Parliament or health visitors with a Government policy decision—both pre-date legislative action by many years. (Voluntary hospitals can be traced back as far as 1120 and may be even earlier.) Here we are concerned with the role of the State, because in the main it brings two new or relatively new elements—that of compulsion, especially in some of the public health legislation referred to later, and in its ability to ensure free or reduced cost services for those deemed unable to afford them.

To trace the developments of the role of the State in these services one can best simplify the history by fitting the events[2] into three broad periods of advance—a process which is fraught with danger on purely historical grounds, because social policies have rarely if ever developed logically or neatly in rigidly defined periods. It is possible, however, with this caution in mind, to discern three such periods—the first which was devoted to environmental services and protection, the second devoted to the services protecting the growing human organism, and lastly the period of developing curative services. We want to examine each briefly in turn.

The Industrial Revolution was, in part, responsible for the growing urbanization of the population of this country in the early part of the last century. Social reformers of this time soon became aware of the many health problems associated with urbanization; problems which were emphasized and dramatically highlighted by such events as the cholera epidemics of the 1830's. One of the foremost of such social reformers was that strange and yet fascinating character and Civil Servant, Sir Edwin Chadwick.[3] Closely associated with reforms in the Poor Law system discussed elsewhere in this book, he developed an interest in health matters, and as a result produced his own Report in 1842 on the *Sanitary Conditions of the Labouring Population of Great Britain*. His individual work was, in effect, consolidated by the Report, two years later, of a Royal Commission on the Health of Towns.[4] By putting the blame for such health conditions on the urban environment, the Report led to the Public Health Act of 1848, which created a General Board of Health, and in areas where health conditions were very bad, Local Boards of Health. This administrative structure had something in common with that of the Poor Law system developed in 1834 (see Chapter 3) and, in its insistence on *ad hoc* local boards only in areas of special need, it foreshadowed the structure developed in a different service under the Education Act of 1870.

Although public pressure led to the discontinuation of the General Board in 1853,[5] the State was by now embarked on the provision of a range of duties, clean water, clean streets and similar environmental services, which were to lead on to our current and much fuller Public Health Services. The intervening Acts are too numerous to mention, but one must be singled out, the 1875 Public Health Act, which transferred public health responsibilities from *ad hoc* boards distinct from local government, to local government itself, and made it obligatory on local authorities to appoint duly qualified Medical Officers of Health to control these services. This provision is still operative today and all local authorities have Medical Officers of Health who, under the direction of the councils and their health committees, are responsible for all local government health duties.

These environmental services, in the strict sense, have much in common with many other services developed in the last quarter of the nineteenth century. Local authorities were given powers to build and maintain fever and isolation hospitals, not so much for curative as for environmental purposes, to prevent the spread of disease. It is a comment on the use of these powers and on the subsequent growth of towns, that today many of these hospitals, once built for safety outside the towns, are now overwhelmed by the outward growth of the towns they served. Compulsory notification to Medical Officers of Health of certain types of infectious diseases were among the clauses of Acts in 1889 and 1899. Many Acts from 1876 onwards sought to control the pollution of rivers by sewage disposal, and a series of Adulteration of Food Acts, and the Sale of Food and Drugs Act, 1875, sought control of the quality of the foods and drugs we buy and eat. In a sentence, the aim of the whole of this period was to reduce as far as legislative and administrative action could ensure, the disease-producing and spreading elements of the environment. Largely as a result of these moves, the death-rate for the population as a whole, which in 1851–5 had averaged 22·7 per thousand of the population, fell by the end of the century to 17·7 per thousand. The first period of health advance was proving successful and has continued to greater successes today, when public health legislation, although technically not a part of the National Health Service itself, is clearly an important and indispensable underpinning of the efforts of that Service.

The considerable fall in the total death-rate was not mirrored in another statistical index of mortality—infant mortality. For the newly born infant, the first day, month and year of life are the most dangerous he is likely to encounter. Then he is most subject to a variety of health hazards some related to the environment, but many more related to his own health, feeding and the care and attention lavished on him. The Infant Mortality Rate, which expresses the number of children born alive, but dying in their first year, as a ratio of the total number of children born alive[6] had stood at 156 per thousand in the 1850's and remained almost unchanged to the end of the century. The public health services were having little or no effect on this most dangerous year, and the failure here was further highlighted by the revelation that, of the young men volunteering for army service in the Boer War, nearly 40 per cent were rejected by the Army medical authorities as physically unfit for service mainly because of want of proper physical development, defective vision and teeth, and diseases of the heart. This deplorable state of affairs led to the appointment of an Inter-Departmental Committee on the Physical Deterioration of the Young, and in turn to the Committee's most important Report of 1904.[7] This rather neglected Report can be seen as a blue-print for much of the health legislation that followed.

Among the many services to stem from this Report, one might mention the school meals service (1906), the school medical service (1907) and later, after World War I, the development by local authorities of all those services we now know as maternity and child welfare services.[8] By these and other services the care of the expectant and nursing mothers, the baby, the pre-school age and the school child were progressively developed and improved. The underlying thesis of these services was, and still is, that a person properly cared for in the early years of life is more able to lead a healthy life and withstand disease, especially, of course, the diseases of deficiency and malnutrition. The success that these services have achieved is dramatically recorded in the fall of the infant mortality rate which in 1961 stood at 21 per thousand. Their work is not ended, although in content it may be changing somewhat, for the local authorities which provide these services play a vital part in the overall health services of the nation. Some of these services are now listed with education and others with the National Health Service, but no such administrative division should be allowed to detract from their essential unity of purpose and aim, or from their continuing important function today.

The State, therefore, has taken upon itself the control of as far as possible environmental factors and to give, again as far as possible, everyone a good and healthy start to life. Logically and inevitably there remained only one further step—the care of those who despite the other services fall ill. It had been doing something on these lines in the mental, fever and isolation hospital services of local government. It was also providing curative services within its Poor Law Services for those who were poor and sick. The development of the Poor Law is referred to elsewhere, as is the important discussions of the Royal Commission on the Poor Law about the advantage and disadvantages of separate provision for the pauper—especially in education and health service. All we need note here, is that although the State was no complete novice in the curative field, its provision was limited in outlook and in the patients it served. It widened its outlook and its coverage and, it may be suggested, opened a new period of health advance in the provision of curative medical care under the National Health Insurance Act of 1911.[9]

This Act was a double landmark in social advance; it was the first move in compulsory State social security (discussed Chapter 3) and at the same time, it enabled the provision for the first time of free curative services for people other than paupers. Under its provisions, free general medical practitioner services were made available for those (of the manual worker and lower income groups) who were contributors to the National Health Insurance scheme. The contributor applied to go on the list or panel of a general practitioner (or panel doctor) who was willing to have him and who, in return for an annual payment for each patient on his list, agreed to provide the patient with all necessary medical care within the limits of the skill of a general practitioner. This, therefore, excluded free provision of hospital, specialist and other similar services, although it did provide a free pharmaceutical service, and later, under the complicated provisions of 'additional benefits' through Approved Societies, included in some circumstances free or partially free dental and optical services. This 'panel' service was important historically for two additional reasons; the unwillingness of the medical profession to see this service administered by local government led to the creation of an *ad hoc* local machinery known as Local Insurance Committees[10] (which after 1948 became the Local Executive Councils, discussed below) and the development of the system of remuneration, known as the '*per capita* system', which became, for the doctors, an important safeguard against what they saw as the dangers of a salaried service, and as such had to be continued after 1948. The 'panel' limited only to contributors and not to their dependants, was expanded under the 1946 Act to include everyone.

With the Act of 1911 the State was firmly embarked on our third phase, the provision of curative services, and the inter-war years saw the coverage of the service expand with the extension of National Health Insurance to new groups. In the same period the powers of the local government were widened to include the provision of general hospital services under the Acts of 1929 and 1930.[11] At this time we can also see the beginning of a major change in attitudes towards the treatment and care of mental illness. The change began, in the Mental Treatment Act of 1930, to swing away from mere custody towards treatment and cure. A brief account of this development is to be found in Chapter 10 where the development of services for the handicapped, of whom the mentally ill have come to be seen as a part, are outlined and discussed.

Before examining the National Health Service Act, 1946, for England and Wales (the Act of 1947 for Scotland is not discussed in this book) let us briefly summarize the developments of the various health services before the start of the Second World War. In 1939 there was no one body concerned with health services or policy as a whole, although there was by now a Ministry of Health (created in 1919). Local government had responsibilities in the hospital, and preventive fields, voluntary organizations provided hospital services, the Local Insurance Committees provided the panel services and many other organizations, voluntary and industrial were also concerned. For the citizen, he might, as a contributor be entitled to free panel services, but beyond this he could be guaranteed no free care. Full medical care existed only for those able to pay for it. The services existed but were badly organized, badly distributed in relation to the distribution of population, and above all, their availability was gravely limited by the financial barriers of cost.

The Second World War brought advance in several ways. The creation of an Emergency Medical Service made the consultants, hitherto mainly confined to the teaching and metropolitan hospitals, aware of the poor average standard of hospital provision, and thanks to their pressure the Government accepted in 1941[12] the need for a comprehensive hospital service as one of the major aims of post-war Government policy. The Beveridge Report (see Chapter 3) in 1942 took the Government one step further when, early in 1943 it accepted as part of its policy the planning of a comprehensive national health service, available to all and covering all types of medical care.[13] With this decision, the road to the 1946 Act and to the National Health Service was open, a road which war, shortages and the difficulties of discussion with the many professional and other interest groups concerned, made a long and difficult one.[14]

Before looking at the administrative provisions of the Service, it is necessary to outline some of the principles on which the service is based. With the complicated administration of 1939 in mind, a basic aim of any reform had, almost of necessity, to remedy these defects. Central responsibility for health services was laid on the Minister of Health and he was given the duty 'to promote the establishment in England and Wales of a comprehensive health service designed to secure improvement in the physical and mental health of the people'.[15] The Government, as the representatives of the community thus assumed the clear duty of responsibility for the health services of the nation.

The new Health Service was to provide the full range of medical and associated services for those found to need them. This was not a service limited to specific types of treatment—it was comprehensive in the services it provided. The comprehensiveness of the service is not, however, as complete as the Act implies, there are still many health services, e.g. those in industry and the Armed Forces which are not part of the National Health Service.

The Service was to be available to all, with no limit on grounds of age, income, sex, religion, race, nationality, contributions to national insurance, personal merit or worthiness—none of these were to be taken into account. The only criterion to be used in judging whether or not a person should benefit from the Service was to be a medical one—if a person needs medical care then he or she is entitled to it within the limits of the available services. Here, surely, is one of the great principles which distinguish our National Health Service from those of many other countries—it is a service whose use is decided by the doctor or dentist and not by any administrator or administrative regulation. Today this is so much part of our way of life that the boldness and revolutionary nature of this principle is often forgotten.

The relationship between the doctor and his patient must be, if it is to be successful, essentially one of trust, and to ensure this the patient, within certain limits, must be free to choose the doctor he prefers, and the doctor his patient, and further the doctor must be free to choose the course of treatment that he, as the person ultimately responsible for the patient, feels is right. Without such freedoms, medical care might become less and less adjusted to the requirements of each person and his illness, and more and more the standardized provision of an impersonal service. To prevent such a result, the National Health Service sought to guarantee these freedoms, always of course, within the limits of availability. One should perhaps remember that the Service created overnight no extra doctor, nurse, dentist or hospital bed, nor could it guarantee to the citizen services which did not exist.

What, of course, the Service offered to each and every one was the promise of the appropriate medical care without the patient having to weigh up the question whether or not he could afford the medical treatment necessary. Cost of medical care is no longer an element which the Englishman must consider when he goes to his doctor and in this, perhaps, he is most fortunate compared with his fellows in many other countries. The cost of medical care is always unpredictable—you may visit your doctor suffering from a slight but irritating cough anticipating perhaps that your total bill will include only the cost of the consultation and a bottle of cough medicine. Instead, and quite unexpectedly, you may find yourself being recommended an expensive X-ray, some expensive surgical treatment and possibly even a long stay in a sanatorium; your final bill may be hundreds of times greater than expected. The fear of such a major economic setback is removed from the minds of would-be patients when no question of the cost of medical care actually arises. Again, after so many years of the benefits of the Service, we have sometimes to remind ourselves of this great benefit.

If the patient does not pay, how then is it paid for? Essentially the Service was to be paid for by the community in a variety of ways. Through general taxation (income tax and the like) we make available a sizeable proportion of the cost of the Service, with our contributions to National Insurance funds, additional contributions for health purposes are levied, and as local authority rate-payers we contribute towards the cost of some of the services provided in our locality. Payment for service is made by all, not only by those who are ill. Modifications to the Service since 1946 have slightly dented this principle in that for some services charges are levied, although the percentage of the cost so levied is never great and the more expensive services are still almost entirely free.

One other principle is worth recording. In an earlier paragraph mention was made of the right of the patient to choose his own doctor, but in that context it referred only to doctors working for the Service. It seemed to those who drew up the Act, that it would be wrong to compel people to use the National Health Service so they, therefore, did not make use of the Service obligatory but allowed those who wanted to pay for private treatment (and who, of course, could afford it) to do so. It might have been decided to make these private services completely separate from the Service by compelling doctors to choose one or the other and by refusing private patients access to the nationalized hospitals. Instead, most doctors were accorded the right to engage in both State and private medical services, and, perhaps paradoxically, private patient accommodation and treatment can be provided in the State's hospitals. As a nation, we therefore chose to preserve both State and private systems of medical care.

We may sum up the principles on which the Service is based by saying that commensurate with the desire to provide a comprehensive range of services for all who wanted them, and within the facilities available, we have sought to afford the maximum possible freedom to the patient and to the doctor both in their use and rejection of the Service. Without elements of compulsion which in 1946 were seen as unacceptable, and today are still unacceptable to most people, no other solution was possible.

A Service like the National Health Service is, of course, not just principles, but also an administrative structure, and an immensely complicated structure at that. All that can be attempted here is a brief outline of this structure in the hope that the reader will seek more detail elsewhere.

Final responsibility for the Service rests, as we have already noted, with the Minister of Health, but the actual running of the Service is delegated to a variety of organizations. Most of these are accorded a considerable measure of independence of operation subject always to the systems of financial control operated by the Ministry of Health and the Treasury. Not only does the Service involve large administrative organizations to control it, it also covers such a variety of professions and skills that no one organization can have the necessary knowledge or technical ability to see the difficulties and problems of each of these specialities. For the express purpose, therefore, of providing advice to the Minister on these general and specialized matters, the Act created a Central Health Services Council composed of 41 members representing a wide range of specialized interests in the Service.[16] In addition there are a series of specialized Standing Advisory Committees to give advice on the more specialized topics. Both these advisory services give advice when asked by the Minister but can initiate advice when they see fit; their advice is, except in rare cases, published so that the public and Parliament can come to their own conclusions about the Minister's decisions on the advice tendered to him. These bodies enable the many skilled people working in the Service to have some forum for their special problems before the Minister, and the public.

For administrative purposes the Service is divided into three more or less separate sections, the hospitals, the domiciliary services and the local authority services. In 1946 hospitals were owned either by local authority or by voluntary organizations and

97

earlier attempts[17] to achieve some co-ordination between them failed. The planners of the Service felt that if we were to have an efficient and up-to-date hospital service, all hospitals must work together (to avoid competition and deficiencies) within some unified plan. To this end the ownership of most hospitals was transferred to the State and because it was felt that the areas of local authorities were too small and their resources too limited to provide a proper service, a relatively new administrative system was created. The country was divided up into fourteen (later fifteen) regions each centred medically if not geographically on a medical teaching hospital, and a Regional Hospital Board of some twenty to thirty members was appointed by the Minister of Health to 'guide and control the planning, development and conduct of the services in their area'. The members of the Boards, who were given power to create the necessary administration to carry out these tasks, were to be paid no salary and only repaid any expenses or time lost as a result of their service. The Boards, in turn, were to appoint Hospital Management Committees, to be responsible for the day-to-day administration of large hospitals or groups of hospitals. Not far short of four hundred of these were created. Again the members were appointed and unpaid. Whilst geographically part of the regional system, medical teaching hospitals in England and Wales (but not in the later Scottish version of the Service) were given separate administrative control only tenuously related to the Board.

This Service, which was created to provide hospital and specialist services is, therefore, a two-tiered *ad hoc* system, based on regional areas and not on the traditional local government areas, appointed and not elected, and depending almost wholly on the Ministry of Health for its finance. No compulsory charge (except in certain rare instances) is levied on the patient using these services.

The second of the three sections of the Service, is the direct descendant of the Local Insurance Committees created by the National Health Insurance Act, 1911. Local Executive Councils are appointed for almost all areas of county council and county borough councils, and the members represent the professions working in the Service, the local authority's health services and a few other people without such direct affiliations. The use of the word 'executive' in the title suggests, quite rightly, that these bodies have less administrative powers than those in the hospital world. They do not directly control their services, but merely make the services known to the public, arrange for the payment of those in the services and have certain disciplinary functions. They are, in truth, mainly executive and never planning authorities. The services provided include first and foremost the general practitioner medical service—the family doctor service. Everyone is guaranteed (the only guarantee under the Act) the services of a general practitioner if they so wish.[18] It is the duty of the Council to publish lists of doctors and where necessary to put patients in contact with the doctors. With the help of a central committee, the Medical Practices Committee, they share some responsibility for achieving a distribution of doctors more in relation to the distribution of population.[19] It is the second duty of the Council to maintain lists of general practitioners, specially qualified for the work, who are willing to provide domiciliary care of expectant mothers up to and just after confinement. (This is one of the three administrative solutions designed to provide care for the expectant mother and her offspring.)

The Executive Councils have similar duties in relation to the provision of general dental services. The citizen is not guaranteed a dentist but can try to obtain the services of any dentist on the list of the Council. The work of the dentist, unlike that of many of the other professional people in the services is centrally controlled in that, without the prior permission of the Dental Estimates Board, no dentist can begin on the free, or partially free dental treatment afforded by the Service, unless the work be of an emergency or minor character. The Council also maintains lists of qualified pharmacists prepared to dispense the prescriptions of general practitioner services, most of these services are provided to the patient at some compulsory charge, the extent and nature of the charge varying from service to service. The remainder of the cost of these services are provided by the central government.

Local Executive Councils are responsible (in all the services listed) for the remuneration of the professionals concerned. In each case the remuneration is intended to cover not only the 'income' element but also the expenses and costs incurred in providing the services. The Executive Council does not provide facilities of any kind, the professional being expected to pay for all the necessary equipment, facilities, and premises from his remuneration. In no case, therefore, is the remuneration a salary—in all except the general practitioner service, the payment is a fee for each item of service performed. For the doctor, the payment represents an annual fee for each person on the doctor's list, irrespective of what, if any, services the patient receives. The Executive Council have one other important duty—the receiving and hearing of complaints against the professionals and where sufficiently serious, the offending doctor, dentist, pharmacist, or optician may be cautioned or fined. In extremely serious cases, the decision is referred to a central body, the National Health Service Tribunal, who also can remove the professional from the list of those providing services—i.e. in colloquial terms to 'sack' them. This should be distinguished from the disciplinary machinery of the professional bodies like the General Medical Council who can take away the right to be a doctor.

The first two categories discussed are therefore administered under an *ad hoc* system specially created with appointed rather than elected members in control. For the third service, the well-tried facilities of the system of elected local authorities have been used. The two major types of local authority, the county and the county borough, have been given a range of duties under the Act. The services which they *must* provide include the maternity and child welfare services already discussed, a domiciliary midwifery service, a home nursing service, vaccination and immunization for those who want it (although since 1946 neither are any longer compulsory) and an ambulance service. They *may* also provide health centres, preventive and after-care services and home helps. In something of a different category and now covered by separate and more recent legislation, the local authorities are responsible for providing a domiciliary mental health service covering a wide variety of provisions and facilities. The financing of these services is made up partly by grants[20] from the central government, partly from the local authority's own rates and partly from charges levied on the users.

There is, therefore, considerable truth in the allegation often made about the National Health Service than it is three services rather than one. Such a system has led to many difficulties, to some overlapping, competition and in some cases to wastage.

Since 5th July 1948, people in England and Wales have enjoyed the benefits of a comprehensive and largely free National Health

Service. How has it developed and what are its problems? To answer these questions properly demands another book, but one or two general points can be made. In the first place it has largely removed the so-called economic barrier to medical care—it has made a health service, of a good if not first-class kind, available to all who need it and want to use it. This, surely, must be its greatest achievement.

Financially, the Service has proved much more costly than was expected. The cost of the Service in 1961–6 was over £920 millions, a figure which contrasts very starkly with the early estimates of an annual cost of about £180 millions. Soaring costs in the first 21 months of the Service led to attempts by successive Chancellors of the Exchequer to restrict the cost below 'ceiling' figures. This move failed and continuing concern over the cost led to the appointment of the Guillebaud Committee in 1953[21]. Its Report in 1956 represents a vital text for anyone studying the National Health Service. Recent attempts to control costs have included more charges being levied on the patient and much greater emphasis on administrative efficiency and tighter financial control. Value for money in medicine is increasingly a crucial issue in the Service. Financially, too, the preponderance in the cost of the hospital service has caused anxiety, as has the relatively low and modest rate of capital development here and in the other services. As a nation, we have not until recently been prepared to spend enough on our Service to keep it abreast of modern developments.

In 1962, the Ministry of Health published its ten-year plan[22] for hospitals which envisages spending some £500 millions in the following ten years to provide 90 new hospitals and 134 substantially rebuilt hospitals. This was followed in 1963[23] by a similar plan (or rather collection of plans for local authorities) for the health and welfare services of local government.

Despite obvious deficiencies and defects the fact remains that in Britain everyone is assured of the services of a general practitioner, hospital care when needed (although often only after a long wait) and there is available all the ancillary services associated with the doctor. On the other hand, there are criticisms of the Service, for example, that it has become more impersonal in its dealings with the patient, and that he is being processed rather than treated.

For those who work in the Service, it has brought anxious problems of the relationship between professional freedom and

State control, it has raised far too often irritating and frustrating issues of remuneration.[24] But above all perhaps, and especially for some groups, e.g. dentists, nurses and now doctors, it has raised the question of shortage of numbers. It has not yet solved the problem of how to plan (in sufficient time) for the future needs of many of the groups which need long and costly systems of training.

In any balance sheet, the National Health Service has a favourable balance—it has benefitted the society it services—but it is yet far from perfect and many of its problems are only now being seriously considered and remedies sought.

FURTHER READING

B. ABEL-SMITH, *The Hospitals* 1800–1948.
A. LINDSEY, *Socialized Medicine in England and Wales.*
H. ECKSTEIN, *English Health Service.*
C. F. BROCKINGTON, *A Short History of Public Health.*
R. M. TITMUSS, *Problems of Social Policy.*
M. SUSSER and W. WATSON, *Sociology in Medicine.*
Sociological Review: Monograph No. 5, Sociology and Medicine.
H.M.S.O.
Annual Reports of the Minister of Health.
Annual Reports of the Central Health Services Council.
Report of the Committee on the Cost of the National Health Service, Cmd. 9663.
Report of the Royal Commission on Doctors and Dentists Remuneration, Cmd. 939.

As a large and costly Service, the National Health Service is frequently the subject of comment and discussion by many organizations. The student is referred to the many articles, leaflets and booklets appearing from time to time from political parties, professional groups and others. In addition to the professional journals covering specialized aspects of the Service, one journal will well repay study, *Medical Care,* which was first published in 1963.

The reader, interested in current research in the National Health Service, should consult the many and excellent reports of the Nuffield Provincial Hospitals Trust.

NOTES

[1] Of 734 mothers asked 'which one of six main social services has helped your family most?' 82 per cent replied that it was the National Health Service. Cf. P.E.P., *Family Needs and the Social Services*, p. 35 ff.

[2] See C. Frazer Brockington, *A Short History of Public Health.*

[3] See S. E. Finer, *The Life and Times of Edwin Chadwick.*

Notes

[4] *Report of Royal Commission on the Health of Towns,* 1844.

[5] E.g. *The Times* of 1854 said, 'We prefer to take our chance of cholera and the rest rather than be bullied into health.' The reader might consider how far, if at all, the State has the right to 'bully' us into health.

[6] E.g. If, of 500 babies born alive, only 470 were still alive at the end of their first year then the Infant Mortality Rate would be 60 per 1000.

[7] *Inter-Departmental Committee on the Physical Deterioration of the Young,* Cmd. 2175, 1904.

[8] An Act of 1918 made this a responsibility of local government, although an Association of Maternal and Child Welfare Centres had been formed as early as 1906.

[9] For an interesting account of the framing of this piece of legislation and the political debates it created, see W. J. Braithwaite, *Lloyd George's Ambulance Wagon.*

[10] See Braithwaite, op. cit.

[11] Local Government Act, 1929 and Poor Law, 1930. The 1929 Act widened and strengthened powers (previously almost unused and included in the Public Health Act, 1875) for the provision of local authority hospitals.

[12] The Government also commissioned a survey of hospital provision to be undertaken in collaboration with the Nuffield Provincial Hospitals Trust. The findings of these surveys were published in 1945 under the titles 'Hospital Survey—Hospital Services in——Area'. In all ten were published and provide a sad commentary on then existing hospital provision.

[13] See House of Commons Official Report, Vol. 386, c16 ff., 18th February 1943.

[14] For a brief account see A. J. Willcocks, 'A Process of Erosion?', *Sociological Review Monograph, No. 5, Sociology and Medicine.*

[15] The National Health Service Act, 1946, s.1.

[16] Ibid., s.2 and First Schedule.

[17] See Willcocks, op. cit.

[18] It is variously estimated that 95–97 percent of the population exercise this option.

[19] For accounts of the work of this Committee, see the Annual Reports of the Ministry of Health. The Committee cannot compel a doctor to practise in any particular area, but it can forbid him practising in areas which they consider have enough doctors.

[20] Grants for this purpose are included in the 'General Grant'.

[21] *Report of the Committee of Enquiry into the Cost of the National Health Service,* Cmd. 9663. The Committee commissioned additional studies and the reader is referred especially to B. Abel-Smith and R. M. Titmuss, *The Cost of the National Health Service.*

[22] *A Hospital Plan for England and Wales,* Cmd. 1604.

[23] *Health and Welfare—The Development of Community Care,* Cmd. 1973.

[24] The reader is referred to H. Eckstein, *Pressure Group Politics—the Case of the B.M.A.* and the *Report of the Royal Commission on the Remuneration of Doctors and Dentists,* Cmd. 939.

6. SOCIAL POLICY AND THE PHYSICAL ENVIRONMENT

Arthur J. Willcocks

THE Health Services provide those who are ill with services of a very personal and often intimate nature. It is a service which is very much based on the face-to-face contact of those who provide it and those who receive it, and as such it can, naturally, lay strong claims to being a social service. It is, therefore, perhaps natural to designate the provision of services by one person or group to another as a social service, and at the same time, to question how far the provision of a commodity rather than a service can be called a social service. It seems clear that the provision of a commodity either at cost or at a reduced price is not necessarily a social service; grocers, soap manufacturers and the rest do just that. It can be argued, therefore, that the provision of houses is simply an economic function and not a social service or a part of social policy. On the other hand it may equally well be argued that if housing is provided by the community for those adjudged to be in some sort of need then it might be termed a social service and part of social policy. The inclusion of this chapter on the housing and planning services assumes that we are here concerned with elements of social policy, if not with social services.

The need for housing may be interpreted in two broad but different ways. In the first place, families in need of housing may be taken to be those who are unable to find any kind of accommodation, primarily because sufficient numbers of adequately-sized houses do not exist. For any organization seeking to meet need in this sense, the main task must be to provide enough houses for all who need them. Need for housing can, however, be interpreted in a second way—namely that some families are unable to afford the purchase price or rent of available, but otherwise suitable housing. To meet housing needs interpreted in this way, the organizations concerned must either provide accommodation at prices or rents within the means of the families in need, or alternatively, as in some European[1] countries, make loans or grants available to enable these families to purchase or rent existing accommodation. Housing legislation in this country, as we shall see, has tended to be somewhat ambivalent about which of these two types of need it is seeking to meet.

There are three main methods by which a modern family can get houseroom; they may purchase their own house, they may rent accommodation from a private landlord or they may seek to rent a house from the local council. In the last century when there were no council houses, about 90 per cent of the population rented accommodation from private landlords, and the remainder, usually the wealthier people, owned the house they lived in. By 1963, the situation has changed quite markedly with a growing proportion of the population now able to own their own houses, and the newest tenure group, local council housing is of growing numerical importance as the table shows:

TABLE I. TENURE OF DWELLINGS—1958 AND 1961[2]

	1958	1961
Owns, or is buying	39%	41%
Rents from local authority	20%	25%
Rents from private landlord	37%	33%
Other	4%	1%
	100%	100%

Affluence and changing methods of financing house purchase account for the rise of owner occupation, and housing legislation and policy for the growth of council tenancies. Unlike many European countries, housing associations have made no significant contribution to the quantative provision of houses in this country;[3] on the other hand their pioneer efforts in the late nineteenth century showed it was possible to provide cheap yet reasonable accommodation for the lower income groups.

Before examining the history of housing legislation, two general points must be made. The first is that in using the word 'houses' we are not speaking of a standard commodity. Houses vary in many ways; in size, number and arrangement of rooms, in site and surroundings, in structure as detached, semi-detached or terraced, as whole buildings or part-buildings, in tenure, in price and in quality and standard. Although, in one sense, a dwelling must always provide potential shelter for those without accommodation, families have varying needs in terms of all the factors listed, a fact which must be borne in mind in all discussions about housing and housing needs.

The second point is that 'the housing problem' is, in reality, two separate problems. One is the problem of numbers, the provision of sufficient houses for all to have a dwelling of some kind, and this is the 'quantitative' problem. The other is a 'qualitative' problem; that of ensuring that the housing that exists is of the right quality and standard to suit the needs of families of today and this may well mean that the Government must face such issues as what to do with houses so bad in standard and condition as to be classed as 'slums', and with other less bad but still sub-standard houses. As we shall see, Government policy in this country has been concerned at different times with both these problems.

In the strict sense, the interest of the State in housing began in a very tentative way with the public health legislation discussed in Chapter 5. Houses are very much part of the environment, and the drive for protection against environmental health hazards inevitably impinged on housing policy. The first formal interest can be noted in two Acts in 1851, the Common Lodging Houses Act and the Labouring Class Lodging Houses Act, which together made some attempt at regulation. The powers of the Local Boards of Health were further enlarged by the Sanitary Act, 1866, with further powers being added by a series of Acts beginning with the Citizens and Labourers Dwelling Act, 1868 (the Torrens Act).[4] The principles behind these Acts were that if an owner did not keep his house in proper condition, then the State had the right to compel him to do so, and further that if his houses became too dilapidated then all that could be done was to demolish them, compulsorily if necessary.

From these early Acts the powers, first of Local Boards of Health and later of local authorities to regulate, to compel the removal of nuisances and in the last resort to demolish, were steadily expanded. By the end of the century, therefore, the main emphasis of housing legislation could be said to be regulatory, and the mainspring of concern in this field, the health of the public.

Such legislation, of course, left the field of house building free for the owner-occupier, the private landlord and to a much lesser extent, the housing association. It was assumed, that, with some minor exceptions, these groups would provide sufficient houses, and that all the State need do was to supervise the quality of building. This limited role for the State came, however, to be increasingly questioned in the early years of this century and especially after the First World War. Investment in housing as a landlord had been a profitable and safe use of capital—'as safe as houses' was more than a trite cliché, but wider and more profitable investments were becoming increasingly possible, and the return on capital in housing less and less satisfactory. The restriction and control of rents, forced on the Government by rising prices in the First World War and maintained without major change until 1957, made landlordism less and less of an attractive proposition. Houses built for private renting began to decline in numbers quite seriously. Further the virtual cessation of house-building during the war, coupled with the sudden rise in the number of families looking for accommodation when the war was over, posed an urgent numerical problem. There were not enough houses; the need was for more houses quickly, and a new source was required. By an Act of 1919[5] the Government sought a solution, by giving powers to local authorities (except for counties and parishes) to build houses for those in need of accommodation. There was no suggestion, at this time, that the houses built under the Act were only for those unable to afford other types of accommodation.

To give local authorities power to build houses, as the 1919 Act did, is to solve only part of the problem. The cost of building a house is very considerable, representing probably four or more times as much as the annual earnings of an average manual worker.[6] For the private person, expenditure of this kind is rarely possible out of current resources; rather he must borrow the money for this purpose (mortgage) and repay it over a period of years. For the public authority, too, a similar (if not quite so pressing) need exists to spread the cost. This need was, in 1919, reinforced by the long tradition of similar borrowing to pay for other capital items, and by the feeling that, as generations other than the current one, would benefit from the houses, they too should share something of the burden of their costs. Because local authorities might have been discouraged from building houses by the cost, the Government felt it necessary to provide a subsidy as something of an incentive. This subsidy, which was in the form of meeting the losses on local authority house-building activities, was subsequently changed to a fixed amount per annum per house, and has remained since then as an essential part of housing policy. It has been used at various times to encourage building, to direct it to special needs or groups, or to reduce the amount of building. Today, the subsidy is seen by many people as a means of reducing the cost of houses to local authorities and this, in turn, making possible lower rents than would otherwise be possible. For many years after the Second World War in support of this view, local authorities had to add subsidies of their own from the rates, but since 1961[7] this is no longer obligatory for the houses they build.

To return to 1919, this Act was aimed at those in need of housing, in contrast to the next major Act, in 1923, which directed that local authority houses be provided only for those of the working classes. Here was an expression of a principle often discussed today, that the social services are, or should be, directed primarily or mainly to the poorer sections of the community. The reader will find current expressions of this view in many writings on the social services.

It is, perhaps, idealistic to expect too much mixing of the social classes in one area (historically they have always tended to separate geographically), but this Act, and the concurrent expansion of private building for owner occupation had the effect of strengthening this geographical separation. Any cursory survey of development in this period, will show the local authority estates kept apart from similar developments for the private owner. Both were however united in their main aims, to build as many houses as possible with, apparently, little or no regard to the community needs for shops, public-houses, parks and the rest.

The Act of 1919[8] resulted over the following four or five years, in the building by local authorities of about 170,000 houses in England and Wales. The next period of housing legislation lasting from the Act of 1923 to about 1933 produced 580,000 council houses, a total post-first-war addition by local government of 750,000 houses. (This impressive figure has to be viewed against the total number of houses in England and Wales in 1934 of about

10·1 millions.) This sizeable increase to housing stock that local government provided together with 420,000 privately built houses in the same period, led the Government of the day to feel that the numerical problem was nearing solution and that attention ought to be turned instead to the quality of existing houses and especially to the problem of the slums. By an Act of 1930, which was largely nullified until the mid-1930's by depression[9] and subsequent economies in Government expenditure, local authorities were given powers to acquire and demolish houses in the worst conditions, the slums, and to build houses to rehouse those displaced. As a result, in 1933, the building of houses by local authorities for those in need virtually ceased and the emphasis switched to taking out of use old houses and replacing them with new ones.

This drive for slum clearance was, and still is, one of immense importance and it poses one of the basic issues of housing, and of planning. Like all capital goods, a house eventually wears out and needs replacing, but in times of shortage even a poor house is better than none at all and it therefore maintains some economic value. It was, and still is a problem for a democratic country to ensure that these old houses cease to be used and that people living in them are afforded the opportunity of better housing. Because of the newness of much council housing, most of the old houses are inevitably privately rented or less often owned, but as slum clearance proceeds they are being replaced by council housing. If this trend is to continue, then more and more people will become council tenants, but if it is not to be allowed to continue, the problem of compelling the owner or private landlord to demolish and replace old housing must be faced. This today is one of the major housing issues and if linked with similar problems for other less dilapidated houses, especially in town centres, is known as 'urban redevelopment'. The need for this 'urban redevelopment'[10] is one of the basic problems and challenges for local government today.

To return to our history, the outbreak of war in 1939 brought to a premature end the slum-clearance programmes for nearly fifteen years, and at the same time, the widespread destruction of houses by enemy bombing coupled with the cessation of house-building and the increase in population and its mobility, led to a severe housing problem at the end of the war. Thoughts of doing something about old houses, had to be dropped in favour of building as many extra houses as possible. The immediate reaction was the so-called 'pre-fab' building programme whereby nearly a quarter of a million pre-fabricated temporary dwelling units were made available for those in the most urgent need. Many, if not most, of these 'temporary' building still remain and are inhabited in 1964.

Although, in the immediate post-war period, the embargo on building houses only for the working classes was not legislatively abolished until 1949,[11] little official notice was taken of it and local authorities were urged to build for those in need irrespective of social class. Until such time as the supply of scarce building materials and the shortage of building labour improved, and because of the competing demands for these scarce resources from factory, road, school and other building programmes, the building of houses was limited to local authority building for those in need.[12] The number each authority could build was rigidly controlled by the Ministry of Health, and private building was only possible by licence, very few indeed being issued.[13]

As the situation eased in the early 1950's, an effort was made to increase the number of houses built. Private enterprise was gradually allowed more freedom until eventually all building controls were removed, and local authorities, far from being limited, were actively encouraged by much more generous subsidies from the Government. Numbers became all-important, but already by the middle 1950's the emphasis was beginning to change until today, 1964, as far as local authority building is concerned little effort is being made to add more houses. Instead a twin approach to the qualitative programme is under way.

In the first place, local authorities were gradually diverted into slum-clearance programmes, a diversion achieved mainly by a variation in the subsidy system and by direct Government controls. In 1955 the local authorities began to take up the problem they had been forced to drop in 1939, but by now the problem was much worse and more houses were, year by year, descending to the level of slums. By the early 1960's slum clearance was seen as the major part of local authority work in this field, and by 1962, about 65,000 houses[15] per annum were being demolished and their inhabitants rehoused.

At the same time, an attack was developing on that group of

houses which, although not slums, were not acceptable by the standards of the 1960's. Where such houses could be modernized and were likely to have many more years life, a new technique was tried. Improvement[16] and later standard grants[17] were offered by local authorities, on behalf of the Government, to enable their facilities to be modernized. It was hoped that these grants would encourage landlords and owners to take the opportunity to bring their houses up to some more acceptable standard. In simple numerical terms, the response has not been as great as expected, e.g. in 1962 110,000 such grants were made.[18]

TABLE 2. PERMANENT HOUSES COMPLETED IN SELECTED YEARS
—ENGLAND AND WALES

		'000s			
	Built by	*Housing*	*Government*	*Private*	
Year	*Local Authorities*	*Associations*	*Departments*	*Builders*	*Total*
1946	21	–	–	30	51
1948	171	2	3	31	206
1951	142	2	7	21	172
1954	200	15	7	88	309
1957	138	2	6	123	269
1960	103	2	2	162	269
1962	105	2	5	167	279

(Source: Annual Reports of Ministry of Housing and Local Government (and its earlier titles). The figures are rounded and do not, therefore, always total exactly.)[14]

A different approach to the same problem was the reason behind one of the most bitterly contested Acts of the 1950's, the Rent Act, 1957. The First World War had faced the Government of the day with the problems of rapidly rising private rents and they had responded by freezing rents for the duration of that war. This temporary measure was still in force in 1957, having been repeatedly extended by ever more and more complicated and often incomprehensible legislation.[19] As a result the rents charged to many private tenants in the 1950's were totally unrealistic in the monetary values of the time, tenants were unwilling to leave overlarge accommodation and lose the benefits of rent restriction, and landlords were getting little or no return on their investment, certainly too little to enable them to keep their properties in repair and up to date, and too little to encourage fresh capital into this form of investment. The aim of the Government in the 1957 Act was to allow rents to rise to encourage or compel more mobility among tenants, to tie such rent increases to improvement to the property thereby encouraging landlords to modernize, and by making landlordism more profitable, to encourage more capital into this type of housing provision. Improvements in both quality and quantity were sought. As might be expected with so contentious a piece of legislation, the results are hard to evaluate objectively, but such studies as have been made, as for example by the Government itself,[20] suggest that both the Government has been disappointed in some of its achievements and the Opposition proved false in some of their wilder and gloomier predictions. Here, however, we must simply record it as one part of the attack on sub-standard housing.

Before leaving this historical survey to discuss the administrative structure of the housing services, the latest major Act, in 1961, must be mentioned. This Act sought to recast the system of subsidies to local authorities relating them for the first time (and in the limited range of housing to which they now apply) to the financial resources of the individual local authorities and their ability to support needed housing programmes. Secondly the Act gave a belated recognition of the part housing associations might play in providing houses to rent. A fund of £25,000,000[21] was set aside to provide loans to non-profit making housing associations who provide housing to rent at economic cost, i.e. at unsubsidized rents. It was hoped that this relatively small sum would serve to 'prime the pump' and to get capital flowing back into the provision of housing to rent.

Unlike most of the social services discussed in this book, the State is far from being the majority provider of houses, as we have already seen. Central responsibility for this role as minority provider rests with the Ministry of Housing and Local Government, a Ministry which has changed its name and range of functions on several occasions since 1945. Originally part of the Ministry of Health[22] it was separated from the Ministry and has gradually collected the functions of planning and the general oversight of local government. Left with the Ministry of Health are some of the public health elements of housing policy. In housing policy, the Ministry of Housing and Local Government is responsible for general oversight and control of the work of local authorities, but it is not the initiator of the actual provision of houses. This is the duty of local authorities, all of whom, except counties and parishes, have housing duties. Unlike children's, educational and health services, the local authorities are not obliged to appoint special chief officers or committees, and as a result the pattern of local administration is extremely varied. Generalizations about local authority housing services are, therefore, extremely risky and subject to many conditional statements.

With this limitation in mind, we can now discuss some of the local issues in housing and first and foremost, the role of local government in the housing services. Some people are inclined to argue that the duty of the local authority is to provide houses only for those who cannot afford other forms of tenure. This is, in a sense, the working-class restriction of earlier legislation in a new guise (although one should note that private renting may be cheaper than local authority renting though often at a lower standard). Others say that it is the duty of the local authority to house those in need, whether by virtue of a shortage of houses or because their houses are being demolished. For a further group, the work of the local authority is seen as much the same as any landlord and it should be their task to manage their property economically. Finally, there are those who believe that the final aim of local authority housing is nothing less than all houses—that council housing should become the one and only, or at the least the main tenure available.

Some of these issues are relevant to the policy adopted by an individual local authority. Their rental policy, for example, will depend in part on their conception of their duty—to provide a social service for those in need, or to run an economic business. For those who cannot afford the rents charged by the local authority, the council must face the issue as to whether or not they should be subsidized and if so, by whom. It is possible to subsidize housing from local rates, that is from the wider community of the ratepayers, or it is possible to argue that the tenants as a whole should pay and that to make up for those who cannot pay the full amount, others should pay more. To use the analogy of the railways, either the community as a whole subsidizes the uneconomical branch lines, or else the travellers on the profitable main lines must do so. Answers to these questions will depend, to some extent at least, on the political party deciding housing policy.

As a landlord, often on a very large scale, the local authority faces the problems of all landlords, the collection of rents, dealing with defaulters, maintaining its property in good order and so on. But local authorities face two additional problems which must be discussed briefly, the selection of tenants and their welfare.

If one is letting off a part of one's house as a flat, an advertisement will no doubt produce many applicants. Most landlords in this situation presumably use hunch or some other criteria to decide between them. These private choices are not likely to have public repercussions, but for the local authority, political repercussions (especially when favouritism or jumping the queue is suspected) are never far removed from the work of the housing department. Hunch will not do, and instead the local authority must find some objective, or apparently objective criteria which it will use to pick from among its applicants. But the need for a house may be based on a variety of facts, a large family in a small flat, ill health, insanitary conditions and so on, and a major problem that has faced local housing departments has been to rate these factors in terms of priorities. How, for example, does one decide between a family with three young children newly moved into the area and living in one room, and the not so young married couple with no children who have been waiting for a council house (and a family) for ten years? Most local authorities have reduced these factors to points scales and each applicant is allotted a number of points on the basis of his housing situation. This system has the appearance of objectivity and avoids suggestions of political favouritism. It does not however disguise the fact that many of the harder pressed local authorities have to find a statistical wisdom of Solomon to decide between varieties of housing need.

The other major question which falls especially to the public rather than the private landlord is the welfare of his tenants.[23] For the average private landlord his responsibility for the tenant, and his duties towards him are limited to the property, its maintenance and to the regular payment of rent. There are, however people who are convinced that the local authority, as a landlord, has duties beyond this. For all, or at least most of their tenants, the local authority, it is claimed, should have some regard for their social and personal problems. Many local authorities attempt to do this by employing special welfare workers whose job it is to help the tenants when help of this kind is needed. This view is criticised by other commentators on the grounds that, in the first place the landlord is concerned only with the property and not directly with the tenants, and that secondly the tenants of local councils are much the same as many families who are not council tenants and that such services as are needed are provided by other organizations for all, whether tenants or not. Whatever view is held, there is agreement that the local authority may have certain welfare responsibilities for 'problem families'[24] whom they often have to house because no one else will, but that for the rest of the tenants the answer will depend on whether or not they are seen as ordinary families, or as a specially selected group of families more likely to need help.

These, then, are some of the issues which concern local authorities in their housing duties. But housing is, of course, only part of a much wider issue, that of the planning of our towns and countryside. When a house is built, land is put to one of many possible uses—it could have been used instead for part of a park, for farmland, for industrial development, for a road, for a school and so on. There are, clearly, many possible uses for land and in previous centuries it has been the most economically profitable use that has prevailed. The profitable use of the land, however, may not be that best suited to the health of the community or to its needs for schools, and roads none of which are 'profitable'. This is not to claim that the private development of land has been completely unresponsive to the wider needs of the community. There have been examples of attempts to 'plan' the environment with the general well-being of the community in mind. The names of people such as Robert Owen, George Cadbury, Ebeneezer Howard and others spring to mind and one recalls the attempts of late nineteenth-century Birmingham to plan its city centre as a coherent whole. But it is not until the twentieth century, and despite earlier Acts of limited importance, not really until after the Second World War that the use of land to suit community needs as a whole became an important duty of local government.

A series of Reports[25] during the war had explored the need for, and some of the problems of town and country planning, and their findings were reinforced by the need for planning whole city centres in the heavily bombed towns. For towns like Plymouth, Coventry and Exeter, the widespread destruction gave a unique opportunity for a fresh start, and legislatively, this need was recognized in an Act of 1944. But this was a relatively rare situation and what was seen to be needed was a framework for long-term planning and control of the use of land.

The Town and Country Planning Act, 1947 (although considerably amended on its financial provisions for compensation in compulsory purchase and in loss of development value), remains the basis of modern planning. Under this Act county and county borough councils were instructed to prepare 'Development Plans' for their areas, setting out the long-term plans for the use of land. Each piece of land was 'zoned' for one of the many alternative uses of land and once the Plan had been approved by the Ministry of Town and Country Planning (now the Ministry of Housing and Local Government) it became the framework of planning control. Each new building or addition and each change in the use of land, became subject to control by local authorities, whose permission had first to be obtained. The local authorities can only give permission where such developments or changes do not contradict the Development Plan. By this process, a slow and painful move began towards sorting out the use of land on some rational and socially needed basis. It is important to note that this is a form of negative rather than positive control—negative in the sense that all the local authority can do is to approve or reject, it cannot compel development to take place. (Except, of course, when it is itself, the developer, as many authorities now are in their town centres.)

The town and country planning authorities are therefore seeking the socially desirable use of land by the gradual transformation of the areas in which we live and work. But planning is more than this; it has to meet the demands of expanding towns for more space and of the town-dweller to enjoy the countryside.[26] Under the New Towns Act, 1946,[27] and the Town Development Act, 1952, provision is made for planning completely new towns or the expansion of small existing towns. The growing population of the heavily populated towns have, to a certain extent, been 'decanted' into these new or expanded towns, each with, it is hoped, sufficient industry and other employment to provide work for all or most of its inhabitants. This, it was intended, was to stop the ever outward expansion of existing towns, the increasingly longer journeys to work, and, at the same time, to preserve something of the countryside from the devouring appetite of the house-builders.

Social Policy and the Physical Environment

Much could be written about these attempts to plan a 'better environment' but, as any study of the Reports of the Ministry of Housing and Local Government or of local conditions will show, many problems remain. The attempt to contain urban growth by constricting towns within 'green belts' is increasingly under pressure, the regional movements of population still pose serious problems in the receiving areas and the growth of the number of motor cars has thrown a new and very difficult ingredient into the planners' problems. Transport is increasingly receiving public attention—the building of motorways and the Buchanan Report[28] on one side and the delining use of railways and the Beeching Report[29] on the other are both symptoms of this attention. The regional movements of population have been recently studied officially in the *South East Study*.[30] All in all we may justifiably say that the many issues of town and country planning are among the most serious 'social issues' facing central and local government in the 1960's.

The needs of a family for a house are expressed not only in terms of the need for a roof, but also for land on which to put it, and for the provision of the many needed communal facilities of shops, libraries and the rest. Those who have to be housed need a healthy environment, relatively easy access to work, to shops and to schools, and at the same time, the chance to enjoy, if they feel so inclined, the countryside. All these needs and many more are sought by the activities of our housing and town and county planning services.

FURTHER READING

Housing
H. ASHWORTH, *Housing in Great Britain.*
S. ALDERSON, *Housing,* Britain in the Sixties series.
M. BOWLEY, *Housing and the State.*
J. B. CULLINGWORTH, *Housing Needs and Planning Policy.*
    Housing in Transition.
D. V. DONNISON, *Housing Policy Since the War.*
    et al., *Housing Since the Rent Act.*

Planning
W. ASHWORTH, *Genesis of Modern British Town Planning.*
P. SELF, *Cities in Flood.*

Notes

There are, in addition, many studies of life on housing estates from a sociological point of view. For more technical literature on planning, the reader is referred to the appropriate journals.

H.M.S.O.
Annual Reports of the Ministry of Housing and Local Government.
Various specialized Reports referred to in the notes above.

NOTES

[1] See *Housing in the Northern Countries* published in Copenhagen.

[2] This Table is compiled from two sources: (1) 1958 data which applies only to England comes from *Housing Since the Rent Act* by D. V. Donnison, *et al.*; and (2) the 1961 data from a statement by the Minister of Housing in a Parliamentary Debate. Fuller and more accurate data should be available from 1961 Census when published.

[3] E.g. In 1960 of post-war housing, housing associations had provided 26.2 per cent in the Netherlands, 26.1 per cent in West Germany, 29.5 per cent in Sweden, and in England and Wales less than 1.5 per cent. See studies made by Economic Commission for Europe (E.C.E.).

[4] See also Working Classes Act, 1890 and Small Dwelling Acquisition Act, 1899.

[5] The Housing, Town Planning, etc. Act, 1919.

[6] See E.C.E. studies.

[7] Housing Act, 1961.

[8] For the best account of housing legislation and progress in the inter-war years, see M. Bowley, *Housing and the State*.

[9] In an attempt to nullify the effects of economic depression and slump, the Government embarked on a series of reductions in spending.

[10] A perusal of housing and town planning journals of recent years will show how often this problem is being discussed.

[11] Housing Act, 1949.

[12] Unlike many other social services, the housing services are in competition with many other organizations for their basic materials and skills. More houses means fewer hospitals, roads or factories. The reader should see for himself the extent to which house-building and its expansion has had to compete with concurrent expansion in many other fields.

[13] For an account of post-war housing policy, see D. V. Donnison, *Housing Policy since the War*.

[14] For fuller details see the quarterly *Housing Statistics* issued by the Ministry of Housing and Local Government.

[15] At this rate it would take over 215 years to demolish 14 million houses (the approximate number in England and Wales) and many of the houses being built today will have to stand for over 200 years.

[16] Housing Repairs and Rents Act, 1954.

[17] House Purchase and Housing Act, 1959.

[18] An annual rate of 100,000 a year would mean that in a stock of 14 million houses, it would take 140 years to modernize all of them Put another way, the average house would have to be over 100 years old before its turn came for modernization by this system.

Notes

[19] See Norman C. Abbey, *The Rent Acts* 1920–57.

[20] See *The Rent Act* 1957—*Report of Inquiry*, Cmd. 1246 and Donniston, op. cit. (Note 2).

[21] This sum has now (1964) been completely earmarked. Proposals are before Parliament to increase the size of the fund.

[22] Housing was, in the nineteenth century, the responsibility of the Local Government Board which became the Ministry of Health in 1919.

[23] See *Councils and their Houses,* A Report of the Housing Management Sub-Committee of the Central Housing Advisory Committee.

[24] See *Unsatisfactory Tenants,* A Report of the Housing Management Sub-Committee of the Central Housing Advisory Committee.

[25] See *Royal Commission on the Distribution of the Industrial Population,* Cmd. 6153; *Committee on Land Utilization in Rural Areas,* Cmd. 6378; *Expert Committee on Compensation and Betterment,* Cmd. 6386.

[26] See National Parks and Access to the Countryside Act, 1949, and I. L. Gowan, 'The Administration of the National Parks', *Public Administration,* Winter 1955.

[27] Under the Act of 1946, special *ad hoc* bodies were set up (Development Corporations) to build the New Towns. Only when the building was nearing completion were many of their functions returned to local government.

[28] See C. D. Buchanan, *Traffic in Towns,* H.M.S.O.

[29] See *Reshaping of British Railways* 1963, British Railways Board.

[30] See *South East Study* 1961–1981, Ministry of Housing and Local Government.

7. EDUCATIONAL SERVICES

Arthur J. Willcocks

DURING his early years, a child learns much of the basic information and skills necessary for adult life from his parents and from the adults and other children with whom he comes into contact. This is the inevitable and natural process of education, but as the information and skills needed have grown with increasing specialization of work in modern industrialized society, so a new specialized function has had to be developed. People, other than the parent, and with special training, have taken on a formal responsibility for imparting such information and skills to the young child. This latter can be termed 'formal' education as distinct from the 'natural' process of education. Education, taken in its widest sense, is, therefore, a dual function of home and school, and in our modern highly specialized society, a child without both is, to some measure at least, handicapped for adult life; he may be said to be in need. This need has been recognized for many centuries and has been met, in part, in two ways. Firstly voluntary societies, often connected with religious bodies, provided free education, and secondly private organizations have provided similar services for those parents willing and able to pay.

Among the voluntary schools were the 'charity schools'[1] developed in the reign of Queen Anne at the beginning of the eighteenth century to provide an education for the children of the poor. The education they and many other voluntary schools gave was not completely disinterested for they sought to educate these children not only in reading and writing but also in the moral discipline and principles of the Church of England. Such educational aims were given formal statement in the constitution of the National Society for Promoting the Education of the Poor in the Principals of the Established Church in 1811. This Society for the established church had been preceded some three years earlier by the formation of the British and Foreign Schools Society which aimed to educate its children in, among other things, the beliefs of the nonconformist churches.

Any religious organization seeking to secure recruits and converts to its faith must see the opportunities which educating children affords for achieving this aim. Inevitably, therefore, religious bodies, throughout the world and irrespective of faith, have been deeply concerned in education and have always looked with suspicion on any attempt by the State to provide an education unrelated to religion. Whenever a State has sought to develop a public system of education, it has had to face suspicion and often opposition from religious bodies and the history of education in this country is no exception. Here the Churches were pioneers in the provision of education, and as the State developed its own educational services, disagreements and disputes occurred. Any analysis of the parliamentary debates on the 1870[2] or 1902 Education Acts will reveal the extent to which these disagreements monopolized the debates. Even today the echoes of these old controversies can still, on occasions, be heard.

It was not so long ago that Christians were singing:

> The rich man in his castle, the poor man at his gate,
> God made them high and lowly and ordered their estate.

a recognition of the ordered hierarchy of society which has been an important element in the development of education in this country. True education is no respecter of such social class divisions and may even call the existence of social classes into question. It is, therefore, not surprising to find education developing, either accidently or by design, along different streams, one for the upper social classes and another for the lower classes or 'the poor'. The eighteenth and early nineteenth centuries were marked, educationally at least, by a determination to educate the poor under what Defoe called 'the great law of subordination'. The poor were to be educated to the requirements of their station in life and no more. As G. M. Trevelyan put it: 'The typical unit of Elizabethan education was the grammar school, where the cleverest boys of all classes were brought up together; the typical units of eighteenth- and nineteenth-century education were the charity schools, the village schools, and the "great public school" where the classes were educated in rigorous separation.'[3] The development of State

I   121

education has, therefore, not only come into conflict with religious interests but also with those who believed in educating the social classes in 'rigorous separation'.

What, in fact, was the contribution that the State could make, in nineteenth-century Britain, to the provision of education? It could, for example, try to ensure that voluntary organizations provided places for those who wanted them or it could go further and provide school places itself or through local government where they were lacking. This would be contribution enough perhaps, but it brought something no other organization could bring—compulsion. Education is, of course, primarily and mainly for children, but is it unrealistic to expect them to be able to choose for themselves. It is the parents who will, in fact, choose and for them the question, especially in the nineteenth century, was to weigh the economic assets to the family of a child at work, against the short run liabilities and doubtful long-run assets of the non-earning child at school, and in such circumstances many parents could be expected to ignore education. The importance of the role of the State in compelling parents to have their children educated can thus be clearly seen, for no matter how attractive education may be, there must always be the power to compel children to attend to ensure that all get their share of the benefits of education. This, perhaps above all else, was the great contribution of the State in the nineteenth century.

Once the State had entered the educational arena, it is perhaps unfair to expect it to be completely disinterested when other educational bodies have failed to be so. As early as the Health and Morals of Apprentices Act, 1802, the Government in its concern for the pauper apprentice, recognized, however dimly the connection between education and industry. This interest grew as the century progressed (reinforced by many non-statutory experiments) and reached a fuller recognition in the Technical Education Act, 1899. This Act was based on the recommendations of the Royal Commission on Technical Instruction (1884)[4] which sets out the development of technical education up to that date. The Royal Commission came to the conclusion that although England had been ahead in production of her industrial competitors, thanks to superior and more efficient educational systems they were rapidly overhauling us. This suggestion that industrial progress was related to education has always been used since then to justify further educational advances. The State wants better workers, more technologists or whatever it might be and as such it can never be completely disinterested in the education it pro-vides. The careful reader will find evidence of this interest in many recent educational reports, notably that on Higher Education.[5]

Unlike many of the other social services discussed in this book, education is a service which involves the State in conflicts of aim and principle, and it is as well that these conflicts are recognized and borne in mind in considering the development of statutory educational services. In England and Wales the State's first real token of interest in education was made through the religious educational bodies. In 1833 the first of a series of annual grants was given to the British and Foreign Schools Society and the National Society for Promoting the Education of the Poor to en-able them to expand their educational activities. This grant was for £20,000, a figure which contrast starkly with over £1,000 million spent in one year in 1962. It was, however, a beginning and it is important to realize that it was made at the time when many new social ideas and experiments were being canvassed and when the doctrines of laissez-faire were still strongly held.

The next hesitant step came almost forty years later when an Act of 1870[6] made provision for the first state schools. Under this Act, where the provision of school places in any area was insuffi-cient to provide elementary education for all children in the area, School Boards were to be set up to provide schools for those children not provided for. Although democratically elected, the school boards were not part of the local government system, but instead were *ad hoc* bodies with separate elections, membership and financing powers. The financial aid to the voluntary schools was continued by the central government, completely separate from the School Board system.

The system of elementary education thus created, was in reality two systems with the School Boards merely filling the gaps left by the voluntary schools system. In the next twenty-five years the Boards provided some 2·2 million new places and the voluntary schools nearly 1·5 million, and by the end of that period, thanks to other education Acts which strengthened the powers for com-pulsory schooling, virtually all children were getting an elemen-tary education up to the age of eleven. But the system was limited to elementary education and attempts to extend the powers of the

Boards to include secondary education failed. In 1895 a Royal Commission reported on the need for the development of secondary education, and four years later a famous judicial ruling[7] clearly limited Boards to elementary work. It was not, therefore, until the passing of the Education Act of 1902 that further advances were made.

This Act abolished School Boards and gave local authorities throughout the county the responsibility for the educational services. No longer was the role of the State limited to those areas where voluntary provision was insufficient—education was now a responsibility of elected government in all areas. There remained, of course, the fact that voluntary schools still existed and provided a sizeable proportion of the school places. On this point, the Act transferred the grant giving power to local education authorities, thus beginning the process of bringing these voluntary schools under the control of, and operating as part of the State system. Today, although the voluntary schools have some discretionary powers, there is little to distinguish them from the local authority schools. The so-called dual system was beginning to give way to a State system. One should, however, hasten to add that the local authority had no power to compel schools to accept its grants and many schools, now called the independent schools, remained outside the system. We, as a nation, have, as in the health service, sought to provide a comprehensive educational service for all those children whose parents want them to use it, whilst leaving parents the right if they want (and can afford) to purchase educational services privately.

To return to the Act of 1902, the other major step forward was to impose on the new local education authorities the duty to develop a system of secondary education. Thus, in two steps, were the foundations of our current services laid and although there were major Acts in 1918, 1936 and 1944, the basic legislative framework has not been altered. The basic achievement since then has not been so much of Acts of Parliament as in a gradual build up in the numbers being educated and the quality, variety and length of the education provided.[8]

Before turning to the Act of 1944 which is the basis of the modern system in England and Wales it is worth noting a problem of education which the State inherited with the Act of 1902. The aims and content of elementary (or primary as it is now called) education are fairly clear and largely accepted. The teacher, at this stage of education seeks to train the child in the basic skills of reading, writing and numbers. These are the basic tools of any educational system and must remain, whatever improvements may be added or new methods adopted, the basic elements of primary education.

But to move beyond primary education into secondary education is to enter the field of controversy and difference of opinion— what exactly does one teach a secondary school child? For an interesting discussion of this question, and for the foundations of our present secondary system, the reader is referred to one of the many famous Reports on Education in this century, the Hadow Report of 1926.[9] Is secondary education intended merely to reinforce the learned basic skills, is it to prepare the pupil for examinations leading to higher education, or is it to fit him for life, work and leisure?

Writing in 1926, the Hadow Committee had been able to say that 'the years between 11 and 14–15 form the opening phase of secondary education for a small minority of children and the closing phase of elementary education for the great majority'. Today, thanks to the system developed under the Education Act of 1944 the recommendations of the Hadow Committee for secondary education for all graded according to the abilities of the child, is more of a reality than ever before. In most areas three separate types of secondary education exist. For those children of high intellectual ability whose aptitude is for conceptual and academic education, the grammar school seeks to provide the 'proper' education. For those of good mechanical aptitude, able to think in mechanical terms, the secondary technical school should provide the 'proper' education. For the remainder, and indeed the bulk of our school population, the 'average' child, the 'proper' education was to be found in the secondary modern school.[10]

This tripartite system of education developed under the 1944 Act, but stemming from Hadow and earlier, seeks to answer the question: What is secondary education about?. It sets fairly clear aims for grammar and technical schools, but transfers the burden of the question to the secondary modern school. What do we teach 'Half our Future' adults?[11] This tripartite system also reveals perhaps the most contentious question in the education field in recent years, the methods and age of selection—the 11+. Can one decide the type of education best suited to each child with sufficient accuracy at this age? Need one in fact select so early or even at all?

In recent years, local authorities have responded to the problems of secondary education in two ways. In the first place, many have tried to improve the efficiency and painlessness of the actual selection process. Secondly, many authorities have tried to break down the rigidities alleged to exist in the three parts of the system, and to obviate some of the differences in social prestige attached to one part and not to another.[12] Comprehensive schools, bilateral schools, O-level courses in secondary moderns and the so-called Mason plan in Leicestershire have all sought to overcome these problems. With the recent appearance in fairly quick succession of the Crowther, Robbins and Newsome Reports,[13] it seems as though secondary education is once more in a period of change—if, that is, it can be said to have ever really found a settled solution to its basic problem—What is secondary education?

To return to the Act of 1944, it imposed on local education authorities the duty to provide an educational service through three progressive stages primary, secondary and further and 'to contribute towards the spiritual, moral, mental and physical development of the community by securing that efficient education throughout these stages shall be available to meet the needs of the population . . .' (s. 7). The role of the State has therefore progressed from providing only primary education to something much bigger and more ambitious. Whilst the duty of the State has thus advanced, it has been able to do so by the precaution of compelling the parent of every child 'to cause him to receive efficient full-time education suitable to his age, ability and aptitude, either by regular attendance at school or otherwise' (s. 36). Education is therefore, in theory at least, directed not to any specific interest or viewpoint, but to the personal characteristics of every child, his age, ability and aptitude.

At this point educational administration must be briefly examined. In 1870 education had been made the responsibility of elected *ad hoc* School Boards, but from 1902 onwards it became the duty of local government and has remained so, with some changes, ever since. Education is therefore clearly established as a matter of local concern and responsibility. Today in England

and Wales, education is the responsibility of the major local authorities, the county and county borough councils, of whom there are 144. Each county and county borough is responsible for the full range of educational services as described below, and carries out its duties through education committees to which all educational matters must, by the Act, be referred and through Chief Education Officers (or Directors) and their staffs.

In the areas of county councils there may be two types of exception to these general statements. Where a minor local authority has a population beyond a certain figure, it may claim, as of right, to provide primary and secondary education for its area. It is, in the language of the Act, an 'excepted authority'; today in 1964 there are about 55 such authorities. Secondly, a county council may decide to delegate some of its educational functions to divisions of its county area (which need not necessarily be coterminous with existing local government boundaries) and create 'divisional executives' for these functions. Some 150 or more of these exist today, although their use varies very widely from county to county.

Central responsibility for the work of these local education authorities and for national educational policy was given, by the Act of 1944, to the Ministry of Education, a department previously without ministerial status. However, since then, in 1964, to form a closer link between higher education and other forms of education a new department has been created called the Department of Education and Science. It includes among its responsibilities contact with the *ad hoc* University Grants Committee which acts as the spokesman for the universities, and also distributes Government money among the universities. Although the new department does not control the curricula of individual schools or colleges some attempt is made to advise, help and to raise standards through a rather unique system of inspectors. These inspectors (H.M.I.s) aim to influence rather than to compel and their reports form an interesting commentary on the work of our schools.

Only a brief account of developments in primary and secondary schools is possible here.[14] Free primary and secondary education is now available to all, secondary education is provided in a greater variety and with greater regard to the needs of each child than ever before, the length of the school life has been lengthened from nine to ten years, and voluntary attendance beyond that considerably increased. The post-war 'bulge' in the birth-rate, the increase in the length of school life and the numbers staying on beyond the compulsory age, has meant a considerable pressure for more places. The expected respite that was to follow the passing of the bulge into work or higher education, has not materialized for the rising birth-rate has put fresh and more serious numerical pressure on the schools. New school building has had, therefore, to become a major issue in educational policy—since the war about £900 million worth of new schools have been built and many more are planned or being built. Much has been done to revolutionize not only the content and scope of education, but also the physical structures in which it takes place.

This, however, is not to claim that all the problems have been solved. There are still too many old buildings in use, there is still too much rigidity in some areas in the working of the tripartite secondary system and the aims of secondary education are not always agreed. Beyond all this, the major problem has been and remains the shortage of teachers. The almost continuously rising school population has put a burden on the teaching profession. Its heavy dependence on women teachers has meant further problems; the excess of women over men in the younger half of the population which has meant, in the past, a supply of women who could be expected to become 'career' teachers, has now disappeared, marriage rates remain high and the age of marriage remarkably low. As a result the average woman teacher makes a relatively short contribution to the service after her training and before retiring to marriage and family life. Recruitment must therefore be kept continuously at a high level. It is pleasant, therefore (despite all these changes), to record that we have felt able to increase the length of training for teachers, only one of many steps taken since the late nineteenth century to improve the quality and qualifications of school teachers.

One other problem merits special mention—that of the cost of education. The financing of the day-to-day work of education depends on two main sources of money. In the first place as a local government service, education is financed in part, from local authority rates, i.e. the tax levied each year on the assumed annual value of real property in the area. Secondly, and of much greater financial importance, is the contribution of central government by way of grant to local education authorities. From 1944 to 1959, a grant was paid to local education authorities specifically for education related to the amount they spent on the service, but since the Local Government Act, 1958, and the creation of what is popularly called the 'Block Grant', this specific grant has disappeared. Instead central government makes available to local authorities a 'general grant'[15] to be allocated among their many services as the local council see fit. This general grant is distributed in relation to population and other needs of the area, and is, in national total, calculated on the basis of the expected expenditure on, *inter alia*, educational services. In the early 1960's, with the cost of education exceeding £1,000 million per annum compared with less than £200 million at the end of World War II, financial questions bulk large in discussions about the present and future development and administration of education.

Before discussing the third of the progressive stages of education, some account of special educational treatment must be given. It is the duty of all local education authorities to ascertain the children in their area who are handicapped, blind, deaf, epileptic and so on, and to provide either alone or in conjunction with other authorities and voluntary bodies, special schooling for them. This duty extends, where appropriate to providing education for those in hospital and bedfast at home. Modest in amount when compared with the provision for the non-handicapped children, these special educational services are an important and humane part of the service which seeks the well-being of the handicapped child even if he may never be able to use his education in any truly productive sense. No matter what his handicap he is entitled to some care from the education service.

In discussing the third of the three progressive stages, we leave some of the traditional fields of education and move into new and often exciting territories. The duties of local education authorities under this heading can be divided into two groups; those that are concerned with further formal education and those concerned with the informal leisure time services akin to education. It is the duty of the authorities to make provision for further education in technical, commercial, art and similar colleges either on a full- or a part-time basis. Here there has been considerable expansion since the war, especially noteworthy being the development of some technical colleges into self-governing colleges of advanced technology and eventually into universities. Any annual report of the

Ministry of Education, or some of the reports of special committees will show the extent and the limitations of these developments.

Local authorities along with other bodies including the Workers Educational Association and the Extra-Mural Departments of Universities, have been responsible for making provision for adult education. Local authorities have played their part as well in the expansion of grants for those attending universities and other institutions of higher education. Nor should the expansion of universities and the establishment of new universities be forgotten, but the credit for this lies with central government and with the University Grants Committee.[16]

Only a brief reference is possible to some of the other types of further educational services. Firstly there are the Youth Services of the local authority which provide youth clubs, centres and services for the young people of its area. This is neither an exclusive nor a compulsory duty for local government; much valuable work is done in this field by voluntary youth groups of all kinds. Some wear uniforms and others do not; some are attached to churches, some have special interests;[17] indeed the total picture is one of immense variety and of a new lease of life engendered by the Albemarle Committee Report,[18] and the subsequent interest and money devoted to the Service by the Government. It is a service to which many adults give long hours of valued voluntary service, and one in which there is increasing scope and opportunity for professionally trained staff. In the absence of any attempt to fulfil the plans of as long ago as 1918 for day continuation colleges, i.e. colleges to which young teenage workers would be released from work one day a week for general education, the youth service must seek to help bridge the gap between school life and work.

Another of the informal further educational services is the community centre movement, in which an attempt is being made to foster community feelings and to give local groups and neighbours a convenient centre for meeting their general and specialized interests. Many local authorities have built community centres and have provided full-time community centre wardens.

It is perhaps a measure of the indefiniteness of our definitions of education that this account moves farther away from education into peripheral, but none the less important services which may or may not be part of the educational service. One such service, which is discussed in Chapter 4, is the Youth Employment Service. Is this an educational or an industrial service? In 1944 the Ince Committee seemed unable to provide a clear answer to this question, and so the service remains in some places part of education, and in others part of the services of the Ministry of Labour. Also important among these peripheral services are those listed as 'ancillary' services. The School Medical and Dental Service is an important example of such an ancillary service. The School Meal Services is similarly listed, as are the duties laid on local authorities to provide transport to school in certain circumstances, boarding schools if thought appropriate, and clothing for children too poorly clad to attend school. Ancillary services these may all be, but in each case and in total, they provide a necessary precaution for enabling the educational services to function properly.

Education, as can be seen, includes a very wide range of services, not all of them, perhaps, meriting the title of social services. Although we in this country tend to refer to them all as social services, many other countries do not list education as a social service, contenting themselves by referring to the social services associated with education. Whilst in theory education is devoted to the age, ability and aptitude of the individual child, then it must have a strong claim to be called a social service. At the same time it is, unquestionably, a major and complicated piece of administrative machinery, involving both local and central government, and posing for citizen and educator alike, questions of high opportunity often at great cost.

FURTHER READING

General
K. LINDSEY, *English Education.*
W. K. RICHMOND, *Education in England.*
H. C. DENT, *The 1944 Act.*
W. O. LESTER-SMITH, *Education in Great Britain.*
     These books are by way of general introduction. The reader is referred to the numerous books on special aspects of education. No attempt is made to list them all, but the following are suggested:
O. BANKS, *Parity and Prestige in English Secondary Education.*
O. STEPHENS, *The Living Tradition.*
J. B. MAYS, *Education and the Urban Child.*

Notes

J. VAIZEY, *The Cost of Education.*
J. FLOUD, A. H. HALSAY and F. M. MARTIN, *Social Class and Educational Opportunity.*

H.M.S.O.
Annual Reports of the Ministry of Education, now the Department of Education and Science.
Annual Statistics of Education in 2 vols., Ministry of Education.
Reports of University Grants Committee.
The Special Reports of aspects of education already noted above, i.e. Hadow, Crowther, Newsom and Robbins.

NOTES

[1] See M. G. Jones, *Charity Schools Movement.*
[2] One speaker on the 1870 Bill said that the House of Commons was like 'a fine herd of cattle in a large meadow deserting the grass which is abundant about them and delighting themselves by fighting over a bed of nettles in one corner of the field,' quoted by E. Eagleshaw, *From School Board to Local Authority.*
[3] G. M. Trevelyan, *English Social History,* p. 162.
[4] *Royal Commission on Technical Instruction,* 1884, Cmd. 3981.
[5] *Report of Committee on Higher Education* (Robbins), Cmd. 2154.
[6] The Elementary Education Act, 1870. For an interesting account of the development of this system, see Eagleshaw, op. cit. He suggests that the Act might properly have been called 'An Act for the Secular Education of the Children of Poor Labourers'.
[7] The Cookerton Judgement, 1899.
[8] See *The Education of the Adolescent* (Hadow) *Report of Consultative Committee for the Board of Education,* 1926. This shows that the development of secondary education was extremely patchy and, in most areas, implied grammar school education for the lucky few.
[9] See Hadow, op. cit.
[10] *Half our Future* (Newsom) *Report of the Central Advisory Council for Education* (England), 1963.
[11] See Newsom, op. cit.
[12] See O. Banks, *Parity and Prestige in English Secondary Education.*
[13] See Newsom, op. cit. and Robbins, op. cit., 15 *to* 18 (Crowther) *the Central Advisory Council for Education* (England), 1959.
[14]   TABLE 1. NUMBER OF PUPILS ATTENDING SCHOOL JANUARY 1962.
ENGLAND AND WALES
'000's

Primary Schools	4,130
Secondary Schools	2,836
Special and other	80
Direct Grant	123
Independent	495

Total 7,663
(Source—Annual Report for 1962 of Ministry of Education.)

Notes

[15] The General Grant is intended to cover not only educational expenditure but also that of many other services in local government.

[16] See the *Report of the University Grants Committee.*

[17] See J. M. Brew, *Youth and Youth Groups.*

[18] *Report of Committee on Youth Services* (Albemarle), Cmd. 939, 1960.

PART THREE

Social Provision to Meet Special Needs

INTRODUCTION

THE services that have been considered so far have been those which most citizens use at some time during their lives, as school-children, as patients, as retirement pensioners, etc. Some members of the community, however, have needs which they and their families are unable to meet without additional forms of help. Others, because of their difficult or anti-social behaviour, are brought to the notice of the authorities for special care, treatment or control. That some groups have special claims on the community because of handicap or infirmity has been recognized for many centuries, but recently in this and many other countries there has been increasing emphasis on their individual needs as *persons* with physical, mental or social handicaps, rather than on the problems they may have in supporting themselves in an industrial society.

These services, perhaps more than any others, are inadequate and present a most confusing picture over the country as a whole. This seems to be partly due to the difficulty the ordinary rate-payer and taxpayer has in understanding some of the more subtle needs of those who may suffer a handicap; partly because the rapid increase in scientific knowledge is only just beginning to show ways in which some people can be helped (e.g. the great advances in prosthetics which has so greatly contributed to the mobility and independence of some physically handicapped people); partly because problems affecting only a very small number of people are not always realized by the rest of the community unless the imagination of the general public is caught as in the case of the 'thalidomide babies'; partly also because some forms of unconventional or anti-social behaviour naturally rouse antagonism and social ostracism.

As has already been noted, much of our modern social service provision has developed out of voluntary effort and it is in meeting special needs that voluntary organizations find one of their most fruitful fields of activity today. The stage of development of these services for groups with special needs is also reflected in the fact that much of the relevant legislation is worded in such a way that it permits widely differing interpretations by local authorities or other bodies charged with responsibility. Moreover, some at least of this legislation is permissive not mandatory.

Complete uniformity may not be desirable but unevenness in the standards and scope of provision can lead to considerable hardship.

8. OFFENDERS AGAINST THE LAW

Richard L. Silburn

IT may seem odd to find in an introductory volume on the administration of the social services, a section on the Delinquency services. After all, if we were asked to name one or two social service institutions we would almost certainly think of, say, a Welfare Centre, or a Children's Home, before we would mention a Borstal Institution or an Approved School.

Moreover the delinquency services differ markedly from most, if not all, other social services in that they are imposed upon the recipient by a court of law; whereas most social services are gladly used by those eligible to make use of them, many of the persons found to be in need of the delinquency services make enthusiastic and vigorous efforts to *avoid* taking advantage of them! The delinquency services are usually considered more as a selection of possible forms of punishment to be meted out to wrongdoers, than as an elaborate series of reformative measures attempting to cope with one of the most intractable of social problems.

But, imposed or otherwise, it is reasonable to regard the forms of treatment devised for the young offender as bona fide social services; they constitute an important part of national social policy and social expenditure; the men and women who staff the various services and institutions share, fundamentally, the same attitude towards their reluctant clients as do their colleagues in other, more obvious, forms of social work. This has not always been the case; on the contrary, the way that society has dealt with those who broke its laws has undergone some drastic changes in modern times.

Until the nineteenth century few people doubted both the justice and wisdom of severe punishment of the criminal; it was just because the suffering of the prisoner was an expiation for his crime, and it was wise because the fear of harsh punishment deterred others from committing crimes.

The two most frequently imposed punishments for serious offences were the death penalty and transportation to one of the convict settlements overseas. During the earlier years of the nineteenth century public opinion reacted against the almost indiscriminate passing of the death sentence, and changes in the law limited execution to fewer and fewer offences. At the same time, it became more difficult to transport offenders; after America gained her independence it was of course no longer possible to send criminals there, and the law-abiding colonists in Australia became increasingly reluctant to allow more and more convicts to be sent to the Australian penal settlements. Thus, by the 1840's, the question of what to do with convicted criminals became a serious problem; the Victorian answer was to build a large number of prisons, and sentences of imprisonment became the standard method of punishing convicts. Although the régime in the prisons was rigid and harsh, it was probably from about this period in mid-century that traditional retributive theories of punishment were first doubted, and an interest in the possibility of reformative treatment was seriously indicated. This concern for reform rather than retribution has slowly gained ground ever since, and although the principle of reform is still not universally or unambiguously accepted it is today the major concern of the penal system. The major interest of the reformers was, at first, the treatment of juvenile offenders, and although penal reforms have by now been proposed which affect offenders of all ages, it has always been in the treatment of young offenders that the pioneering work has been done. For example, the first experiments with the placing of young offenders under the supervision of a responsible person who can advise and befriend them took place in America in the 1840's and 1850's, and rather later in this country; out of these early experiments developed what we know today as the probation service. Again at the beginning of the twentieth century in England what we now know as a Borstal institution for young men was first tried out, as an alternative to imprisonment. Slowly but surely, the treatment of juvenile offenders has become less primitive, and society's attitude towards them has become more sensitive and understanding; indeed, something of a social service attitude has become implicit in the law itself. According to the Children and

Young Persons Act, 1933, for example, the duty of the juvenile court is to 'have regard to the welfare of the child or young person', and if he is found guilty of criminal offences the court must secure 'that proper provision is made for his education and training'. This humane theme—sometimes called the 'principle of guardianship'—has very recently been extended. Under the Children and Young Persons Act of 1963, the age of criminal responsibility has been raised, with effect from the 1st February 1964, from eight to ten years. That is to say, no child of less than ten is deemed capable of committing a crime; what would be criminal behaviour in an older person, is in the case of such a child behaviour which may demand our concern, and maybe the attention of the Children's Department, and the Child Care Service, but it is *not* a matter for the Courts. The principle of guardianship extends to offenders over the age of ten; indeed all young people are examined and treated in a manner quite different from older offenders. The juvenile courts are physically separate from the ordinary courts, the procedures adopted are different, and the task of the magistrates is different as well.

The young offender is not to be judged or punished in the same way as the adult criminal, but is to receive special attentions appropriate to his age, temperament and experience; moreover, 'the fundamental principle . . . has long been accepted, that the penal treatment of young offenders should be primarily remedial'.[1]

The first remedial consideration is that the young offender should be protected from any contaminating or disruptive influences with which he may be in contact, particularly the company of older and more experienced criminals. From a penal point of view this means that imprisonment is, as a rule, not a recommended form of treatment for those under 21; indeed under the Criminal Justice Act, 1961, no offender under 17 may be sent to prison by any court, unless there are special circumstances so compelling that the court can find no appropriate alternative to imprisonment. Those between 17 and 21 may only be imprisoned if the court is satisfied that there is no appropriate alternative and here, too, the court will only sentence to imprisonment with reluctance. One of the immediate aims of modern penal policy is to provide suitable and varied alternatives on such a scale that it will never be necessary for anyone under 21 to be committed to prison. Our concern must be with the alternatives which are now available.

The period since the war has witnessed a considerable extension of the traditional methods and institutions, and the creation of new and experimental techniques for dealing with juvenile offenders. A magistrate or judge can now choose an appropriate form of treatment from a varied range of alternatives, some of which interfere with the offender's normal mode of life in only the slightest degree, whereas others may involve total supervision and control in an institutional setting for a period of time, as long as 2 or 3 years.

Let us first examine those forms of treatment which do not involve removing the offender from his normal home background.

ATTENDANCE CENTRES

Section 19 of the Criminal Justice Act, 1948, as amended in 1961, provides that if a person aged 10 and under 21 is found guilty by a magistrates' court of an offence for which a person over that age could be sentenced to imprisonment, and if an attendance centre is available to the court for persons of his age and sex, the court may order him to attend the centre for a period of not less than 12 hours (unless the offender is under the age of 14 and the court considers 12 hours excessive) and not more than 24 hours. A person ordered to attend an attendance centre who fails to do so, or commits a breach of the Attendance Centre Rules that cannot adequately be dealt with under the Rules, may be brought back to Court, and the court may deal with him in any way in which he could have been dealt with in the original proceedings.[2]

The establishment of attendance centres was first suggested and discussed before the Second World War, but it did not become part of our penal legislation until 1948, and the first attendance centre was not in fact opened until 1950, as an entirely new treatment method.

The method of the attendance centre is simple; it is to deprive the offender of a certain amount of his free time when he is brought 'for a period under discipline and, by teaching him something of the constructive use of leisure, to guide him on leaving the centre to continue organized recreational activity by joining youth clubs or other organizations ... a period of physical training is usually followed by a lecture, employment in handicrafts or other instruction. The boys remain under firm discipline throughout the period of attendance'.[3]

An attendance centre normally operates on Saturday afternoons, and each session usually lasts for 2 hours. Thus a maximum sentence of 24 hours involves the offender in the forfeiture of 12 otherwise free Saturday afternoons which must be spent in the uncongenial surroundings of the attendance centre; in all other respects, however, he is free—he lives at his home quite normally, goes to school or work like everyone else, and is not subject to any supervision outside the centre during his sentence, nor is he subject to any form of after-care upon completion of his sentence.

The Home Secretary bears the legal responsibility for providing attendance centres, and the entire cost of organizing and running them is borne by the Exchequer. The actual establishment and detailed administration of an attendance centre is carried out by the local police authorities, who take on this additional task at the Home Secretary's request. Thus, in nearly every case, attendance centres are organized by the local police authorities, are in the main staffed by policemen as a normal overtime duty, and are frequently held on police premises or, by arrangement with the Local Education Authority, on school premises.

So far most of the effort has been concentrated on junior attendance centres which are available for those under the age of 17; in March 1962 there were 44 such centres, nearly all of them in large towns, and all of them dealing only with boys. There has so far not been enough demand to justify the establishment of attendance centres for girls. In 1958 the first senior attendance centre, for those aged 17 and under 21 was opened in Manchester. This centre is not run by the local police force but has been delegated to the Prison Commissioners, and is consequently staffed by prison officers. The curriculum of this centre is only marginally different from its junior counterparts. . . . 'The first hour of attendance being devoted to cleaning, scrubbing and carrying out internal decoration, and the second in strenuous physical education.'[4]

Although no one would pretend that committal to an attendance centre is an agreeable experience, none the less punishment through loss of leisure is clearly a fairly mild and unrigorous form of training, which imposes only a very minor restraint on the offender's freedom of action. This form of treatment, like any

143

other form, will be more effective on some people than on others, and a basic problem facing all magistrates and judges is to decide which specific treatment is most likely to be most effective for the particular offender they have before them at any given moment It is always very difficult to determine how effective any form of penal treatment is, but one way of getting a useful impression is to examine the careers of all those who have undergone a specific form of treatment (such as an attendance centre), to find out how many are re-convicted within a given period of time after their release. If those who are re-convicted can then be shown to share some significant characteristic, then whenever an offender comes before the court and he is seen to have that observed characteristic, it is a fair bet that that particular form of treatment is not likely to be very effective with him, and that some other form of treatment may prove to be more effective. In this way the attendance centre (and every other form of treatment as well) ought to be reserved for the sorts of offender whom experience shows to be those most likely to respond favourably to it.

The Cambridge Institute of Criminology has completed a research project and published a report on the junior attendance centres which throws some light on to the question of the sort of offenders best suited to this form of treatment; they are those 'with little or no experience of crime, coming from a fairly normal background'. Those who have already been convicted of a number of offences, or who have a particularly unstable home background, might be in need of the long-term support of a probation officer, or perhaps even a period of training in a residential institution, but were much less likely to benefit from a few hours spent at the attendance centre. The attendance centre is for the person who is only beginning to develop anti-social tendencies, whose 'minds are then most likely to be open to the effects of punishment and the influence of the attendance centre staff in teaching them to respect the law and property of others'.[5]

THE PROBATION SERVICE

The probation service is probably the most generally well known of the penal methods at the Court's disposal; it is a method which has been developing since the middle nineteenth century, and by now it is well tried, and universally recognized to be 'a major instrument of policy in the field of the prevention of crime and the treatment of offenders'.[6] The declared aim of the probation service has always been, in the words of the 1907 Probation of Offenders Act, 'to supervise the probationers . . . to advise, assist and befriend them'. The detailed methods by which this aim has been fulfilled have undergone a gradual but important process of development; arising out of the voluntary, well-intentioned but fundamentally inspirational efforts of the Police Court Missionaries, it has since developed into a highly professional case-work service, requiring a wide range of special abilities, systematic and prolonged training, and practical experience.[7]

A court can, with the consent of the offender, make out a probation order which will apply for a minimum of 12 months and a maximum of 3 years, during which time the offender promises to be industrious and of good behaviour, and to follow the advice and guidance of his probation officer. This usually involves him in reporting regularly, probably every week, to his probation officer, who will meanwhile visit the offender's family at frequent intervals to encourage in them the will to assist the offender in every way that they can. Thus the existence of the probation service enables the court to place an offender under systematic and expert supervision, providing support and encouragement for a fairly long period of time, while the offender continues to live and work in his home environment, his normal routines are not unduly disrupted, and he is not moved into the 'unnatural' atmosphere of a residential institution. The offender on probation is given personal and individual treatment, and the sensitive probation officer is able to provide a type and degree of support appropriate to the needs of the offender.

Overall responsibility for the probation service in England and Wales is borne by the Home Secretary; there is a probation division at the Home Office, and the Home Secretary appoints a Probation and Advisory and Training Board, which acts as a specialist advisory committee.

From an administrative point of view, the probation service is particularly interesting, because there are three different forms of administration currently in operation. In London, the service is under the direct administrative control of the Home Office, and so it is centrally organized; in England and Wales outside London it is organized by special *ad hoc* committees and in Scotland the probation service is administered by the larger local authorities. We are thus able to make a direct comparison between these three administrative forms, all applied to one service.

Let us first examine in more detail the administration by *ad hoc* committee in England and Wales outside London. The country is divided into 103 probation areas, each area normally consisting of a number of petty-sessional divisions combined together. Each area is controlled by a probation committee of magistrates, who may co-opt such other interested parties as they choose, and who are responsible for appointing and paying the salaries and other expenses of the probation officers within their area, and for general supervision of their work. Thus the probation officer is in fact as well as theory, the servant of the court, and the particularly close relationship which exists between the magistracy and the probation service is built into the very nature of the administrative structure itself.

Less clearly defined, however, is the relationship between the probation committee and the local authority; this becomes a matter of considerable importance because the expenses authorized by the probation committee are paid for by the local authorities within the probation area with a 51 per cent subsidy from the Exchequer.

The local authority, although it accepts considerable financial responsibility for the probation service, has no direct executive control over the service. Indeed, the local authority is not even officially represented on the probation committee; yet it cannot refuse to pay its share of the costs of the service, nor indeed can it query the budget of the probation committee. There are a few minor items of expenditure where the local authority must be consulted in advance, but this is the whole extent of the local authority's official influence.

The Morison Committee examined in detail the workings of all three administrative systems mentioned above. They were unanimously agreed that the probation service 'is, essentially, a social service of the courts . . . the probation officer is, and feels himself to be, the servant of the courts because the great bulk of his work, in particular his work of supervision, is placed upon him by decisions of judges and magistrates to whom he is very often, although not necessarily, personally known'.[8] The Committee was therefore more favourably inclined towards administration by the *ad hoc* committee of magistrates typical of England and Wales. Arguments in favour of a nationally organized system, which would certainly permit economies in the running of the service 'are wholly outweighed by the desirability of preserving the employer-employee relationship between magistrates and probation officers . . . this relationship has been of prime importance in the growth of the probation system. It has fostered the courts' interest in probation and it has encouraged probation officers in their work by the assurance that the employers are people who are in daily touch with their practical problems'.[9] Moreover, the Committee criticized the administration of the London service (which is embryonically a national service) 'as having the remoteness of a government department . . . in consequence, some officers have become dissatisfied and dispirited'.[10]

The Association of Municipal Corporations, in giving evidence to the Committee in the course of the inquiry, argued strongly in favour of the local authority taking the service over. This suggestion was rejected partly on the grounds that it would not result in a more efficient service, and partly perhaps because their examination of the Scottish service led them to conclude 'that a principal cause of the failure of the probation service to develop in Scotland as it should have done is that it has been regarded not as a court service but as a relatively minor local authority service'.[11]

It would, of course, be quite unfair to argue from the example of the probation service that there are no services which would not be better run by an *ad hoc* committee than by either the State or the local authority; quite clearly there are many services run most efficiently by both sorts of authority. What we can see, however, is that the most suitable form of administration depends very largely upon the particular nature and character of the service involved.

Needless to say, no form of administration is without its drawbacks, and the system of largely independent probation areas certainly has its share. To the extent that each probation area is an administratively separate unit, we have not so much one probation service as 103—one for each area. In the smaller areas, where the staff is correspondingly small, this raises a number of immediate practical difficulties; a sudden fluctuation in the volume of work can seriously overload an already over-stretched staff, and even the difficulties of arranging a holiday rota, or coping with an epidemic of 'flu become complicated and distracting. Even more important from the long-term point of view is the unsatisfactory career structure that a fragmented service offers. There are only two senior grades, and the prospects of promotion, particularly within one area, are extremely limited; the danger is that this will act as a disincentive to many able young men and women, of the calibre looked for in recruits to the service. The Morison Committee recognized these difficulties and recommended that whenever possible the probation area should, by a process of amalgamation, be enlarged until each area could employ a minimum of one principal and at least six other officers. This would increase the number of promotion places available, as well as overcome the sort of day-to-day problems posed by a very small staff. This movement towards a greater regionalization of the probation service should not, of course, interfere with the essential character of the administration.

Neither probation nor the attendance centre involve removing the offender from his normal home environment, and even while under supervision he can continue to live and work in the community quite normally. In many cases, however, the court may well feel that the offender's best interests may be served by committing him for a period of residential training. In cases of this description there are a number of different sorts of institution which the court can choose; each one provides its own special form of training and so each one is most appropriate for a specific sort of offender.

THE DETENTION CENTRE

The detention centre involves the shortest removal from home, and like the attendance centre was a new form of treatment first introduced in the Criminal Justice Act of 1948. 'The purpose of the centres is to provide a method of treatment for young offenders who do not require a long period of residential training of the kind provided by approved schools and Borstals, but with whom milder measures have failed or are inappropriate.'[12] Originally the detention centres were established to fill the gap between the distinctly reformative measures mentioned above, and the alternative of a short term of imprisonment. Indeed it is hoped that very soon detention in a detention centre will replace entirely the short-term imprisonment of anyone under 21. Perhaps for this reason detention centres are administered by the Prison Department of the Home Office, and the regime is explicitly disciplinary in character. It aims to provide a 'short, sharp shock'. 'The keynote of the regime is brisk activity under strict discipline and supervision. . . . Particular attention is given to the inculcation of standards of personal cleanliness, obedience and good behaviour.'[13]

In the 12 years since the first centre was opened the centres have not resisted change and development; indeed 'the system has already shown some flexibility in expanding the original conception of a regime based primarily on deterrence to include elements of positively personal training . . . it will be well able to maintain the same brisk and exacting regime, which will . . . be both more rigorous and more constructive than is possible for short sentences in local prisons.'[14] The Eighth Report on the Work of the Children's Department adds that 'the staff are trained to take a personal interest in the boys and to make a real effort to find out what is wrong with them and how it may be put right'.[15]

From the outset the detention centres were the subject of research and in 1958 Doctor Grunhut, of Oxford University, published a report on their effects. Based upon an analysis of those who pass through the centres but are none the less subsequently re-convicted, he concluded that 'punitive detention appears suitable for boys with a more or less substantial criminality not due to deep-rooted personal factors or seriously adverse home conditions for whom detention is the first experience of any form of institutional treatment'. That is to say, that those who had already been to an approved school, or Bostal, and consequently were familiar with the normal rigours of any residential establishment were less likely to respond favourably to the specific rigours of the detention centre.

The first centres achieved a success-rate sufficiently high to encourage the Government to plan for a rapid expansion of detention centre facilities. By February 1963 there were 13 centres, one for girls, two for boys between 14–17, and ten for boys between 17–21. The detention centre has established itself as a permanent feature of our penal system, and is consequently subject to recurrent examination and criticism. Already, in a number of official publications, suggestions have been advanced for the amendment of the law relating to the centres. Public discussion and controversy seems at the moment to be concentrated on whether the standard sentence of 3 months (10 weeks with full remission) is long enough to make any lasting difference to a boy. After his release from a detention centre, the offender comes under the supervision of a probation officer for a 12-month period, and it may well be that an efficient after-care service can contribute much to a youth's readjustment to the environment.

THE APPROVED SCHOOL

It is sometimes forgotten that an Approved School is exactly what it says it is—a school that has been approved by the Home Office. It is *not* a children's prison, nor is it an old-fashioned reformatory, but it is an educational establishment providing an educational service for a specially selected group; the people who staff an approved school are not warders or gaolers, but schoolmasters, albeit schoolmasters of a rather special kind.

An approved school exists for the benefit of those between the ages of 10–17, who are either so unstable themselves, or whose home background is so unstable or unhappy that the Court thinks it best that they should be removed from their normal environment, and should spend some considerable amount of time in sustained residential training. A child may be committed if he has been found guilty of an offence punishable in an adult by imprisonment, or if he is beyond the control of his parents, or if he is in need of care and protection. Although he need not necessarily have broken the law, he is usually suffering the same sort of difficulties and stands in the same danger as the law-breaker, so no distinction is made between offenders and non-offenders within the approved school.

The approved school provides a service of education and rehabilitation;

> the aim is to base the process of rehabilitation on understanding of each child's personality, history, abilities and aptitudes, and on knowledge of the family situation. This process calls for a stable environment in the school, enabling remedial influences to be brought to bear and progressive training to be given; it requires contact with the home to be maintained, and after-care to be thoroughly prepared for and carried out.[16]

Needless to say the particular abilities, needs and circumstances of the individual offender will vary quite enormously, and a great deal of harm would be done if children committed to an approved school were to be allocated haphazardly to the nearest available school, there to be subject to a quite uniform treatment. There must first of all be a careful and systematic examination of the child's character, experience and problems, on the basis of which an informed decision can be made as to which type of approved school he would be most likely to respond—where he would receive the education most suited to his talents and interests, in an environment most suited to his personality and temperament. This preliminary examination and decision is made at one of the 5 classifying schools (four for boys, one for girls) to which every-one committed to an approved school is sent for a short period (about 5–6 weeks) before being sent on to a training school. There are 121 approved schools in the country, of these about a quarter are run by the Local Authority, the other three-quarters being run by voluntary organizations of one kind and another. They are however all inspected, approved, to some extent supervised by, and partly paid for by the Home Office.

The approved schools are unusual in that so large a proportion of them are maintained by voluntary bodies of one kind or an-other; on the other hand, this very fact gives some indication of the variety of approach that one is likely to find and underlines the importance of a satisfactory initial classifying system.

Although an approved school is certainly a school, it is equally certainly very different from any other sort of school; for a start its pupils are almost invariably unstable and difficult, and they are frequently very backward; moreover the school is operating all the year round and does not have the same holidays as a normal school. Again new pupils may arrive at a school at any time, not just at the beginning of a term, and they may stay at the school for anything from 12 months to 3 years. Finally, approved schools are boarding schools; any boarding school has a number of diffi-culties of organization and discipline that arise out of its very nature, but a boarding school of difficult, and often resentful children, has its own special difficulties of administration and teaching, particularly as 'the main task of the approved schools is the readjustment and social re-education of the child in prepara-tion for his return to the community'[17] and the normal educa-tional curriculum is a supplementary task.

It is not possible to discuss any of the special problems in detail but a brief mention ought to be made of some of the outstanding difficulties.

Discipline is a problem in any boarding institution, and the character and degree of discipline desirable in an approved school raises a number of difficulties. For a start, discipline must be seen to have a quite different function in an approved school from that in a detention centre. There discipline is a central part of the very training process itself, the centre is an explicitly disciplinary institution; in an approved school this should not be the case. Discipline ought to be firm enough to ensure the smooth and efficient running of the establishment, clearly defined so that each inmate knows exactly what is allowed and what is not, and should contribute towards establishing a sense of security and confidence in the lives of boys and girls who have neither.

Another problem which inevitably worries the managers of an approved school is the problem of absconding. All approved schools are open institutions without bolts and bars, and all the pupils are there at the court's insistence rather than of their own volition, so it is only natural that from time to time some of them are going to run away. The pupil who runs away in a fit of homesickness or despondency, does not present any real problem. Much more serious is the person who runs away persistently, particularly if while at liberty he commits further offences, or who has a background of persistent truancy. In the last resort, the managers of the school may have to take the boy back to court, where he can be transferred, if the magistrates think fit, to a Borstal.

Perhaps the most intractable, and in its long-term effects, the most serious problem is that of institutionalization; everyone who spends a considerable period of time in an institution runs the risk of becoming so used to life in an institution, so used to its customs and regulations, so used perhaps to the companionship, that he comes to depend upon the institution, and is unable to readjust to the reality of the outside world which demands a measure of independence and responsibility. If a period in an approved school results in the pupil becoming institutionalized then, upon release, he will be less rather than more capable of coping with the stresses of life, more likely to repeat his delinquency and so find himself in the familiar and (for him) reassuring atmosphere of another institution, be it Borstal or prison. To send a child to an approved school is to run the risk of setting in motion an almost irresistible process of institutionalization, during which the pupil passes through every form of penal institution yet devised, finishing up as a recidivist, an 'old lag', a menace to himself, and an expensive nuisance to society.

BORSTAL TRAINING

Nowadays Borstal is so well known and familiar a method, that it is easily forgotten how daring and far-sighted was the first experimental institution, established in 1908 in the little Kent village of Borstal. Both in principle and in practice the Borstal marked a sharp break in the traditional methods of the penal system as it had been developed under the stern Prison Commissioner, Edward Du Cane. Even more revolutionary was the development of the Borstal system under Sir Alexander Paterson between the wars, a development which attempted to embody Paterson's view that 'you cannot train men for freedom in a condition of captivity'. The Borstal system, although administered by the Prison Department, is, in most important respects, different in purpose and method from a prison, and the view that a Borstal is only a junior prison, although quite widespread, is quite wrong.

A Borstal exists to provide long-term training for anyone between 15–21, found guilty of an offence punishable by imprisonment; but an offender will only be committed to a Borstal if the court is quite satisfied that a spell of Borstal training is the only suitable sentence. Indeed so seriously is this decision to be taken that it is not within the power of the magistrates in a summary court to sentence anyone to Borstal; they may recommend Borstal, but must pass the offender on to the higher Court of Quarter Sessions for the sentence to be passed.

The sentence itself is a long one—it lasts for 4 years, of which not more than two are to be spent in the institution, the remainder being spent on licence, that is to say at liberty, but under some form of supervision, probably under a probation officer. Indeed, the very length of the sentence causes its own problems; in nearly all cases it is substantially longer than the maximum prison sentence for the same offence. Thus the offender sentenced to Borstal may feel that, by being sent to Borstal he is being punished more severely, and only because of his relative youth. This resentment can be expected to interfere with the training programme, because of the resistance to the influences of the institution that will arise.

The Borstal tries to achieve three things: to build up the characters of the inmates, in much the same way as a public school tries to build up the character of its inmates. There is usually a house-system in a Borstal; this, it is hoped, breaks the institution up into smaller and more personal units, and encourages the development of community spirit, social consciousness and other character-building sentiments. Secondly, the Borstal attempts to develop in the inmates the habit of hard and consistent work. Each boy is expected to do a normal day's work in the Borstal; exactly what form this will take varies from one Borstal to another; it might be domestic work within the institution itself, it might be working the land, or in a Borstal workshop, or even (as in one famous institution) it may be land-reclamation. Whatever it is, the aim is to accustom the boys to the routine of a normal day's work. While in the institution the boy may undertake a training course, so that upon his release he has some vocational qualification.

Thirdly, the Borstal carries on the education of the offender; there are compulsory evening classes for a set number of hours a week, and for the backward, there will be extra tuition during the day. In addition there are more informal educational programmes encouraging the cultivation of constructive hobbies, ranging from amateur dramatics to a cadet force, or the young farmers.

All of these aims are pursued within the disciplinary structure of the institution. As we have already seen, some formal discipline system is necessary in any institution; in a Borstal an attempt is made to encourage in the boy 'the will to do well, putting it up to him to choose right, not forcing, through fear of punishment, the right choice upon him'. In other words there must be a fairly flexible discipline system, one which makes the individual very largely responsible for his own conduct, within clearly prescribed limits. Any tendency towards a rigid, inflexible or repressive system must be resisted.

Of late there have been a number of experimental developments within the Borstal system. For example, group-counselling has become a standard feature of many institutions. More use is being made of such initiative-training programmes as the Duke of Edinburgh's Award Scheme, and the Outward Bound Schools.

Contact between the Borstals and outside organizations is increasing; sports fixtures are arranged between the Borstal and outside clubs and schools, etc. In this and other ways any feelings of isolation, of being cut off from the outside world, are reduced.

The Prison Department now control 24 Borstal Institutions; 4 of these are for girls and the other 20 are for young men. There is a tremendous variety of opportunities and great differences between the regimes operating in each institution. Twelve of the male Borstals are open establishments, whereas the other 8 are closed, although even here the degree of security and supervision varies enormously.

A POSTSCRIPT ON PRISONS

It is difficult to conceive of the prison system as a part of the Welfare State at all; there appears to be an appalling muddle and confusion within the prison service as much as within Government circles, or in the opinions of the general public, as to what the prison service is attempting to do, and how it ought to go about doing it. Moreover innovations in the methods used within the prisons, and ambitious schemes for the modification of present methods are often frustrated by the physical and administrative conditions in which such schemes must operate.

For a start, most of our prisons were constructed over 100 years ago and were constructed according to a particular and punitive vision of what a prison should be like which was common at that time. Thus most of our prisons are large, forbidding buildings, depressing to look at and providing few civilized (and civilizing) amenities. The number of people sentenced to prisons, Borstals and detention centres has greatly increased in recent years; in 1956, for example, there were just under 20,000 people in a prison, Borstal or detention centre, and by 1962 this figure had increased to just over 30,000. Thus, buildings which are intrinsically unsuitable for a constructive reformative purpose are made even more unsuitable because of woeful overcrowding; the living conditions of many prisoners are quite disgracefully inadequate, while the staff are so overburdened with the administrative problems of running an establishment under conditions of this description that they have neither the time nor the stamina to be able to embark upon any constructive programme of reform.

One administrative body—the Prison Department of the Home Office—is responsible for the organization and running of the Prison Service. The prisons under the control of the Commissioners are classified according to their particular function. There are four main classifications as follows:

(1) *Central Prisons.* These take prisoners who are serving long or very long sentences; these prisons are overcrowded, so that it may be necessary for such prisoners to spend a substantial part of their sentence in a local prison before being transferred to a central prison. In 1962 there was an average population of 1,885 in central prisons.

(2) *Regional Prisons.* These emphasize the role of training in the sentence. They provide a range of training facilities for selected prisoners who are serving a sentence for at least twelve months. Some regional prisons are 'open', that is to say, the prisoners are not locked up, but live a very much more normal life. This may require a considerable amount of self-discipline and self-control as the temptation to walk out through the open doors must constantly be overcome. In 1962 there was an average population of 2,024 in regional prisons.

(3) *Corrective Training Prisons.* These provide training facilities for a special group of prisoners who are given a specific sentence of corrective training. These are usually young prisoners who have a long record and who have probably served a number of short sentences, and for whom corrective training is often the last opportunity they will get to take advantage of constructive assistance within the prison system. There are very few separate Corrective Training Establishments; more usually they form a section of some other prison, very often a regional prison.

(4) *Local Prisons.* These are the majority of prisons, and it is here that most prisoners must serve their sentences. In 1962 there was an average population of 16,170 in local prisons. It is here that the overcrowding is worst, the conditions the most primitive, and the prison staffs' task is the most thankless. These prisons are sometimes very large indeed, in some cases holding over 1,000 inmates.

Thus it can be seen that there are several different kinds of prison offering a range of different treatments; and within each category there are differences between one prison and another. However, it cannot be denied that for the majority of prisoners, particularly those serving short sentences in a local prison, imprisonment is a very negative form of treatment. The prison is too large and impersonal for any degree of personal contact except between inmates, while the sentence is too short for any reformative influences to be brought to bear.

There are, however, a number of encouraging signs, which indicate that there are important changes taking place within the prison service. For one thing a number of new prisons are being built, and the design of these prisons shows a determination to avoid the monolithic and depressing atmosphere of the older prisons.

Within the prisons new methods are being experimented with; for example, group-counselling is becoming more widespread in an attempt to encourage the prisoner to discover for himself problems common to most prisoners. The special contribution that can be made by the psychologist and the sociologist is increasingly respected, and plays an increasingly important role in the treatment provided.

Most encouraging of all, however, is evidence of the changing attitude of the prison staff towards their job. No longer does the prison officer regard himself merely as a turn-key, imposing a rigid but senseless discipline. Increasingly he sees his task as a very much more demanding and sensitive one; he sees his role as being a crucial part of a reformative system and himself as having a genuine and complex social-work function.

All these trends which are gathering pace and momentum every day, suggest that the prison system is entering upon a period of important developments which may well produce some fundamental reforms in the system as we know it today.

CONCLUSION

Although it is very easy to talk glibly about the 'Problem of Crime' it can now be seen that no easy answer has been found to the problem. On the contrary it has, it seems, been found necessary to initiate and elaborate a complex series of social and public services, some institutional, some intensely personal; some deeply involved in an attempt to train or re-educate, others with a more negative, punitive function. Each of these services has its own particular administrative structure, and its own problems of staffing and control. Thus the apparently straightforward task of stopping people from breaking the law has given rise to a complex of detailed and specialized provisions which seems likely to become more rather than less complicated, and to employ more and more people with ever more refined and sophisticated skills and techniques.

Some critics have little sympathy with this tendency; for them the treatment of the criminal is simple. They recommend a return to some of the traditional, usually somewhat violent, methods which were common (and largely ineffective) a hundred and more years ago. They can see no virtue in the apparently 'soft' methods of today, methods which seem to think more of the criminal than of his victim. These critics do not appreciate that the victim is best protected if the offence is unlikely to be repeated, and that therefore it is more valuable to prevent an offender repeating his offence than it is to make him suffer; but it is also very much more difficult. All human behaviour is hard to understand and control, and human misbehaviour is particularly difficult. The criminologist and the penologist, the social worker in the field and the research worker in the laboratory must constantly bear in mind that any proposed form of treatment of the criminal treads a delicate line between the undeniable necessity for social control on the one hand, and unwarrantable interference with personal liberty on the other.

This delicate operation ought not to be entrusted to the clumsy, the inexperienced, the simple-minded or the bigoted. We must therefore welcome the announcement by the Home Secretary in April 1964 that he was setting up a Royal Commission to investigate thoroughly all forms of penal policy and treatment. It will, of course, be some years before such a Commission can complete its investigations, but it is encouraging that patient and expert scrutiny, rather than reiteration of prejudice and unproven assumption, marks official attitudes towards the penal system.

A NOTE ON LEGAL AID

It has often been noted that the costs of legal advice and representation are very high, but that equally many people involved in proceedings do themselves less than justice by being unrepresented by a lawyer; it would certainly be a very serious situation if the courts failed to ensure that justice was done, or innocent people were inhibited from using their courts because of the high costs of litigation. To overcome this problem the Legal Aid and Advice Service was established in 1948; under this service anyone whose means do not exceed certain defined limits, can obtain advice from a solicitor, and if necessary, representation in any court for a very reasonable cost. The regulations governing this service ensure that frivolous or unnecessary litigation is discouraged, but at the same time that no one with a genuine and tenable complaint is derived of his rights because he cannot afford to assert them (see Chapter 13).

SUGGESTED READING

WINIFRED ELKIN, *The English Penal System.*
HUGH J. KLARE, *Anatomy of Prison.*
LIONEL FOX, *English Prisons and Borstal System.*
B. BEHAN, *Borstal Boy.*
PETER WILDEBLOOD, *Against the Law.*
T. FYVEL, *Insecure Offenders.*
JOAN KING, *The Probation Service.*
H.M.S.O., *The Sentence of the Court.*

NOTES

[1] *The Treatment of Young Offenders, Report of the Advisory Council on the Treatment of Offenders,* H.M.S.O., 1959, p. 7.
[2] *Non-Residential Treatment of Offenders under* 21, H.M.S.O., 1962, para. 11.
[3] *Report of the Committee on Children and Young Persons,* Cmd. 1191, para. 288.
[4] *Report of the Prison Commissioners for* 1962, Cmd. 2030, para. 86.
[5] *Report of the Committee on Children and Young Persons,* Cmd. 1191, para. 291.
[6] *Foreword to the Report of the European Seminar on Probation,* London, 1952, published by U.N.O.
[7] For a discussion of Casework and Probation, see the *Report of the Departmental Committee on the Probation Service,* Cmd. 1650, para. 53–9. (This report is known as the Morison Report.)
[8] Morison Report, para. 158.
[9] Ibid., para. 169.
[10] Ibid., para. 232.
[11] Ibid., para. 246.
[12] *Report of the Committee on Children and Young Persons,* Cmd. 1191, para. 30.

[13] *7th Report on the Work of the Children's Department*, H.M.S.O., 1955, para. 195.
[14] *The Treatment of Young Offenders*, H.M.S.O., 1959, para. 27.
[15] Ibid., para. 157.
[16] *8th Report on the Work of the Children's Department*, H.M.S.O., 1961, para. 184.
[17] *Report of the Committee on Children and Young Persons*, Cmd. 1191, para. 451.

9. THE PHYSICALLY HANDICAPPED

Joan L. M. Eyden

THE acceptance by the State of some responsibility for those who are physically handicapped goes back at least to the Act of 1531 (discussed in Chapter 2), and was incorporated in the famous Poor Law of 1601, but this legislation was concerned only with the destitution of those who were handicapped. Special provision by religious foundations certainly goes back many centuries earlier, but again was primarily concerned with the material needs of those they sought to help. The leper houses of the Middle Ages were mainly the result of fear not of compassion and were attempts at isolating the leper from the rest of the community and not at giving him the care and treatment he required.

THE WELFARE OF BLIND PERSONS

The establishment of a School for the Blind at Liverpool in 1790 for instruction and industrial training was perhaps the first institution of a more modern character to be founded. The curriculum included music, basket-making, the manufacture of window cord, tarred cloth, etc. One early pupil became an organist, others taught music in schools. The establishment of similar schools in Bristol (1798) and in London (1799) coupled with the founding of such societies as the London Indigent Blind Visiting Society (1834) led by degrees to a comprehensive welfare service for this group of handicapped people.[1]

Throughout the nineteenth century the local societies for the blind continued to develop, providing a wide variety of services according to the particular interests and concern of their founders. A great advance in the education and training of the blind was made after the general adoption of the Braille method of reading. The Royal National Institute for the Blind was founded by Dr. Thomas Rhodes Armitage in 1863 under the title British and Foreign Blind Association. Its first task and in one sense its original motive was to co-ordinate embossed reading methods, and by the end of the century it had done much to promote the use of Braille in substitution for a variety of other codes. Gradually this Institute extended its interests to education and later to employment and the prevention of blindness and is now recognized as the main national organization in the field of welfare for the blind. It co-ordinates the work of other bodies in this field although there are some local regional and national organizations usually providing some particularly specialized service which are completely independent.

The development of Blind Welfare into a comprehensive service is the result of a fruitful partnership between statutory and voluntary activity. As early as 1834 the Royal Commission on the Poor Law noted with approval the use being made of the early Schools for the Blind by some overseers of the poor for their destitute blind and commended their action in paying for such persons from the poor rate.

With the provision of universal elementary education in the last decades of the nineteenth century the State was forced to look even more closely at the educational needs of the handicapped child. A Royal Commission on the Blind was set up in 1885 with the following terms of reference: 'the investigation of the condition of the blind, the various systems of education existing at home and abroad, the employments open to them, and the means by which education might be extended and the number of persons qualified for suitable employment increased'. In 1886 its terms of reference were widened to include the deaf and dumb and its report issued in 1889 led to the Elementary Education (Blind and Deaf Children) Act, 1893. Under this Act the duty of providing for the education of these children passed from the poor law authority to the local education authority, and parents had a duty to see that their handicapped children received education between the ages of 5 and 15. Moreover, special schools became eligible for grant aid. Although some of the larger education authorities provided their own special schools for handicapped pupils under this and subsequent Acts, it has been the practice for many to discharge their obligations through the use of voluntary schools or schools provided by other authorities.

Apart from education, perhaps the most important step in providing a universal and comprehensive system of blind welfare in this country was taken in 1919 when, after the report of a Departmental Committee set up in 1914, the newly established Ministry of Health issued a circular which required local authorities to compile a register of blind persons in their areas if they wished to benefit from certain grants-in-aid.

This was followed in 1920 by the Blind Persons Act—the first statute concerned with the general welfare of a specific group of physically handicapped persons. This Act imposed on every County Council and County Borough the duty of framing to the satisfaction of the Ministry of Health and of putting into operation at least a minimum scheme of service for the blind in its area. The Minister suggested that such schemes should include the care of children under school age, the education and training of children, young people and adults; employment in workshops or through home-workers schemes; the augmentation of wages; the provision of hostels and homes; of home teaching and the giving of financial assistance to the necessitous blind. The Blind Persons Act, 1938, amongst other things laid down that all domiciliary financial assistance to the blind and their dependents must be given under the Blind Persons Act not under the Poor Law. The establishment of an accurate register of blind persons was an essential part of all schemes made under these Acts and provided important information about the number, age, and onset of blindness by means of which realistic provision could be made.

An important feature in the Acts of 1920 and 1938 was that local authorities, if they wished, could discharge their responsibility for all or any part of their schemes through voluntary organizations whom they could reimburse from public funds for the services provided on their behalf. As a result, during the 1920's and 1930's blind welfare developed rapidly throughout the country, but with great diversity of provision and organization.[2] In 1939 the amount spent per head per annum on blind welfare by County Councils varied from £6 to £33 and by County Borough Councils from £12 to £50. It would seem that by this date at least a minimum nation-wide service had been built up for all members of this handicapped group, but that in seeking to provide a service capable of giving or restoring the maximum amount of 'contributive citizenship' to all members, blind welfare was only partially successful, differing strikingly in quality from area to area.

In spite of this inequality, however, blind welfare services were considerably in advance of comparable provision for any other physically handicapped group. The responsibility of the local Education Authorities for the provision of special education for various groups of handicapped children (extended and revised by a number of Acts including the Education Act, 1944) has already been noted. Apart from this, until the Second World War, services for other handicapped groups were almost entirely provided by voluntary organizations.

THE WELFARE OF DEAF AND DEAFENED PERSONS

Permissive powers were given to local authorities by Section 67(b) of the Poor Law Act, 1930 to make contributions to voluntary bodies for the purpose of placing deaf persons in work and by the Education Acts to grant aid trade schools and instruction centres for deaf young people.

The deaf depended until recently on the Missions for the Deaf which, originally and still essentially religious in character, inevitably found themselves undertaking more and more work of a social character where the difficulties of communication could be met and overcome by providing social clubs, outings, sports, as well as religious services.[3] Mission workers were increasingly called upon to act as interpreters for the deaf at work, in courts of law and in all kinds of official and unofficial situations.

The National Institute for the Deaf, founded in 1911, attempted to co-ordinate through affiliation the work of the local missions which, in 1939, numbered 82 grouped into 5 regional associations. Like the organizations for the blind, those for the deaf were reluctant to give up local autonomy in order to achieve a more unified and effective organization. By 1939 it was becoming apparent that the needs of the deaf and even more the needs of the deafened or hard-of-hearing were not being adequately met by existing voluntary organizations and support was growing for legislation which would give more security and assistance to these handicapped groups, but the outbreak of war led to the temporary abandonment of efforts to obtain such a development.[4]

The Physically Handicapped

For many years a great variety of voluntary effort, some of it ephemeral, some lasting and most of it local in character had attempted to meet some of the needs of the crippled. War-time conditions brought an impetus to the development of more comprehensive services from another quarter. The increasing demands of the war effort made it imperative that workers and potential workers were used efficiently and to the maximum extent. The conditions of severe unemployment characteristic of the 1920's and 1930's gave way to an unprecedented demand for labour of every kind. Many handicapped people had the opportunity for the first time of proving what they could do as industrial workers. Moreover, it was essential that ways should be found of getting back to their maximum working capacity as soon as possible those who were injured or ill. Although a series of rehabilitation departments in military orthopaedic hospitals had been set up during the war of 1914–18, they developed very little between the wars. The British Medical Association Committee on Fractures in 1935 and the Delevigne Committee on the Rehabilitation of Persons injured in Accidents in 1939 had paved the way for further experiment and rapid development in medical rehabilitation, particularly after the introduction of the Emergency Hospital Service, and physiotherapy and occupational therapy made rapid strides. In 1941, Mr. E. Bevin as Minister of Labour introduced a pilot scheme for the training and resettlement of disabled persons. The success of this led the Government to set up an Interdepartmental Committee on the Rehabilitation and Resettlement of Disabled Persons under the chairmanship of Mr. George Tomlinson, which subsequently reported in 1943 and led directly to the passing of the Disabled Persons (Employment) Act, 1944.

The Act marks a most important stage in the development of a comprehensive service for all the disabled. The aim is to help men and women who are substantially handicapped by some kind of disability to obtain suitable employment or work on their own account. It is an *employment* Act and therefore it covers only those who are capable of productive work of some kind. A striking feature of the Act is that it applies to people with all types of disability for a disabled person is defined for the purpose of the Act as one who 'on account of injury, disease or congenital deformity is substantially handicapped' in getting or keeping suitable employment or work. The test in every case is whether there is a substantial handicap to employment or work which would otherwise be suitable. Those so handicapped and whose disablement is likely to last at least six months are eligible for registration under the Act. This register of disabled persons is one of the basic features of the whole scheme, but there is no obligation on any person to register unless he wishes to receive help under the Act. The Ministry of Labour is responsible for the keeping of this register as well as for implementing the other provisions under the 1944 Act. At each of the local offices of the Ministry there is a disablement resettlement officer whose responsibility it is to assist disabled persons who are capable or likely to become capable of remunerative employment to find suitable work and to receive appropriate training and other help where necessary. These officers are part of the staff of the employment exchanges and may devote all or a proportion of their time to this service.

The Act makes provision for the setting up by the Minister of courses of industrial rehabilitation for those who are not fit enough to return to work immediately after leaving hospital or who want to test their fitness to do a particular job. The aim of Industrial Rehabilitation Units is to restore employment confidence by providing mental and physical 'toning up' and an opportunity of gradual adjustment to working conditions. They also provide opportunities for testing vocational aptitudes—often extremely important if the disabled person has to start a completely new working life as a result of his disability. Courses usually last for 6 weeks but may be as long as 12 weeks where this appears to be advisable. The committee of inquiry set up in March 1953 on The Rehabilitation Training and Resettlement of Disabled Persons under the chairmanship of Lord Piercy, reported in 1956 that 15 I.R.U.s had been set up under the 1944 Act; each unit had a number of workshops, a gymnasium, a garden, a schoolroom and accommodation for interviews and for general administration. One unit, that at Egham, was fully residential, two had hostels attached, and the rest were non-residential, but suitable lodgings were arranged where necessary. In commenting on the process of rehabilitation and the evidence received from the British Medical Association and other bodies, the Committee accepted it as a fundamental principle that 'the rehabilitation process is to be conceived, not as divided naturally or essentially into definite stages, but as a single process in which the emphasis at the beginning is on the medical aspects, and the emphasis at the end on the work aspects'.[5]

After a period of industrial rehabilitation, many disabled people are able to return to employment, either to their old jobs or directly to new ones. Others, however, need training as a disabled person's prospects of satisfactory resettlement through employment will be much improved if he has skill and experience to offer which are in good demand in the labour market. Facilities for training the disabled can be provided under two enactments. The first is the 1944 Act, restricted to disabled persons who are in need of training in order to render them competent to undertake employment of a kind suited to their age, experience and general qualifications. The second is the more general Employment and Training Act, 1948, under which the Minister of Labour may provide courses for 'the purpose of assisting persons to select, fit themselves for, obtain and retain employment suitable to their age and capacity'. At the time of the Piercy Committee's report there were 16 Government training centres, and 4 centres for the severely disabled run by voluntary organizations with the financial support and technical advice of the Ministry of Labour. The disabled can also be helped to take professional courses of training or study if such courses are necessary for their satisfactory resettlement. Allowances for trainees, and where necessary their dependents, are paid by the Minister and the official policy has been to fix these at a point in excess of unemployment and sickness benefit, but below the average wage that would be payable generally to trainees on first entering employment in their training trade or occupation.

It is hoped that by these methods it will be possible for the great majority of disabled who are employable to obtain work in open industry on their merits as workers, but to facilitate this the 1944 Act requires every employer with 20 or more workers to employ a quota, at present 3 per cent, of registered disabled persons. An employer who is below his quota may not without a permit engage an able-bodied worker, nor may an employer discharge a registered disabled person without reasonable cause if such a discharge would leave him below his quota. The Piercy

Committee in discussing the working of the scheme commented:

> . . . its main value has been that it has provided a sound basis for publicity among both employers and workpeople to show the industrial value of disabled persons. As one of the witnesses put it the quota scheme 'builds up a sense of public responsibility towards the disabled'. Investigations have shown that the quota has become generally acceptable to industry, and although it may be largely unnecessary in a time of full employment the Committee believes the educational importance of the quota scheme to be such that it should continue.[6]

That this type of education is necessary is often evident. Joan S. Clarke tells the story of the lame girl who had a job in a store. One day the manager saw her walking across the floor and as a result discharged her. The girl pointed out that she was lame when he engaged her, to which he retorted: 'Maybe, but if I'd known I wouldn't have engaged you.' Mrs. Clarke comments: 'The manager's arbitary discrimination against this girl had no reference to her handicap, which did not prevent her being an efficient saleswoman nor from having an appearance sufficiently pleasing for him to have engaged her. He had a fixed objection to bodily defect, and to this the lame girl fell a victim.'[7]

As a supplement to the quota scheme the Minister of Labour has powers to require that vacancies in certain 'designated' occupations shall be filled by registered disabled persons, irrespective of the size of the employer's establishment and that a permit shall be obtained by an employer who wishes to engage a non-registered person for these types of employment. So far two occupations, those of car park attendant and electrically operated passenger lift attendant are the only ones which have been so registered.

In spite of the great emphasis in recent years on the need to help the disabled to take their place in industry on normal terms, there has also been the recognition that some are unable to do this. The Tomlinson Committee in 1941 said: 'The use of institutional or sheltered employment must be limited to that small group who cannot hold their own on level terms and under competitive conditions.' The Piercy Committee endorsed this and added that

> even if sheltered employment is found to be the only means of providing disabled persons with a livelihood at any point of time, it should always be in the mind of those responsible that sheltered

employment is only second best to competitive employment. . . . Nothing, in the Committee's opinion, could be worse than the prospect of a group of disabled people, some of them young on entering a workshop, remaining the whole of their working lives in a sheltered environment as a matter of course, and incidentally perhaps causing others with far better claims to sheltered work to be excluded.[8]

Sheltered employment may be provided under the 1944 Act for registered disabled persons who by reason of the nature or severity of their disablement, are otherwise unlikely to obtain employment. Such sheltered employment is provided by voluntary organizations, local authorities and a non-profit-making company (Remploy) set up by the Minister of Labour. Mention has already been made of the establishment of workshops for the blind by voluntary associations and some local authorities under the Blind Persons Acts. Voluntary organizations also provided a variety of sheltered workshops for other groups of handicapped. Local authorities, however, had not provided sheltered employment for the physically handicapped other than the blind except for two village settlements and two workshops as part of the after-care provisions for tuberculosis persons under the National Health Service Act, 1946. The Piercy Committee considered that the responsibility for the employment of all types of disabled should be with the Ministry of Labour and recommended that the provision by local authorities of sheltered employment whether for the blind, the general classes of the handicapped or the tuberculous should be under the powers given under the Disabled Persons (Employment) Act, rather than other relevant legislation. This was implemented by the Disabled Persons (Employment) Act, 1958.

Remploy Limited was established in 1945 as the Disabled Persons Employment Corporation Limited, and in its early years had considerable difficulties in establishing itself without running at a considerable loss. As a result of recommendations made by the Organization and Methods Division of the Treasury the position of Remploy has become much more secure and stable. However, as the Piercy Committee pointed out, Remploy is operating a social service for the disabled, one which seeks to demonstrate that, given suitable conditions of work, even the badly disabled person may make some effective contribution to the country's production, but 'it is unreasonable having regard to the difficulties . . . to expect this social service to operate without a loss'.

From this brief account of the Disabled Persons (Employment) Act, 1944, and its implementation, it is obvious that the last twenty years has seen a revolution in the employment position of disabled persons. The absence of large scale unemployment except in certain areas of the country has certainly aided the absorption of many more handicapped people into open industry than at one time would have been thought possible. There is still much to be done, and the emergence of large scale unemployment might make some of the provisions of the Act such as the quota scheme unenforceable. Yet the fact that in 1960 some 644,140 out of 693,000 on the Disabled Persons Register were employed, besides an unknown number of handicapped people in regular work who for one reason or another had not registered is no mean achievement. During the same year, 1960, the Disablement Resettlement Officers placed 79,664 of the registered disabled in ordinary employment and 1,203 in sheltered workshops.[9]

THE WELFARE OF DISABLED PERSONS

Good medical and industrial rehabilitation and settlement into suitable employment solves many of the problems, personal and social as well as economic, of the handicapped and their families. The implementation of the Disabled Persons (Employment) Act, and the nation-wide provision of rehabilitation incorporated into the National Health Service, however, still left many needs unmet. More adequate provision for financial aid was made, of course, by the National Insurance Act, 1946, and the National Insurance (Industrial Injuries) Act, 1946, and Part II of the National Assistance Act, 1948, already discussed in Chapter 3.

It was the National Assistance Act which for the first time made statutory provision for general welfare services for all groups of the handicapped, extending to the deaf and the crippled, etc., the possibility of the same kinds of help which had been developed for the blind under the Acts of 1920–38. These Acts were repealed by the National Assistance Act, but the duty of providing welfare services for the blind continued under it. Section 29 of the National Assistance Act, 1948, empowers County Councils and County Boroughs to make arrangements for promoting the welfare

of persons who are blind, deaf or dumb, and others who are substantially and permanently handicapped by illness, injury or congenital deformity. It is suggested that schemes under the section
may include an information service, the provision of social and
occupation centres, workshops, hostels, home worker schemes
and 'giving such persons instruction in their own homes or elsewhere in methods of overcoming the effects of their disabilities'.

It is clear from this that if local authorities implement to the full
this legislation in close co-operation with voluntary organizations,
all groups of the handicapped or their families should have a comprehensive service to which they can turn to meet any of their
specialized needs. Unfortunately this has not been the case. The
duty of providing services was continued under the National
Assistance Act only for the blind. Guidance to local authorities on
the provision of welfare services for other classes of handicapped
persons was issued by the Ministry of Health in circular 32/51 in
August 1951, and local authorities were invited to submit schemes
to the Minister for approval, but the submission of such schemes
and their subsequent implementation were not made compulsory
until 1960. Moreover, such phrases as 'methods of overcoming
the effects of their disabilities' are liable to very different interpretations. As a result the development of services for the deaf
and other categories of handicapped persons over the past sixteen
years has been patchy and inadequate.

Reference has already been made to the Committee of Inquiry
into the Rehabilitation, Training and Resettlement of Disabled
Persons under the chairmanship of Lord Piercy. It was appointed
in 1953 with the following terms of reference—'To review in all
its aspects the existing provision for the rehabilitation, training
and resettlement of disabled persons, full regard being had to the
need for the utmost economy in the Government's contribution
and to make recommendations.' The report of the Committee,
issued in 1956, emphasized the widening of the concept of rehabilitation. In a debate in the House of Commons on the 13th December 1957, on future planning for the disabled in the light of the
Piercy Report, the need was accepted 'to ensure the full development of their potentialities so that they might take their proper
place in life and to treat each handicapped person as an individual,
not as a representative of a group or type of disability'.

The Piercy Committee pointed out that the total amount spent by local authorities in England and Wales for the year ending 31st March 1955, on services for the disabled other than the blind and partially-sighted was only some £250,000 as compared with £2·4 million spent in the same period on the blind and partially-sighted. By 1956, moreover, 36 local authorities out of a total of 146 had not made schemes for such services and others were only just at the beginning of their development. Having due regard to the plea for economy expressed in its terms of reference, the Committee concluded that developments in the welfare field could only take place gradually, having regard to the nation's ability to pay for the services, but it considered it essential that local authorities should be grant-aided by the Exchequer in their expenditure on services provided by them under Section 29 of the National Assistance Act. This recommendation of the Committee was accepted in principle by the Government. Specific grants in aid were superseded by a block grant from the Exchequer towards local authority services under the Local Government Act, 1958, but in calculating this block grant some allowance is now made for a contribution towards the welfare services.

Moreover, since 1960, the Minister of Health has required all local authorities to make schemes for the handicapped in their area. Progress in recent years in the development of these provisions can to some extent be gauged by the rise in expenditure and the increasing numbers of disabled served. Thus, although the number of registered blind persons was virtually stable between 1957 and 1961, the numbers of deaf people registered with local authorities has risen from 17,826 in 1957 to 22,906 in 1961, and those in the general classes from 64,700 to 100,157 in the same period. Nevertheless, the fact that in 1962 541,616 physically handicapped people (excluding those with eye defects) were registered as disabled persons with the Ministry of Labour and that 300,000 children were deemed by the Ministry of Education to require special educational treatment on account of physical disabilities other than blindness, indicates that the number of people registered with the local authorities is only a small proportion of those who may need the help of the services which can be provided under the National Assistance Act, 1948.

Another administrative development which should perhaps be noted here is that the Local Government Act, 1958, provided for the delegation of welfare services under Section 29 of the National

Assistance Act together with certain services under the National
Health Service Acts by the County Councils to non-County
Boroughs, Urban and Rural District Councils of 60,000 or more
inhabitants. This has meant that another group of local authorities
are involved in the provision of welfare services for the handicapped and the reorganization of the local government of the
Greater London area will add still more.

The establishment of statutory services for the disabled has had
a far-reaching effect on the voluntary organizations. In many instances the local authorities have endeavoured to secure their co-
operation on something like an agency basis through which the
voluntary bodies have been assisted by public funds. As the services have developed, however, the Piercy Report considered that
'comprehensiveness of service throughout the country is difficult
to organize on the basis of voluntary effort. . . . Moreover a major
statutory service of a professional or economic character could not
be in fact economically run or conveniently controlled on such
a basis of delegation'. Nevertheless, the Committee held that 'the
future of voluntary services lies in making the fullest use of its
natural suitability for the exploration and development of the
fields of work and the fact that the voluntary work equally naturally can supply that personal interest and care which is more
difficult to provide through the ordinary machinery of the public
welfare service'.[10]

From what has already been said it is clear that both voluntary
and statutory provision will need to be increased if the needs of
the handicapped are to be more fully met.[11] In 1962 the Minister
of Health asked all County and County Borough Councils to plan
the development of their health and welfare services for ten years
ahead and to provide schemes complementary to the ten-year plan
for hospital development brought out in 1962. The report, *Health
and Welfare, The Development of Community Care*,[12] issued in 1963,
collated all these plans and shows that in the case of the physically
handicapped the local authorities hope to extend their services
considerably in some directions. Thus there were 40 purpose
built or specially adapted occupation centres for the physically
handicapped in 1963, with 17 more under construction, but plans
for as many as 185 additional ones by 1973. However, only 11 new
homes providing 322 places of residential accommodation for
young handicapped people is planned—a development which the

Ministry of Health recognized to be inadequate. One of the biggest and continuing shortages in these services is likely to be in personnel in the supply of social workers. Although plans for the increased training of social workers suggested by the Working Party on Social Workers in the Local Authority Health and Welfare Services are being put into operation, there is some doubt as to whether the local authorities will reach their targets in the next ten years owing to the difficulties of recruitment. This shortage of qualified workers is, however, not peculiar to this field and will be discussed further in Chapter 13.[13]

FURTHER READING

Services for the Disabled 1961, issued by the Ministry of Labour and National Service, published by H.M.S.O.
THOS. FERGUSON and A. W. KERR, *Handicapped Youth*
J. D. KERSHAW, *Handicapped Children.*
I. R. and A. W. G. EWING, *New Opportunites for the Deaf Child.*
Report of a Working Party Commissioned by the British Council for the Rehabilitation of the Disabled; The Handicapped School Leaver.

NOTES

[1] See Madeline Rooff, *Voluntary Societies and Social Policy*, Part 4, for further information.
[2] See J. F. Wilson, 'Voluntary Organisation for the Welfare of the Blind', in *Voluntary Social Services*, A. F. C. Bourdillon (ed.).
[3] See J. D. Evans, 'Voluntary Organisation for the Welfare of the Deaf' in Bourdillon, op. cit.
[4] Joan S. Clarke, *Disabled Citizens*, Chapter V.
[5] *The Rehabilitation and Training of Disabled Persons*, 1956, H.M.S.O., Cmd. 9883 (The Piercy Report).
[6] Ibid.
[7] Clarke, op. cit.
[8] Piercy Report, loc. cit.
[9] See *Report of the Ministry of Labour and National Service for* 1960.
[10] Piercy Report, loc. cit.
[11] See J. H. Nicholson, *Help for the Handicapped*, published by the National Council of Social Service.
[12] *Health and Welfare, The Development of Community Care*, H.M.S.O. Cmd. 1973.
[13] *Social Workers in the Local Authority Health and Welfare Services*, 1959, H.M.S.O. (The Younghusband Report).

10. THE MENTALLY DISORDERED

Joan L. M. Eyden

THE development of services for the mentally ill and handicapped has had a very different history from those for the physically disabled. To some people this may seem surprising while others may wonder why one would expect these services to develop along the same lines. The need to make provision for the care and treatment of the mentally disordered has been complicated by the fear aroused in the community by the occasionally bizarre and at times dangerous behaviour of some patients. The custodial measures taken by society to allay this fear have led to problems concerned with the liberty of the individual and thus involved the judicial system. It is only in the mid-twentieth century that the emphasis in community provision has shifted from the protection of society to the care and treatment of the patient suffering from mental disorder.

The history of provisions for the mentally disordered is a long and complicated one, and one in which the State has been interested for many centuries—unlike its almost complete disregard for the fortunes of the physically handicapped. This interest, however, was originally concerned not with their care and well-being but with their right to hold and control land. The Act *De Proerogativa Regis* (1324), differentiated between the 'lunatic'—'one who aforetime hath had his wit and memory but happen to fail of his wit,' and the 'natural fool'—'one that hath no understanding from his nativity and so is, by law, presumed never likely to attain any'. This attempt at differentiating between the mentally ill and the mentally subnormal related only to their capacity to hold and administer land and in subsequent centuries there was considerable confusion, legal, social and medical between lunacy and idiocy, a confusion which perhaps was justified in the light of some modern theories as to the nature of certain forms of mental defect.

The main concern of the State and the public was with the potential danger to the community of those who were sometimes thought of as being possessed by devils. Bethlehem Hospital was established in 1246 as a religious foundation for the care of the insane and after considerable reforms survived the closing of the religious houses by Henry VIII along with St. Bartholomew's and St. Thomas's Hospitals. It later earned notoriety as Bedlam, a place of entertainment, until 1770 when amongst other reforms an apothecary was appointed as the first resident medical officer. In spite of some outstanding exceptions, few doctors were concerned with the nature of mental illness until the twentieth century.[1] Although it is true that by the eighteenth century public concern was beginning to be felt for the treatment of the lunatic, custody and restraint were still the time-honoured methods of dealing with the insane whether in public institutions or private asylums. Destitute lunatics could be sent to the workhouse under the Poor Law, while others could be sent to gaols or houses of correction under the Vagrancy Acts. There was legal sanction for the practice of chaining these unfortunate people if they were considered to be 'dangerous lunatics'. The nineteenth century saw a series of inquiries and acts which sought to meet the urgent need of safeguarding the interests of patients and was thus primarily concerned with the removal of flagrant abuses and the improvement of madhouses, asylums and workhouses. The emphasis on custody made it imperative that procedure for the detention and protection of patients should be carefully regulated. K. Jones[2] points out that the enlightened interest of doctors and philanthropists might have resulted in the establishment of a new and constructive attitude towards the whole problem of the care and treatment of the mentally disordered in the middle of the nineteenth century. Yet this promise was not fulfilled. The latter part of the nineteenth century continued to be dominated by two public prejudices—'the fear of the insane and the fear of illegal detention of the sane'. K. Jones quotes a letter to *The Times* on 5th April, 1877, signed by 'A Lunatic's Victim', which deplored the tendency of the present law '. . . to protect the liberty of the lunatic at the expense of the lives, limbs and comfort of the sane'.[3]

The Lunacy Act, 1890, was a consolidation of former Acts concerned primarily with the prevention of ill treatment and of illegal detention. Its provisions emphasized the legal aspect of insanity and confirmed the rigid structure of institutional care based on legal certification which resulted and which tended to inhibit the development of a more constructive attitude during the first decades of the twentieth century.

Meanwhile there was increasing interest in the problems of the mentally defective. Until the Idiots Act, 1886, no special arrangements were made for this group of mentally disordered people. If they were unable to support themselves and became destitute they, like pauper lunatics, might be sent to the workhouse, or if they appeared to be a danger to their neighbours they could be dealt with under the Lunacy Acts. The Act of 1886 made it possible for local authorities to make special provision for idiots by building separate institutions, but little was done as the measure was a permissive one only. Similarly local authorities were given permissive powers to provide education in special schools or classes for feeble-minded children by the Elementary Education (Defective and Epileptic Children) Act, 1899—some six years after powers had been given for the provision of special education for blind and deaf children.

This interest in the mentally defective was part of an increasing general concern about the growth of 'a social problem' group. The study of eugenics was attracting increased interest at the beginning of the twentieth century and the importance of the hereditary and natural factors in mental defect and disease, coupled with limited recognition of environmental factors, led to a demand for the provision of institutions for the segregation of mental defectives and the supervision of those remaining in the community to prevent them from becoming parents. The Mental Deficiency section of the National Conference on the Prevention of Destitution in 1911 emphasized this point and called for further legislation. According to Dr. C. W. Saleeby: 'The problem of mental defect and disease is the great omission from Mr. Lloyd George's superb scheme of National Preventive Medicine: it must now be dealt with by legislation.'[4]

The outcome was the 1913 Mental Deficiency Act which gave local authorities, working through mental deficiency committees the duty to ascertain in its area all persons 'subject to be dealt with', to provide institutional care and guardianship; and to provide for the supervision of mental defectives in the community. The social repercussions of mental deficiency were recognized in that the definition of deficiency was primarily an attempted estimation of social functioning. The classification of those affected, idiots, imbeciles and feeble-minded was based on the extent of mental defect and the need for supervision and control; a fourth category, the moral imbecile, was added as an attempt to bring within the scope of statutory regulation a number of those who were deemed members of the 'social problem group' and who might otherwise not prove able to be dealt with. This category led to much controversy amongst doctors, lawyers and members of the general public, because of difficulties of definition. The Act of 1913 required proof that mental deficiency had existed 'from birth or an early age' before a person could be dealt with, but the Mental Deficiency Act, 1927, amended this to 'before the age of 18 years'. Another important innovation in the Act of 1913 was the setting up of a Board of Control which took over all the powers and duties of the existing Lunacy Commissioners and became responsible for the supervision of the local authorities in the exercise of their powers under the Act and for the protection of all defectives. These Acts remained the basis of provision for mental defectives until the National Health Service Act revolutionized the machinery of administration.

K. Jones points out that between the wars parallel movements took place in mental deficiency work and in the care of the mentally ill. 'In both cases, there was a swing away from the concept of permanent detention, and a desire to find means of integrating patients more closely with the society which had previously been concerned only to reject them; but they were distinct movements, and there was comparatively little contact between them up to 1939.'[5] Because under the Lunacy Act, asylums could only take certified patients they tended to give only custodial care, and thus new theories and knowledge about mental illness and new method of treatment tended to be developed outside them. Treatment of neurosis, for instance, was given mainly in private consulting rooms and in out-patient clinics of voluntary hospitals. The Mental Treatment Act, 1930, by creating categories of voluntary and temporary patients made it possible for the local authority asylums, in future to be called mental hospitals, to make progress in the treatment as well as the care of the mentally ill. Moreover, the authorities were also given permissive powers to provide psychiatric out-patient clinics at general or mental hospitals, and to make arrangements for after-care. The Act was hailed as a breakthrough in the treatment of the mentally ill, but although progress was made during the 1930's and 1940's, the stigma of certification and indeed the stigma attached to mental illness itself remained very strong and continued to work against the early treatment and hospitalization of mental patients.

Thus, even by 1948 when the mental hospitals were beginning to be affected by the administrative changes discussed below, voluntary patients still numbered only 21,788 and temporary patients 527, while certified patients amounted to 145,799. By 1958 these figures had changed to 62,704; 351; and 78,625 respectively —a considerable improvement on the eve of the Mental Health Act, 1959.

The National Health Service Act, 1946, already discussed in Chapter 5, affected the development of provisions for both the mentally ill and the mentally defective, because for the first time it brought the institutional care of both these groups under the same administration as other hospitals. The newly appointed regional hospital boards became responsible for the care and treatment of all patients, thus giving recognition to a movement towards integration which had been gathering momentum. A report on 'The Future Organization of the Psychiatric Services', published in June 1945, stressed that 'the argument for treating psychiatry in all essentail respects like other branches of medicine' was 'strong and conclusive . . . there is everything to be said for making the administrative structure of psychiatry exactly the same in principle and even in major detail as that of other branches of the health services'.[6] As the Minister of Health became the central authority for mental health the Board of Control retained only its quasi-judicial interest in protecting the liberty of the subject. Local authorities lost all their hospitals but were given wide powers capable of very varied interpretation for prevention, care and after-care of patients.

In spite of the administrative changes brought about by the National Health Service Act, it became increasingly obvious that the existing law relating to mental illness and mental deficiency was out of date and needed revision. Accordingly a Royal Commission was set up in 1954 and its report, published in 1957, recommended far-reaching changes.[7] It advocated the repeal of the existing Lunacy, Mental Treatment and Mental Deficiency Acts and their replacement by a single legal code embracing all form of mental disorder. The Commission hoped that in most instances those suffering from mental disorder would have access to treatment both as out-patients and in-patients in exactly the same way as those suffering from any other illness, and that the practice of the formal designation of certain hospitals for the reception of mentally disordered patients would be discontinued. The report, however, recognized that some provision had to be made for the compulsory admission of patients to hospital for care and treatment in certain circumstances, but it advocated that this should be primarily an administrative procedure on medical recommendation instead of legal certification, with the safeguard of a right of appeal to a specially constituted tribunal. The categories of patients who in specified circumstances could become subject to compulsory powers, it was suggested, should be mentally ill patients, psychopathic patients or patients with a psychopathic personality, and patients of severely subnormal personality.

The recommendations of the Commission were welcomed by most professional and lay opinion, although there was considerable controversy over some points of detail—notably the responsibility to be placed on the medical profession to recommend compulsory admission and the definition of the categories of patients subject to compulsory powers. There was also discussion, particularly in Parliament, about the suggested extended responsibility of local authorities and how far these should be mandatory. The report of the Commission strongly endorsed the recommendation of many witnesses that there should be a shift of emphasis from hospital care to community care and that 'the local authorities should be responsible for preventive services and for all types of care for patients who do not require in-patient hospital treatment or training or who have had a period of treatment or training and are ready to return to the community'.[8]

The Mental Health Act, 1959, implemented most of the recommendations of the Commission. It repealed almost all of the existing legislation in this field, including the complicated arrangements for certification. Administratively, the Act completed the change already initiated by the National Health Service Act and abolished any legal or administrative distinction between mental hospitals, in the future to be called psychiatric hospitals, and any other hospitals. The only exceptions were the 'special' hospitals providing maximum security conditions for specially dangerous patients which were to be administered centrally by the Minister of Health. The Act ensured that the normal method of admission for treatment should be completely informal.

However, the Act provided for two forms of compulsory admission—for observation and for treatment. Section 25 (2) states that:

> An application for admission for *observation* may be made in respect of a patient on the grounds—
> (a) that he is suffering from mental disorder of a nature and degree which warrants the detention of the patient in a hospital under observation (with or without other medical treatment) for at least a limited period; and
> (b) that he ought to be so detained in the interests of his own health or safety or with a view to the protection of other persons.

The application for admission has to be founded on the written recommendations of two medical practitioners, and the patient may be detained for a period not longer than 28 days.

Section 26 provides for the compulsory admission for *treatment* in respect of a patient on the grounds that:

> (a) that he is suffering from mental disorder being—
> (i) in the case of a patient of any age, mental illness or severe subnormality;
> (ii) in the case of a patientient under the age of twenty-one years, psychopathic disorder or subnormality; and that the said disorder is of a nature or degree which warrants the detention of the patient in hospital for mental treatment;
> and
> (b) that it is necessary in the interests of the patient's health or safety or for the protection of other persons that the patient should be so detained.

Again the application for admission has to be founded on the written recommendations of two medical practitioners, and in both instances can be made either by the nearest relative of the patient or by a mental welfare officer.

The definitions and classification of mental disorder in the Act differ in a number of important respects from those in the report of the Royal Commission. Thus, in Section 4, psychopathic disorder means 'a persistent disorder or disability of mind (whether or not including subnormality of intelligence) which results in abnormally aggressive or seriously irresponsible conduct on the part of the patient, and requires or is susceptible to medical treatment'. A new category is added, that of subnormality which is defined as a state of arrested or incomplete development of mind (not amounting to severe subnormality) which requires or is susceptible to medical treatment or other special care or training of the patient.

The Act makes a number of provisions for the easy discharge of patients who are subject to compulsory powers and there is also the possibility of appeal to a Mental Health Review Tribunal. Part V of the Act is concerned with the admission of patients concerned in criminal proceedings and the transfer of patients under sentence, and gives the courts power to provide for the more flexible treatment of offenders suffering from mental disorder.

Local health authorities, the County and County Borough Councils, are given wide powers to provide residential accommodation, day centres for training and occupation, and other ancillary services, and for the appointment of mental welfare officers, thus defining in greater detail the power given to authorities under Section 28 of the National Health Service Act.

Since the Act was passed there has been considerable progress in the mental health field, a modernization of many more hospitals, the use of informal procedures for more than 80 per cent in-patients—the provision of more occupation and training centres for the mentally subnormal, hostels for all groups of the mentally disordered and an energetic policy for the recruitment and training of mental welfare officers. The plans of local authorities for the next ten years envisage a continued expansion of facilities for the community care of the mentally disordered. Similarly the plans of the regional Hospital Boards are designed to hasten the replacement of the large mental hospitals of the past by smaller modern psychiatric units, many of which will be part of general hospitals.[9] However, there is considerable concern over some of the provisions of the Act and their implementation. In spite of modernization programmes and a more hopeful attitude towards the care and treatment of patients, there are still persistent criticisms of the regime in some hospitals and of the attitude of some staff. There is a continuing shortage of recruits of good calibre for all grades of staff and the idea of the hospital as a 'therapeutic community' is one which is still not always understood. Many local authorities are only at the beginning of their plans of development and it is feared by some people that the early discharge of patients from hospital may have adverse effects on the patient, his family and public opinion because of the inadequacy of alternative care and supporting services. For a variety of reasons such as the siting of some hospitals, failure of administrative arrangements, shortage of trained staff, there is not always the degree of co-operation necessary between hospital, local authority and general practitioner services. It is also suggested that the arrangements for the compulsory admission of patients to hospital are not always adequate, or if the power is there, that there is some failure on the part of those responsible to use it adequately to prevent intolerable strain on family and neighbours.

Some disquiet is also felt over certain of the basic assumptions of the Act and plans for the future. Is it necessarily always in the best interests of the patient that he should be discharged at the earliest possible moment, or that provision for the care of the mentally subnormal should be integrated with that of the mentally ill and both with the care of the physically ill? Is there a danger that essential differences in need may be glossed over?

Nevertheless, in spite of the continuing discussions, there is no doubt that the Mental Health Act, 1959, 'a piece of delicate legislative engineering animated by a high social purpose,' as the Minister of Health called it, was a landmark in the provision of services for the mentally disordered and provided a framework within which the resources of the community could be mobilized to maintain and improve the mental health of every individual.

NOTES

[1] See K. Jones, *Lunacy, Law and Conscience, 1744–1845.*
[2] K. Jones, *Mental Health and Social Policy, 1845–1959.*
[3] Ibid.

[4] National Conference on the Prevention of Destitution, 1911: *Report of the Proceedings of the Mental Deficiency Section.*

[5] K. Jones, *Mental Health and Social Policy, 1845–1959.*

[6] *Royal Medico-Psychological Association: Report of Medical Planning Committee—A Memorandum on the Future Organisation of the Psychiatric Services,* 1945. Quoted Jones, *Mental Health and Social Policy.*

[7] *Report of the Royal Commission on the Law relating to Mental Illness and Mental Deficiency,* 1954–57, Cmd. 169.

[8] Ibid.

[9] *Health and Welfare; The Development of Community Care,* Cmd. 1973. *Hospital Plan for England and Wales,* Cmd. 1604.

See also:

H. FREEMAN and J. FARNDALE, *Trends in the Mental Health Services.*

P.E.P., Vol. XXIX, No. 468, *Psychiatric Services in 1975.*

M. ROOFF, *Voluntary Societies and Social Policy,* Part III.

11. THE ELDERLY

Joan L. M. Eyden

ALTHOUGH the needs of the elderly, unable to support themselves because of increasing illness and frailty, have long been recognized, it was not until the last decade of the nineteenth century that public attention began to be directed towards the urgent necessity of providing more adequate assistance for old people. Friendly societies, savings banks and charity were insufficient to meet the need and the only means of subsistence for many was through the receipt of poor relief. Before 1890 no distinction as to the age of paupers was made in the official Poor Law returns, but in that year the figures in what became known as 'Mr. Burt's Return' showed that old age was a major cause of poverty.[1] This finding was confirmed by subsequent returns and other investigations such as that of Charles Booth. Booth, indeed, was so concerned about his findings that he argued the case for a universal State pension at the age of 65 in *Pauperism and the Endowment of Old Age*, published in 1892. So controversial an issue aroused much discussion. A Royal Commission on the aged Poor, set up under the chairmanship of Lord Aberdare, failed to agree and its report published in 1895 was inconclusive. Subsequently an Expert Committee was appointed in 1898 to consider schemes making provision for old age. After examining more than a hundred schemes the Committee also found themselves unable to make recommendations and it was not until another committee, appointed in 1899 (the Chaplin Committee), reported more favourably on the possibility of a pension scheme and after much public agitation and concern, that the Old Age Pension Act, 1908, was finally passed (see Chapter 3). Thus the first major step was taken to make more adequate provision for the elderly outside the Poor Law.

In recent years the social problems connected with ageing have attracted more and more attention. There are a number of factors involved—the greater number of people living into their 70's and 80's, the greater affluence of society which has led to the expectations of higher standards for all members, the increase in mobility which has often led to the isolation of the older generation from the younger members of the family.[2] Moreover, the rapid development of industrialization and the pace of social and economic change has meant that flexibility, enterprise and new ideas are more highly prized in modern society than experience, tradition and stability, with a consequent denigration of the conbution which elderly people can make to the community. Thus not only has the economic and material dependency of the elderly increased quantitatively, but greater social and personal insecurity and lack of status has led to a new quality of need.

In the preceding chapters reference has already been made to a number of ways in which general social provision endeavours to meet some of the needs of elderly people. Because age brings increasing infirmity and a slowing up of activity, few elderly people are able to support themselves by continued employment and thus income maintenance during retirement is a major problem. Private superannuation schemes encouraged by fiscal policy, national insurance, including the graduated pensions scheme, and national assistance are, of course, primarily designed to help the elderly to obtain the basic necessities of life. Although a large proportion of retired people enjoy a reasonable standard of living by modern standards, yet there is considerable public disquiet as recent inquiries suggest that a percentage of old people have not shared adequately in the growing national prosperity.[3] The development of a conventional retirement age of 65 for men and 60 for women, moreover, poses further problems for many elderly people who are able and willing to work either full or part-time. Not only does the tempo of modern industrial life not permit the easy absorption of elderly people into suitable employment, but superannuation and insurance schemes do not give much encouragement to delayed retirement. Thus the problem of occupation for the active 60 and 70-years-old can be a very real one. Some firms, local authority welfare departments and voluntary organizations have undertaken experimental projects for the employment or occupation of elderly people, but these are still on a very limited scale.

The Elderly

The provision of housing for the elderly has been an important responsibility of local housing authorities in recent years and specially designed flats and bungalows are part of the building programmes of most authorities. The charitable provision of alms-houses and homes for the aged antedate statutory provision by many centuries and there are innumerable trusts today, some dating back to the Middle Ages, some of recent foundation, which attempt to assist elderly people able to live independently. Registration of such trusts under the Charities Act, 1960, should give accurate information as to the extent of this provision in the future. However, in spite of the efforts of local authorities and voluntary organizations there is still a considerable amount of unmet need for shelter suitable for them.

One of the problems encountered in satisfying this need is the variety of accommodation required to meet the very different requirements of elderly people. The 'Problems of Old People' is sometimes talked of as though all elderly people were alike and had the same requirements instead of being a category of unique people differentiated from the rest of the population only by their age. Moreover the rate and effects of ageing vary greatly from person to person, and although there has been a considerable interest in geriatrics by the medical profession in recent years, still very little is known about the factors involved. The kind of housing discussed above is ideal for those who are able to live independently and there is increasing public concern that supporting domiciliary services should be available to enable elderly people to live in their own homes for as long as possible. Some old people, however, do not wish to live alone, and for others this is impossible or unwise because of increasing frailty. Since 1948 the responsibility of local authorities under Part III of the National Assistance Act to provide residential accommodation for those who 'by reason of age, infirmity or any other circumstances are in need of care and attention which is not otherwise available to them' (Section 21), has resulted in the provision of many small homes for elderly people either by adapting existing large houses or by specially built units. In 1948, when local authorities were faced with discharging this responsibility, they had to make use of many large ex-Poor Law institutions as these were the only buildings available to them. Some of these have been successfully adapted to meet modern requirements, some have been closed, but there are many old people still living in sub-standard accommodation of this type.[4] The ten-year development plan for local authority health and welfare services envisages a considerable increase in the provision of residential accommodation. There is a growing demand for this type of care for the frail elderly, partly because of the total increase in the numbers of people in the upper age groups, partly because of the difficulties which many families experience in looking after their elderly relatives in all social groups. The extent to which families are prepared to care for the older generations must not be underestimated, but nevertheless real difficulties are encountered. Although, as seen in the quotation from Section 21 of the National Assistance Act given above, residential accommodation can be provided by local authorities for people who do not come within the retired age groups, yet most of those in need of care and attention are from this group and this section appears to be specifically directed towards meeting their needs.

However, as with the provision for income maintenance and housing, almost all statutory services through which the needs of the elderly are met come under general legislation. Thus the domiciliary services referred to above which help elderly persons to remain in their own homes for as long as possible or give support to families caring for them are provided under the National Health Service Act. General practitioners, home nurses, home helps, health visitors, all contribute to these supporting services, but their assistance is of course not restricted to the elderly. However, in 1962, 50 per cent of all the cases attended by home nurses were patients aged 65 or over at the time of the first visit and 77·6 per cent of the cases served by home helps were those of old age and chronic sickness.[5]

In the voluntary sphere of action there has been a great deal of specific provision for elderly people—clubs, social and occupation centres, holidays, outings, friendly visiting, help with shopping and the care of gardens and other forms of assistance are given in many areas, and show considerable imagination, understanding and enterprise.[6] Much of this work is carried out by or with the collaboration of local Old People's Welfare Committees, but there are many organizations taking part in this work, the Churches, Toc H, the W.V.S., the Red Cross to name only a few. Interestingly enough, much of the impetus for the development of Old

People's Welfare Committees came from the Assistance Board in 1940, when the Board took over responsibility for the provision of supplementary assistance to pensioners from the Public Assistance Committees. Until that time elderly people had a regular weekly contact with the relieving officer who was able to keep a friendly eye on their welfare, especially of those living alone, and arrange for medical care, hospitalization or the provision of other services which might be needed. The introduction of supplementary pensions paid through the Post Office and subject only to half-yearly review, meant that a number of old people were left friendless indeed, and thus the organization of a friendly visiting service was encouraged. The National Old People's Welfare Council, established in 1940, is a national focal point for information and advice on all aspects of the care of the elderly. It brings together in consultation some 50 national voluntary societies, 6 government departments, representatives of old people's welfare committees throughout the United Kingdom and individuals with special experience. It also acts as a pressure group in the interests of old people and its declared aim is 'a co-ordinated nation-wide service for the care of elderly people in need of help —a service comprising both statutory and voluntary assistance, ranging from care in sickness and infirmity to acts of neighbourliness and friendship'. A regional organization brings together the local committees for the exchange of information and ideas and joint action when the occasion demands it. Work with old people relies heavily on the unpaid services of the volunteer, and it gives hope for the future that there appears to be an increasing concern on the part of the Churches and other citizen groups to ensure better care for the elderly. The Ministry of Health's Report, *Health and Welfare: the Development of Community Care*, also reflects this concern as many local authorities are planning a considerable expansion of services which are of particular importance to the elderly during the next ten years.

As in any field of work where there is interested and informed public concern, there is considerable questioning of the aims and methods of the provision for elderly people as well as disquiet over its inadequacy. Should the elderly be treated as a special group and a comprehensive service be developed for them; can more be done to assist the family so that relatives can bear a greater part of the care of the older generation or should they be increasingly relieved of this burden; how much responsibility should the State assume for income maintenance during retirement and at what level, and how much should be left to occupational superannuation schemes; how far should the health and welfare departments develop their provision and what continuing part have the voluntary organizations to play? What seems to be likely, to quote from the 1963 Annual Report of the National Old People's Welfare Council, is that:

> In the years to come the elderly will make heavier demands on the social services than any other group in the population, and the character of these demands will gradually change. With some seven and a half million people over retirement age now, with a steady rise to be expected in their total number, and with an even steeper rise in the number of people over seventy years of age, there will have to be, on the one hand, more occupation and social amenities for the active, and on the other, more services for the household, the infirm and the mentally frail.

NOTES

[1] Gertrude Williams, *The State and the Standard of Living*, Chapter II.
[2] Peter Townsend, *The Family Life of Old People*.
[3] Dorothy Cole and John Utting, *The Economic Circumstances of Old People*; Tony Lynes, *National Assistance and National Prosperity*.
[4] Peter Townsend, *The Last Refuge*.
[5] See Report of the Ministry of Health, *The Health and Welfare Services*, 1962.
[6] National Council of Social Service, *Age is Opportunity*.

See also:
B. SHENFIELD, *Social Policies for Old Age*.
I. M. RICHARDSON, *Age and Need—A Study of Older People in North East Scotland*.

12. CHILDREN AND THE FAMILY

Joan L. M. Eyden

INTRODUCTION

STATUTORY authorities and voluntary organizations have for long been interested in the welfare of children. As already noted, charities from the Middle Ages onwards provided for the care and education of poor children, while the Poor Law made particular reference to the need to apprentice pauper children so that 'they may get their living when they shall be of age'. In the nineteenth century the Factory Acts developed from attempts to prevent the ill treatment and abuse of pauper apprentices.

Provision for children in our society has developed partly from a philanthropic concern for the welfare of those who are helpless and so obviously unable to fend for themselves, partly from concern for the workers and citizens of tomorrow upon whom the future safety, prosperity and well-being of the community depends. These two motives in the nineteenth century gradually offset concern lest State intervention should weaken the responsibility of the family for its members. The idea that children had rights even against their parents gradually gained ground. The report of the National Children's Homes in 1884, states, 'It is quite time that the doctrine of parental rights should not be allowed any longer to be a doctrine of children's wrongs.'

During the past hundred years society has demanded higher and higher standards of education and child-care and social, fiscal and industrial policy has increasingly recognized that children are no longer an asset but a social and economic liability to a family. Thus two main trends can be distinguished. Firstly, there is the provision of special services for those children who are neglected, deprived of a normal home life or specially underprivileged in some way. Secondly, there are those services which have developed to help families to meet the normal needs of the child and adolescent in a rapidly changing industrial society. Many of the latter began as services for the deprived and underprivileged, as attempts to do something to modify the educational, economic and social inequalities of the poorest sections of the population, but have gradually been incorporated into present-day health, education and welfare services available for all citizens on like terms. Thus the activities of the Ladies Sanitary Reform Association of Manchester and Salford of 1862, and the mothers' clubs and milk depots of the early years of this century contributed to the maternal and child welfare services which are now used by over 60 per cent of all families spread through the whole range of occupational groups.[1]

Similarly, the school health service, the provision of school meals, of nursery schools, of holiday homes and school camps and the like began as attempts to improve the physical condition of children in the elementary schools, first by voluntary effort and later by education authorities. They have become increasingly accepted as ancillary educational and health services and used by a large proportion of families.

In spite of the development of the major services, it seems likely that some children will always need special services and special care. The provision of schools for handicapped children, of occupation and training centres for mentally subnormal children, and of child-guidance clinics for those with behaviour problems has been steadily increasing, particularly since the Second World War, although there is still a shortage of facilities in many areas. It has, however, been the neglected and homeless child who has attracted particular concern and compassion.

CHILDREN IN NEED OF SPECIAL CARE

Apart from schools for poor children, dating from the Middle Ages, and the provision under the Poor Law already mentioned, one of the earliest institutions for the care of infants was the Foundling Hospital opened in 1747 by Captain Coram for abandoned and unwanted babies. This institution received a subsidy from Parliament from 1756 to 1770—an early example of partnership between voluntary organizations and the State.

During the nineteenth century many schools and orphanages were founded, often small and local in character, but towards the end of the century the great national children's organizations began to develop; the National Children's Homes and Orphanages; Dr. Barnado's Homes, 1870; the Waifs and Strays, 1881; and perhaps most significantly, the National Society for the Prevention of Cruelty to Children, founded in 1884 as a result of pioneer work in America and in Liverpool. Similarly, as has been noted, it was in the same century that legislation initiated by Lord Shaftesbury and other like-minded philanthropists succeeded in establishing some protection of children through the Factory and Mines Acts, and the Education Acts. Successive Poor Law enactments endeavoured to improve the lot of the pauper child, particularly after the vigorous criticism of current practice contained in the report of the departmental committee of 1894.

These developments reflected a growing interest and concern for children, but it was not until 1889 that the first Act was passed specifically for the prevention of cruelty to, and the better protection of children and began the long line of Acts of which the 1963 Children and Young Persons Act is but the latest. The Act of 1889, although limited in scope by modern standards, was referred to in Parliament as the Children's Charter. Subsequent Acts in 1894, 1904, 1908 and 1933, besides liberalizing the treatment of youthful offenders and setting up Juvenile Courts, widened the powers of the courts in regard to children and young people neglected, ill-treated or in moral danger, and made it possible for children 'in need of care or protection' to be committed to the care of a 'fit person' which, under the 1933 Children and Young Persons Act, could be the education department of a local authority. The year 1926 saw the first legal recognition of adoption by the Adoption Act of that year and the protection of children, fostered privately for reward which had developed from the Infant Life Protection Act, 1872, was incorporated in the Public Health Act, 1936.

As in other areas of social welfare, the two world wars led to the acceptance of an increase in responsibility by the State for children. For instance, the 1914–18 war led to the Maternity and Child Welfare Act, 1918, and to the institution of a special welfare service by the Ministry of Pensions for war orphans, and the 1939–45 war saw an extension of care by the local authorities and the

Ministry of Health through the operation of the evacuation scheme and all that that implied.[2]

The general dislocation of family life caused by war-time conditions led to a much greater need for substitute care for children by voluntary societies as well as public authorities. The subsequent quantity and quality of alternative care gave rise to mounting public anxiety voiced particularly by Lady Allen of Hurtwood in her letter to *The Times* in July 1944. The death in 1945 through ill-treatment and neglect of Dennis O'Neil, boarded out by a local authority in whose care he had been placed under a 'fit person' order, precipitated action. In March 1945 an inter-departmental committee, under the chairmanship of Miss Myra Curtis, was set up 'to inquire into existing methods of providing for children who from loss of parents or from any cause whatever are deprived of a normal home life with their own parents or relatives; and to consider what further measures should be taken to ensure that these children are brought up under conditions best calculated to compensate them for the lack of parental care'.[3]

The report of the Committee the following year (and that of its Scottish counterpart, the Clyde Committee) showed the multiplicity of authorities, both voluntary and statutory, responsible for the care of deprived children; the startling variations in methods and quality of care; and the almost complete lack of trained social workers and residential staffs in the whole of this important field.

The recommendations of the Committee for a simplification of administration and a clear-cut public responsibility for any child deprived of a normal home life, the need for boarding-out as a more acceptable method of alternative care than the children's home or institution, and the urgent necessity for providing professional training of a high standard for child-care workers was embodied in the Children Act, 1948, and its subsequent implementation. The Committee urged the necessity for a special local authority committee to be set up to take responsibility

> based in part on the need we feel for emphasising the function of home-finding as something separate and distinct from the education and health services given to all children; but in part also on our desire that it should have its own executive officer with the standing of an important administrative official of the council, in direct touch with the responsible committee. . . . We desire, how-

ever, to see the responsibility for the welfare of the deprived
children definitely laid on a Children's Officer. This may indeed
be said to be our solution of the problem referred to us. Throughout our investigation we have been increasingly impressed by the
need for the personal element in the care of children.[4]

This recommendation was accepted by the Government and the
1948 Act made it the duty of the major authorities to appoint a
Children's Committee, with a special department headed by a
Children's Officer. It was the responsibility of the authority

> to receive into their care, where it appears to the Local Authority
> that their intervention is necessary in the interests of the welfare
> of the child, any child in their area under the age of 17 years who
> has no parents or guardians or has been abandoned or lost, or
> whose parents or guardians are prevented, for the time being or
> permanently, by incapacity or any other circumstances from pro-
> viding for his proper accommodation, maintenance and upbring-
> ing.

This duty was to continue until the young person reached the age
of 18 years and was not to cease even if for a time he was being
cared for by another service. Normally the Act did not authorize
a local authority to keep a child in their care, unless committed
under a 'fit person' order, if any parent or guardian desired to take
over the care of the child, but the authority could assume *by
resolution* the parental rights of deceased parents or incapable or
unfit parents who had the right of objection and subsequent
referral to the Court. Thus the new Children's Committees took
over responsibilities which had been previously discharged by the
Public Assistance Committees, the Education Committees and to
some extent by the Public Health Committees. Centrally the Home
Office became responsible for the public care of all children deprived of a normal home life and set up a Children's Department
for the discharge of its duties under this and allied legislation. It
was expected that voluntary organizations would continue to play
an important part in the new service and both the Curtis report
and the Act of 1948 envisaged that in future the local authorities
and the voluntary organizations would work in close partnership.
Every voluntary home had to be registered with the Home Office
and regulations could be made in regard to their conduct.

Since the Children Act, 1948, the child-care service has developed rapidly. Jean S. Heywood comments:

The new Children Act of 1948 provided a framework based on principles of administrative unity, individual need and the value of the natural family which were new in the legislation for deprived children. These principles themselves, and the insight of the new administrators, stimulated a development in the service which led very quickly to change, to awareness of the best form of treatment for the child and later to an emphasis on the conditions leading to deprivation, and the prevention of them.[5]

These developments were in accordance with the conditions for good substitute care laid down by the Curtis Committee:

> If the substitute home is to give the child what he gets from a good normal home it must stupply—
> (1) Affection and personal interest; understanding of his defects; care for his future; respect for his personality and regard for his self esteem.
> (2) Stability; the feeling that he can expect to remain with those who will continue to care for him until he goes out into the world on his own feet.
> (3) Opportunity of making the best of his ability and aptitudes, whatever they may be, as such opportunity is made available to the child in the normal home.
> (4) A share in the common life of a small group of people in a homely environment.[6]

The rapid development and subsequent publication of research into the physical, emotional and social growth of infants typified by the work of Dr. John Bowlby (discussed in *Maternal Care and Mental Health*, published by W.H.O. in 1951) has had a profound effect on the aims and methods of work of children's departments.[7] Dr. Bowlby's publications came at a time when the new service was still very much in a formative stage and affected its development in a number of ways.

Thus in the attempt to give children the best substitute family care, following the recommendations of the Curtis Committee, workers have stressed the advantages of fostering in a 'normal' home. This policy was endorsed, for quite different reasons, in the sixth report from the Select Committee on Estimates, July 1952; boarding-out seemed the cheapest as well as the best form of public care. In England and Wales at the end of November 1949, out of 55,255 children in care 19,271, or 35 per cent, were boarded out. Notwithstanding a substantial rise in the total number of children in care, the proportion boarded out rose to 44 per cent in 1954, 45 per cent in 1958 and 52 per cent in 1963, with a total in care of 64,807 in 1963.

Secondly, because the impossibility and indeed the undesirability of providing for all children in this way necessitated the continuation of some form of group care, children's departments have developed the small residential family unit scattered through the area and usually in charge of a married couple as house parents, as the typical pattern of residential care, although the large 'Home' is still used of necessity in some areas.

Thirdly, the increasing recognition of the importance to a child of his own parents, inadequate though they may be, led to renewed efforts to care for neglected children within their own families, and thus prevent the break-up of families whenever possible. The Curtis Committee were aware that the problem of children neglected or inadequately cared for in their own homes needed investigation, but were precluded by their terms of reference from considering it except incidentally. Other non-official bodies, however, were carrying out their own inquiries. The work of the Pacifist Service Units, with 'problem families', the investigation of the Women's Group on Public Welfare and subsequent report on 'Children neglected in their own homes', helped to focus attention on the possibility of preventative measures and of working with the family to prevent its break-up.[8] The latter report made a clear recommendation 'that local authorities should be made responsible for providing a comprehensive service of care for all children living in their area'. Children's departments inevitably became involved in work with families. The demands on the new service were such that every effort had to be made to ensure that only when it was essential in the child's interests was he received into care whether on a temporary or long-term basis. The exploration with the parents of the factors leading to the application for admission, and of alternative solutions, often led to the child remaining with his family with the use of other supporting services or being cared for by relatives. Under the 1948 Act local authorities also had a duty under Section 1 (3) to restore a child to its own home as soon as possible consistent with the welfare of the child and although the authority did not have the same duty to work towards the restoration of a child committed to its care by the courts, many children's committees undertook an increasing amount of work with the families of children in care with a view to rehabilitation, and continued after-care on the child's return home. Moreover, Section 2 of the Children and Young Persons Amendment Act, 1952, specifically imposed upon local authorities the duty of making inquiries upon the receipt of information suggesting that any child or young person might be in need of care or protection unless they were satisfied that such inquiries were unnecessary.

Thus, during the 1950's, there was increasing emphasis on work with families primarily through a more co-ordinated and intensive use of existing services. In a circular issued jointly by the Home Office, the Ministry of Health and the Ministry of Education in July 1950, the local authorities were asked to develop co-ordinating machinery so that full use was made of existing services to help children neglected or ill-treated in their own homes.

> If effective help is to be given at an early stage, it is essential that there should be co-ordinated use of the statutory and voluntary services. . . . Without co-ordination information may not reach the service which could be of most assistance until valuable time has been lost. If the right help is not given in time, children who might otherwise have remained with their parents may have to be removed from home because deterioration had gone too far.

The circular suggested that local authorities should designate an officer to be responsible for holding meetings and case conferences bringing together the relevant central and local government officers and workers from voluntary agencies. In reply to a question in the House of Commons on 6th March 1964, the Joint Under Secretary of State for the Home Department stated that out of 145 local authorities concerned, 132 had designated officers who called regular meetings and in 62 cases out of the 132 it was the Children's Officer who was the designated officer. In some areas where there has been a willingness to co-operate in working out joint plans on the part of the departments concerned, the co-ordinating machinery has worked reasonably well. There have, however, been criticisms that some more radical method of providing help for multi-problem families is needed; so many organizations may be involved that co-ordinating machinery can be clumsy, slow and ineffective and is often not brought into use until too late.

The experience of the first ten years working of the Children Act, 1948, and of co-ordinating committees, as well as the continuing work of health visitors, school welfare officers, the N.S.P.C.C., and other problem family workers, suggested that further provision was needed and so the Departmental Committee set up in 1957 under the chairmanship of Viscount Ingleby to inquire into the working of the law relating to juvenile courts and the care and treatment of young delinquents, was asked in its terms of reference to consider 'whether local authorities responsible for child care under the Children Act, 1948, in England and Wales should, taking into account action by voluntary organizations and the responsibilities of existing statutory services, be given new powers and duties to prevent or forestall the suffering of children through neglect in their own homes'. In their report in 1960 the Committee examined the existing provisions and discussed the factors involved, suggesting that 'much of the difficulty which at present exists, apart from that attributable to the shortage of skilled casework staff, is due to inter-service rivalries and above all to failure to analyse the different processes involved . . . it is most important too that arrangements should be made for making the services known to the public and for giving advice so that individuals know where they can apply for help'.[9]

Among their suggestions were that arrangements for the detection of families at risk should extend over the widest possible front; the improvement of facilities for the investigation and diagnosis of the problems in such families and greater publicity about the services available. The Committee considered that local authorities should have a duty to make such arrangements, power to do preventive casework and to provide for material needs that could not be met from other sources. They hoped that a number of experimental schemes would be worked out including the provision of 'family advice centres' or 'family bureaux'.

The Children and Young Persons Act, 1963, among other things already noted in Chapter 8, confirms and extends the power of County and County Borough Councils as children authorities, to take action to prevent or remove conditions that may result in children come into or remaining in care or being brought before a juvenile court, whether as offenders or as in need of care or protection. Under Section 1 it is the duty of the local authority to ensure that the necessary advice, guidance or assistance which can include assistance in kind or exceptionally in cash, is provided, both generally and in particular cases, either directly through one or other of their own services or indirectly through a voluntary organization. One of the biggest problems which authorities are facing in implementing this new legislation is the shortage of qualified professional staff.

ADOPTION

One of the ways of providing the security of a good alternative home for a child permanently deprived of a normal home life with his own parents has been by adoption.

Mention was made earlier of the Adoption Act, 1926, which for the first time provided for the legal adoption of infants. Since the beginning of the century there has been growing concern about *de facto* adoptions. Two adoption societies, The National Children's Adoption Association and the National Adoption Society were pioneers in arranging formal and well-considered adoptions even before the First World War, but the absence of any legal backing gave rise to considerable anxiety because of the insecurity of the arrangements. The 1926 Act gave courts the power of transferring parental rights and duties irrevocably from the natural parents to the adopting parents and local authorities were given supervisory functions. In the ensuing decades adoption societies multiplied and varied considerably in quality. Among other things, the Adoption of Children (Regulation) Act, 1939, provided for the registration of Adoption Societies, and the Adoption of Children Act, 1949, introduced further safeguards and attempted to strengthen the relationship between the child and his new parents. The rapidity with which opinion about adoption changed is seen from the fact that within a year or two of the consolidating Act of 1950, a further study of the law was undertaken, resulting in the report of the Departmental Committee on the Adoption of Children (the Hurst Committee), published in September 1954. The Act of 1958, which was the outcome of its recommendations, sought to ensure that the rights of all parties concerned were considered fairly, the natural parents, the child, and the adopting persons; but it categorically declares that the adoption must be 'for the welfare of the infant' giving precedence to this above all other consideration. The adoptive parents take over all rights from the natural parents, and the adopted child has the same rights as a born child. Other clauses in the Act, and regulations made under it, seek to ensure that adequate inquiry is made as to the suitability of the adoption, supervision undertaken, and that the risks of third-party adoption are minimized.

The Curtis Committee recognized that adoption was one of the best ways of providing for the alternative care of children when there was no prospect of a return to the natural parents and the latter gave consent, but the number of children so available is limited and there have always been many more couples anxious to adopt a child than there have been children available. Since legal adoption first started there has been a steady increase in the number of children adopted each year except for an abnormal period during the 1939–45 war, and the immediate post-war periods, and now between 16,000 and 17,000 children are legally adopted annually.

The extension of adoption and of child life protection has added to the work of the Children's Departments.

SERVICES FOR THE FAMILY

P. M. Bromley, in the Preface to the second edition of *Family Law*, 1962, comments, 'more Acts of Parliament relating to family law must have appeared on the statute book since the first edition of this book was published in 1957 than during any other period of five years in the history of English Law.' This interest in the family as a legal entity has been parallelled by a similar sociological interest in the family as a primary social group and by the change in the concept of the relationship between the family and the State already noted. It has been pointed out that in the nineteenth century the responsibility of the family for its members was considered absolute and only gradually did the State intervene.

The Royal Commission on Population in its report published in 1949 deplored the fact that 'in the process of social advance the family had tended to be overlooked or given only a minor place in social policy'.[10] The Commission touched on the historical attitudes towards the family and welcomed the development that had taken place in social provision, but advocated that 'family services should be developed so that help can be given to mothers of young children, through home helps, sitters-in, day nurseries, nursery schools and other means, not only in emergencies but in the normal running of the household' (para. 659). 'The measures of family welfare we have recommended in previous chapters are no more than are justified in fairness to parents and children; but their adoption may well have an effect beyond the immediately practical help they would give . . . measures of family welfare would help to raise the status of the family in national life' (para. 587).

This emphasis on services designed to meet the needs of the *normal* family has already been briefly noted. Moreover, the community has in some measure sought to help the family with its responsibilities not only through services in kind but also by financial provision. At the end of the eighteenth century the Speenhamland system of allowances in support of wages took account of the dependency needs of children in a large family and Pitt, the Prime Minister, commented: 'This will make a large family a blessing, not a curse, and thus will draw a line of distinction between those who are able to provide for themselves by their labour, and those who, having enriched their country with a number of children, have a claim upon its assistance for support.' The fear of a return of some of the disastrous but unintended effects of the Speenhamland system precluded any repetition of this form of help to large families until over a century later.

Dependents' benefits were not at first part of the national insurance scheme and indeed the sick insured person had to depend primarily upon assistance from the Poor Law for his wife and children until 1948. Eleanor Rathbone campaigned for many years for some system of children's allowances to help to mitigate the growing economic burden of a family but had very little public sympathy. One of her supporters, however, was William Beveridge and the introduction of a national system of Family Allowances was one of the assumptions he made in presenting his recommendations for reforming social insurance. The Act of 1945 was epoch making in that for the first time the State made an allowance out of the Exchequer funds to families with two or more dependent children without any test of means.

Child dependency had, however, already been recognized in another way. As early as 1909 fiscal policy gave special consideration to income-tax payers of small means with dependent children, and this use of the fiscal system as an instrument of social policy related to the family has grown steadily since then. It is of some interest to realize that this measure gave direct economic help to families in a middle income range. Lower income families where the actual need was greatest were not affected by this concession as the family income was too low to be liable to income tax. They had to wait for nearly forty years for any comparable assistance through the institution of Family Allowance payments.

Stemming from the nineteenth century, social workers had always been concerned with the family as a unit, but the development of social provision along specialized lines and the break-up of the Poor Law tended towards the meeting of individual need and the fragmentary treatment of the family group. The physical separation of the members of many families during the war years, the isolation of a proportion of elderly people, the loneliness often experienced by young wives and mothers, particularly as a result of new housing areas, and greater physical and social mobility accounted for new public interest in the family as a social group.

From the point of view of those concerned with the social services renewed interest in the family as a social entity was at least in part intensified by the problem of the 'problem family'. The existence of families who always seemed to be in need of help from many agencies and whose way of life seemed, at least to the outsider, to be disorganized and hopeless in spite of a growing affluence on the part of other members of society and increased social provision were a challenge which has led to some re-thinking of the aims and effects of much modern social provision and of social work methods. The experimental work of the Family Service Units specifically concerned with these multi-problem families, the residential training centres for mothers and young children such as Brentwood and The Mayflower, the increasing information gained from such inquiries as the studies reported by Dr. Blacker in *Problem Families, Five Inquiries*, by A. F. Philp in *Family Failure*, and from the work of the co-ordinating committees already referred to, have emphasized the importance of family relationships to individuals and the strength of family ties.

The strains and stresses to which all families are subject to some degree are particularly evident in those which have been called 'problem' families. It is the interaction of a multiplicity of adverse factors which seems to result in their pathological condition. Thus it is perhaps understandable that in the search for preventative measures which might reduce the number of unsatisfactory tenants, of families in need of temporary accommodation, of children becoming delinquent or having to be taken into care through the social disintegration of the family, the kind of measures advocated go beyond provision of services for families thought to be particularly 'at risk'. Illustrative of this is the reference by the Home Secretary in a special foreword to the Report of the Work of the Children's Department of the Home Office, 1960–1 headed *Against the Evils of Delinquency*, to the establishment of family welfare centres by local authorities under the Children and Young Persons Act, 1963, discussed earlier. He went on to say, 'The value of marriage guidance counsellors has been well established; there is a field of home behaviour where family welfare counsellors can perhaps give equal help to parents who know things are going wrong but are not sure what to do for their children.

Most social workers in the course of their day-to-day work inevitably find themselves involved in cases of behaviour difficulties on the part of children and of marital disharmony. It is of interest to notice that the London Charity Organization Society which pioneered much social work from its inception in 1869, changed its name in 1946 to the London Family Welfare Association partly in order to stress the fact that in the middle of the twentieth century the promotion of family well-being by the methods of social casework was the primary aim of the society. Most similar organizations followed suit and now provide a family social work service in many towns.

The Probation Service has for long been concerned with matrimonial conciliation and the Departmental Committee on the Social Services in Courts of Summary Jurisdiction, noted in 1936 that 'the general practice of courts throughout the country is to employ a probation officer as a conciliator'. It was not, however, until after the report of the Denning Committee (1943) and the Harris Committee (1948) that an impetus was given to the development of a marriage guidance service which could provide help at an earlier stage in incipient marriage breakdown than most probation officers were able to do. As a result of the Harris Committee government grants are now given to the National Marriage Guidance Council, which has some 100 local councils in England

and Wales, the Catholic Marriage Advisory Council with some 50 local centres and the Family Discussion Bureau. This last was set up in 1948 as an experimental project in the field of marriage welfare by the Family Welfare Association in conjunction with the Tavistock Clinic.

Marriage Guidance Councils, as well as other religious and educational organizations interested in the well-being of the family are increasingly concerned to develop educational work aimed at helping the husbands, wives and parents of the future to be more aware of the difficulties and opportunities of family life. These developments can be seen as part of a more general movement to help the family to adjust to the rapid economic and social change characteristic of the mid-twentieth century.

To sum up: in recent years there has been a renewed interest in the family as a social unit and a greater awareness of the family as a group of interacting people with physical, social and emotional needs that must be met at least in part within the context of the family. This greater awareness is beginning to have an influence on some aspects of social policy and its implementation, not only in those services most directly concerned with children and their parents, but also in those services for the physically and mentally handicapped and for the elderly where the concept of 'community care' is based on the help and support of the family by supplementary community provision. The working out of this concept is still in its early stages, but there are a number of people who consider that most services of the future should be 'family' centred rather than 'individual problem' centred.

SUGGESTED READING

M. HOPKIRK, *Nobody Wanted Sam.*
D. V. DONNISON, *The Neglected Child and the Social Services.*
A. F. PHILP, *Family Failure.*
A. F. PHILP and NOEL TIMMS, *The Problem of the Problem Family.*
HILDA LEWIS, *Deprived Children.*
D. V. DONNISON and MARY STEWART, *The Child and the Social Services.*
SHEILA FERGUSON and HILDA FITZGERALD, *Studies in the Social Services.*
L. G. HOUSDEN, *The Prevention of Cruelty to Children.*
MARGARET KORNITZER, *Child Adoption in the Modern World.*
R. H. NICHOLS and F. A. WRAY, *The History of the Foundling Hospital.*
M. DE M. RUDOLF, *Everybody's Children.*
A. F. WILLIAMS, *Barnado of Stepney.*
M. WYNN, *Fatherless Families.*
KENNETH BRILL and RUTH THOMAS, *Children in homes.*

NOTES

[1] P.E.P. Report, *Family Needs and the Social Services.*

[2] See R. M. Titmuss, *Problems of Social Policy*, and Ferguson and Fitzgerald, *Studies in the Social Services.*

[3] *Report of the Care of Children Committee*, 1946, Cmd. 6922.

[4] Ibid.

[5] Jean S. Heywood, *Children in Care.*

[6] *Report of the Care of Children Committee*, para. 427.

[7] See also John Bowlby and M. Fry, *Child Care and the Growth of Love.*

[8] T. Stephens, *Problem Families*. Women's Group on Public Welfare, *Children Neglected in Their Own Homes.*

[9] *Report of the Committee on Children and Young Persons*, 1960, H.M.S.O., Cmd. 1191. (The Ingleby Report.)

[10] *Report of the Royal Commission on Population*, 1949, H.M.S.O., Cmd. 7695, para 406

[11] Ibid , para. 659.

PART FOUR

13. POLICY, ADMINISTRATION AND PERSONNEL

Joan L. M. Eyden

IN the preceding chapters an attempt has been made to give a brief outline of the development of social policy in this country and the present organization and scope of the social services. The rapidity of economic, political and social change, tends to make the attempt to look at present-day social institutions difficult because any description or comment may be out of date as soon as it is made. Moreover, there is an inevitable time lag between the development and identification of social needs and the adaptation of policy to meet them. Thus arises the criticism, for instance, that the Welfare State was an answer to the social problems of the 1930's not of the post-war era. Whether this is altogether true is a matter of opinion. What is clear is the necessity constantly to change and adapt social provisions to meet new demands, new needs and altered circumstances.

As new social policies are developed decisions have to be made about the way in which these policies are to be implemented, whether new instruments of policy should be created or existing organisations charged with new responsibilities, what financial resources are necessary and how these can be made available and what personnel is required. The previous chapters provide many instances of the way in which the power of the State exercised through various Government organs is used to curtail the freedom of action of individuals or groups on the grounds of the welfare of others. Much factory and public health legislation is of this 'negative' or 'regulatory' kind. Factory owners must observe a wide range of safety and hygienic precautions in the interests of their workers and they must provide certain amenities; members of the public may not commit 'nuisances' under the Public Health Acts, and householders in designated areas may only burn smokeless fuels.

Compulsion of another kind is found under the Mental Health Act, 1959, under which patients suffering from mental disorder may in certain circumstances be admitted to hospital under compulsory powers for observation, treatment or care, or again since the end of the nineteenth century children have had to undergo full-time education. An example of the use of regulation in a somewhat different situation is the power which the Medical Practices Committee has under the National Health Service Act, 1946, of temporarily closing certain areas to new or additional medical practitioners in order to obtain a better 'spread' of doctors throughout the country.

Social policy may be implemented through Government encouragement of private enterprise or public consumption to develop along certain lines or in particular places. Thus, as already noted, by the use of the fiscal system encouragement is given to the development of superannuation schemes on an occupational basis; firms may be attracted to new towns or 'development' areas by financial inducements. Or, again, better nutrition among the young is encouraged by free or cheap welfare foods, and by subsidizing school meals. During and after the war the food subsidies played a considerable part in both helping the poorer member of the community to obtain a fair share of scarce food and in encouraging the consumption of foods particularly important on nutritional grounds. It is not, however, clear whether the progressive rise of taxation on cigarettes is meant to act as a disincentive to smoking on health grounds, or is a convenient way of raising money!

The greater part of the previous chapters has, however, been concerned with the implementation of social policy by more direct or positive means. The State, as has been demonstrated, increasingly has taken responsibility for providing services to meet certain needs of individuals and groups within the community. In discharging this responsibility the State has used three main organizational methods by which policy has been translated into service; new organs of government, central, regional or local, have been created for the express purpose of carrying out the new policy; central or local government departments have been given further powers entailing the extension of existing functions or

creation of new functions; in some instances voluntary organizations have been used as agents or been encouraged to work in
close partnership with statutory services. The result is a complex
pattern of administrative organization.

Just as complex is the pattern of financing the social services.
Four main ways of meeting the cost of the services can perhaps
be distinguished; by money from the national exchequer raised
primarily by direct or indirect taxation and providing the greater
part of the cost of the Health Services, Family Allowances,
National Assistance, etc., and grants towards the National Insurance Fund and the expenditure of local authorities; by contributions to the National Insurance Fund from insured persons and
employers with which may be coupled the special health service
contribution paid by all insured persons; by the rating of property
which finances a substantial part of the local authority services;
and by direct payment by the consumers or users of the service,
often after a means test, as in the case of accommodation for the
homeless and the elderly, for children in care, for certain services
provided for the handicapped, for home helps, etc. Voluntary
organizations are financed in a variety of ways—donations, sub-
scriptions, money-raising events, income from trust funds and
increasingly by subsidies from central and local government
departments. It is estimated that the endowed charitable trusts
own in aggregate securities and money worth some £200,000,000,
besides a vast amount of land.[1] The income from these and from
other sources is unknown but must be added to the public current
expenditure on social services (including housing) of more than
£4,000 millions in 1962–3.[2] One of the difficulties of making a
precise estimate of the amount even of public money that is spent
on the social services arises from the differences in definition.
Thus the Annual Abstract of Statistics and the Monthly Digest of
Statistics issued by the Central Statistical Office include in their
figures of consolidated current expenditure an item called 'the
social services and housing'. However, this includes approved
schools and remand homes, but not prisons and Borstals, the care
of children deprived of a normal home life but not the probation
service.

The fact that so large a proportion of the national income is
now devoted to the provision of the social services, both statutory
and voluntary, means that all members of the community have a

vested interest both as taxpayers and as beneficiaries in seeing that these are administered efficiently. This is something which is very difficult to assess because of the problem of criteria by which to judge results and partly because of the complexities of the administrative machinery. In the rest of this chapter the structure and staffing of the social services are briefly discussed under the following headings: *ad hoc* bodies, multi-purpose authorities, voluntary organizations, co-operation and co-ordination, and personnel. Other divisions could have been used, but these seem the most useful for our purpose.

'AD HOC' BODIES

The social reforms of the nineteenth century and the foundations of the Welfare State show a number of examples of the establishment of new administrative bodies specially designed to carry out some new aspect of social policy on an *ad hoc* basis. The elected local Boards of Guardians for the administration of the Poor Law in the unions of parishes created under the Poor Law Amendment Act, 1834, the local Boards of Health under the Public Health Act, 1848, and the School Boards established under the Education Act, 1870, are all illustrations of the way in which new experimental and specialist authorities had to be created owing to the absence or inadequacy of existing bodies. Centrally the establishment of strong bodies capable of the effective oversight of local developments had a chequered career because of the fear of bureaucracy. For instance, the Poor Law Commission set up under the 1834 Poor Law Amendment Act, to organize the parishes into unions and to attempt to impose a uniform nation-wide system of poor relief based on deterrent principles was replaced by a Poor Law Board which had less authority. The semi-independent central boards with plural executives was a traditional device in English government and was used extensively in connection with the mid-nineteenth-century social reforms as, for example, in the creation of the General Board of Health, the Charity Commission, the Lunacy Commission and many others, as well as the Poor Law Commission itself. The key minister for co-ordinating the new departments of central control was the Home Secretary, but his jurisdiction was loose and ill-defined, and as David Roberts points out, 'The Victorians' experiments in semi-independent, non-political boards reflected their fear that administrative decision would be made the handmaid of party bias or be caught in the maelstrom of factional politics.'[3] It was not until 1871 that a properly constituted central department to control local government and public health was established when the Local Government Board replaced some of these *ad hoc* central bodies. Others, reorganized and with new powers lasted for many years. Thus, for instance, the Lunacy Commission, given a new lease of life by the 1890 Lunacy Act, was replaced by another *ad hoc* body, the Board of Control in 1913, which was not finally abolished until the Mental Health Act, 1959. The Prison Commission existed until April 1964, when its duties were taken over by the Home Secretary.

With the reform and reorganization of local government which began with Municipal Corporations Act, 1835, and completed by the Local Government Acts, 1888 and 1894, most of the local *ad hoc* bodies were abolished and their functions absorbed into new multi-purpose authorities. The School Boards survived until 1902, and the Boards of Guardians until 1929.

In spite of this trend towards multi-purpose authorities, the twentieth century has seen the emergence of new specialist bodies fashioned to meet particular needs. An outstanding example was the creation of the Unemployment Assistance Board under the Unemployment Act, 1934, in an attempt to place responsibility for giving financial help to the chronically unemployed and their families on a semi-independent, non-political body, after the bitterness caused in some areas by the implementation of the household means test by local Public Assistance Committees. As outlined in Chapter 3, the Board was given additional responsibility for providing financial help in 1941 and was renamed and reorganized by the National Assistance Act, 1948. The members of the Board are appointed by the Crown and are responsible to Parliament for policy through the Minister of Pensions and National Insurance; the work of the Board, which is staffed by Civil Servants, is carried out through regional and area offices.

The National Health Service Act made provision for the establishment of other *ad hoc* administrative bodies—the Regional Hospital Boards and the Executive Councils. These are responsible to the Ministry of Health, the former for the organization and administration of the hospital, consultant and certain other services—an experiment in regional government by an appointed (not elected) body broadly representative of local authorities in the region, and of professional and consumer interests.[4] The local Executive Councils are a compromise solution for the employment of general practitioners and dentists in the National Health Service. They are representatives of the professional and consumer interests involved and like the Regional Hospital Boards are appointed by the Minister of Health. Both Boards and Councils appoint their own staff and have considerable administrative powers although major development plans involving large items of expenditure have to be approved by the Minister of Health and in some instances by the Treasury.

Again within the health field, the Regional Mental Health Review Tribunals set up under the Mental Health Act, 1959, provide an illustration of special bodies, composed of medical, legal and lay members, appointed by the Lord Chancellor to carry out a semi-judicial function. Although concerned with the discharge of mentally disordered patients from compulsory hospital care or guardianship, they are independent of the administration of the National Health Service.

Another interesting example of an *ad hoc* body designed especially for the carrying out of post-war social policy is the New Town Development Corporation. The decision embodied in the New Towns Act, 1946, to provide additional centres for the growing population required some machinery which could undertake the planning and establishment of these new urban areas. Each new town was to be developed by a special agency—a public corporation whose members were appointed for specified periods by the Minister of Town and Country Planning (a function now exercised by the Ministry of Housing and Local Government). The New Town Corporations have power to borrow money from the Treasury, to acquire and develop land, to select their own staff, but have to work in close partnership with the appropriate local authority for the provision of the necessary public services. The time will come (it has already in some cases) when the New Towns will cease to be new and the Corporations will disappear.

MULTI-PURPOSE AUTHORITIES

The previous section has already indicated that, in spite of the continual emergence of new *ad hoc* bodies to provide specialized services, the trend during the past century has been towards the development, both centrally and locally, of multi-purpose authorities. The central government departments, headed by a minister responsible to Parliament and staffed by Civil Servants, are responsible for the more detailed development of policy, laid down by Parliament, and its implementation over broadly defined areas of government. Within these broad areas their functions are often extremely diverse. At first sight it would seem that the Ministry of Education and the Ministry of Health, especially since the latter was shorn of its general oversight of local government in 1951, have the most specialized and homogeneous functions—the development of the education and health services respectively.[5] Nevertheless the functions of the Ministry of Health, first created in 1919, are confused because of the complicated division of responsibility for the National Health Service between Regional Hospital Boards, Boards of Governors of teaching hospitals, Executive Councils and local authorities. In addition the Ministry of Health has responsibility for the oversight of the welfare services of County and County Borough Councils under the National Assistance Act and of certain environmental provisions under the Public Health Act, 1936, the Clean Air Act, 1956, etc., which locally are the responsibility of the Borough and District Councils. Interestingly enough the only direct provision of services by the Ministry of Health is the maintenance and administration of the 'special' hospitals such as those providing maximum security for certain mentally disordered patients.

The responsibility of the Ministry of Education which replaced the old Board of Education in 1944 was almost entirely concerned with the oversight of the education service provided by local authorities—including nursery, primary, secondary and special schools, colleges of further education, various ancillary services, youth clubs and community centres. It provided few direct services itself, and in April 1964 it was renamed the Department of Education and Science, and has also become responsible for the encouragement of scientific research and for the needs of universities. The latter remain autonomous corporate bodies, and the specially appointed and unique University Grants Committee remains responsible for advising the Government about the financial needs of the universities, but through the Secretary of State for Education and Science instead of directly to the Treasury.

The Home Office and the Ministry of Housing and Local Government are examples of government departments with a great variety of functions, especially the former, which are primarily concerned with the general oversight of local authority and other services.[6] Since the demise of the Prison Commission in April 1964, the Home Office now has direct responsibility for the provision and administration of all prisons and Borstals.

Much of the work of the departments already mentioned is carried out centrally, although regional offices are often maintained to facilitate contact with local authorities.

The Ministry of Labour and the Ministry of Pensions and National Insurance are, however, primarily concerned with the provision of direct services to the public and not with the oversight of local authorities. The Ministry of Labour, through its regional offices and its nation-wide network of employment exchanges, provides most comprehensive coverage. The Ministry of Pensions and National Insurance also maintains a regional and local administrative structure, but the greatest part of its activity is centred on its huge record office. Because of its use of the Post Office and of the Employment Exchange as paying agents, and because eligibility for benefit is laid down by regulations under the Insurance Acts and not by an individual assessment of need, there should be less necessity for the Ministry of Pensions and National Insurance to maintain a comprehensive local office system, but in fact many queries about contributions and benefits have to be sorted out. Since 1953, when the Ministry of Pensions and the Ministry of National Insurance were amalgamated, the combined department has to make arrangements for the special welfare services provided for war pensioners and their dependents.

The Board of Trade, the Commissioners of Inland Revenue and other central government bodies all have a part to play in the implementation of social policy, but the bodies already mentioned are perhaps more intimately concerned with those social problems which are the main topic of this book.

Locally the development of multi-purpose authorities has been very evident particularly in those cities and towns of County Borough status which are indeed responsible for all local government functions. In County areas, responsibility for local government is divided mainly between the County Councils and the Borough or District Councils, Parish Councils now having very little power. There has been a tendency for new local services to be given to the major authorities and for some developing services also to be transferred, as with the provision of maternal and child welfare and other domiciliary services which became the responsibility of the County and County Borough Councils under the National Health Service Act, 1946. Nevertheless, the minor authorities still have important responsibilities for environmental services, for housing and a number of amenity services. Moreover, since the Local Government Act, 1958, some of the larger Borough and District Councils have had delegated responsibility for certain personal health and welfare services.

The increase in the number and scope of the services run by local authorities has meant a development of specialized departments and sub-departments. In some instances the administrative organization used to implement a particular legislative provision is dictated by the Act itself or by regulation made under the Act. In others, particularly where permissive rather than mandatory powers are concerned, the local authority is free to decide the means whereby the service will be provided. County and County Borough Councils have to appoint education, health and children's committees, each with their chief officers and appropriate administrative, professional and technical staff. The provision of residential accommodation and welfare services for the handicapped under Part III of the National Assistance Act, 1948, however, may be implemented by such means as the local authority itself determines, although the Ministry of Health has to approve the schemes put forward by the local authorities. Thus, in some areas, the welfare department is the responsibility of a welfare committee directly answerable to the Council and provides residential accommodation and welfare services for the handicapped. In other areas these responsibilities are discharged by a combined health and welfare committee of the Council and welfare services are provided by a sub-department administered by a chief welfare officer under the medical officer of health. In other areas again, there may be a division of function, the services for the handicapped being the responsibility of the health committee, but a separate welfare committee providing residential accommodation.

Administrative organization has often changed with the development of the social services. Local mental health services are an interesting example. Until 1948, the local administration of the statutes relating to mental disorder could be carried out by a number of different committees of the local authorities. Cases of mental illness were dealt with by the statutory Visiting (or Mental Hospital) Committee and the Public Assistance Committee, the former since 1889 and the latter since 1929, when the administration of the Poor Law became the responsibility of the County and County Borough Councils. Under the Mental Deficiency Act, 1913, the local authority was required to appoint 'a committee for the care of the mentally defective' with the proviso that the Visiting Committee could act as this committee or that the personnel of the two committees could be identical. In practice, these committees were often separate, especially as the Lunacy Act, 1890, and later the Mental Treatment Act, 1930, gave the Visiting Committee much more independence than the mental deficiency committee had under the Mental Deficiency Acts. The Visiting Committee had power to carry out all the functions of the local authority in relation to mental illness except those of raising a rate or borrowing money, whereas the mental deficiency committee and indeed the public assistance committee were subject to the detailed control of the Council. The Feversham Report in 1939 urged that each major authority should set up a mental health committee to undertake all the local authority functions with regard to mental disorder. 'This would be no mere formal alteration in the law. The need for co-ordination is deep and urgent. Central administration, in our opinion, is greatly strengthened by unified control, and the formation of a single committee to deal with all the mental health work of the local authority would be an unqualified advantage.'[8] However, when unification came it was not as far reaching as the Feversham Committee had hoped. Because of the strong pressure which also developed in the 1930's and 1940's for the bringing together of the services for both physical and mental health, the unified mental health committees set up by the County and County Borough Councils under the National Health Service Act, 1946, were sub-committees of the Health Committees. They became responsible for the care and after-care of mentally ill patients under the permissive powers of the Mental Treatment Act as well as Section 28 of the National Health Service Act, for the ascertainment and supervision of mental defectives under the Mental Deficiency Acts, and for the appointment of officers, authorized to arrange for the certification and reception of patients under compulsory powers. However, mental hospitals and mental deficiency hospitals became the responsibility of the Regional Hospital Boards together with other specialist and general hospitals. These local administrative arrangements have not been materially affected by the Mental Health Act, 1959.

Another interesting example of changes in the scope and organization of local authority provision is the evolution of the child care service to which reference has already been made in Chapter 12. Because of the piecemeal development of services for different groups of children in need of care, the Curtis Committee found in 1946 that at least three local authority departments, four central government departments and numerous voluntary organizations had some responsibility in this field. The Children Act, 1948, required local authorities to set up a special Children's Committee with the primary responsibility of providing alternative care for children who for some reason were unable to be looked after adequately at home by their own parents or guardians, taking over duties discharged before by the Health, Education and Public Assistance Committees. Thus the function of these new departments were fairly clearly defined. The joint memorandum, issued in 1950 by the Home Secretary, the Minister of Health and the Minister of Education, considered that local authorities had sufficient powers under existing legislation to help children neglected in their own homes if these powers were fully used and efforts coordinated.[9] Until the Children and Young Persons Act, 1963, however, there was considerable discussion and difference of opinion as to whether Children's Committees had the power to work with families to prevent children having to come into care, although in practice many authorities found themselves undertaking an increasing amount of such work. Section 1 of the new Act lays additional duties on the local authorities and although many different departments and voluntary organizations may be involved in preventive work the Children's Committees are primarily responsible. It is becoming increasingly clear that their function is in the process of changing from departments whose primary responsibility is the provision of alternative care to departments providing a more general social work service for children and their parents. This development inevitably impinges upon much of the personal work done by other departments and voluntary organizations, and thus Section 1 of the new Act, while clarifying the powers of the local authorities adds also to the confusion concerning the division of responsibility within the local authorities and also between them and a number of voluntary bodies.

Other examples could be quoted but these may serve to show how the development of social policy and its implementation not only means the creation of new administrative organs or an alteration or extension of existing ones, but also the repercussions these changes may have on the scope or function of other bodies. One more illustration may be given of the interconnection between different services or organizations when new legislation is passed embodying major changes of policy. The Mental Health Act, 1959, involved the repeal of 71 enactments and 48 minor and consequential amendments to existing law. Statutory changes not only affect central and local government bodies but have their repercussions on voluntary organizations, many of which have been pioneers in the field affected by the legislation in question.

VOLUNTARY ORGANIZATIONS

The relationship between voluntary and statutory social services is a complicated and changing one. The Government has often encouraged the activity of voluntary bodies in some fields of welfare and indeed may enter into a formal contract with an organization to provide a particular service on an agency basis.

As indicated in Chapter 2, in the nineteenth century it was considered that social needs and problems should be met primarily by voluntary organizations or individuals and statutory provision was only slowly developed as a means of supplementing such private enterprise for welfare when it was demonstrated that the latter was insufficient. An example of this is the establishment of local School Boards under the Education Act, 1870, with power to set up elementary schools in those areas where voluntary provision was inadequate. Voluntary organizations have traditionally been pioneers, identifying needs, experimenting with methods of meeting these needs and educating public opinion. The great majority of the services described in the preceding chapters have started in this way. As they have developed they have often made use of the special experience of organizations for a time before providing a comprehensive public service. An illustration of this was the use made of Friendly Societies as approved agents in the administration of the first national health insurance scheme under the National Insurance Act, 1911, and not dispensed with until 1948. Similarly voluntary hospitals were used by the Government to help to provide the Emergency Hospital Service during the 1939–45 war before being 'nationalized' under the National Health Service Act, 1946.

A recent example of the use of a voluntary body as an agent of government policy is the administration of the legal aid scheme, which is the responsibility of the Law Society, and governed by the Legal Aid and Advice Acts, 1949 and 1960. Moreover, this particular example is unique in that it is the only case of a professional association rather than a charitable body undertaking a welfare service on behalf of the Government. More usual are the arrangements which many local authorities make with organizations for the welfare of the blind or other handicapped persons to provide certain services on their behalf under the National Assistance Acts, 1948 and 1962, or with district nursing associations to provide home nursing under the National Health Service Act, 1946. It is noticeable, however, that a number of these arrangements are coming to an end as local authorities gain more experience in these fields of public activity and resolve to establish their own direct service which can thus be integrated more closely with other personal services.

Rapidly changing conditions throw up new needs, cause new stresses and lead to fresh pioneer ventures on the part of the voluntary organizations, both old and new.[10] It is a study in itself to trace the way in which many old-established bodies are prepared to change and adapt to modern demands; others unfortunately linger on providing an inefficient and overlapping service for too long while yet others quietly go out of business. The existence of so many voluntary organizations working often in close partnership with central and local government bodies indicates that there are other functions for such organizations less temporary than the purely pioneer one. The use made by local authorities of special schools and children's homes run by voluntary bodies indicates that these have an important role in providing for the very special needs of small groups, as for children with multiple handicaps, or for minority groups on religious or similar grounds. Again organizations, like the Family Planning Association, can provide services in fields where there is considerable public controversy. An interesting recent development has been the very close partnership which exists between voluntary organizations and local authorities in the Youth Service which provides for a wide variety of leisure-time activities, thus giving an essential freedom of choice to the individual in this important field—a field which is likely to become even more vital with shorter working hours.

There is little doubt that voluntary organizations have as important a part to play today as in the past. They are flexible, able to undertake new work without seeking fresh statutory powers and are able to concern themselves with minority causes. Perhaps one of the continuing contributions voluntary organizations can make is in seeking to affect social policy and the way it is implemented rather than by continuing to act as agents for the State in carrying it out. The report of the Committee on the Law and Practice relating to Charitable Trusts, 1952, suggested that

> Some of the most valuable activities of voluntary societies consist, however, in the fact that they are able to stand aside from and criticise State action, or inaction, in the interests of the inarticulate man-in-the-street. This may take the form of helping individuals to know and obtain their rights. It also consists in a more general activity of collecting data about some point where the shoe seems to pinch or a need remains unmet.[11]

Many of the most energetic organizations today act as centres of information and education about particular problems and needs, and where necessary act as pressure groups to get more or better public provision in their particular fields.

An interesting development in this century has been the greater size and more complicated organization of many voluntary bodies. In the same way that statutory bodies have provided a more comprehensive and uniform service over the country as a whole, so too voluntary organizations have tended to become more national in coverage. Sometimes the pattern is one of a national organization with a central office and regional or local branches with more or less independence. Sometimes the central organization affiliates semi-autonomous local bodies which fulfil certain conditions; or yet again fully independent local bodies come together in a standing conference for the interchange of information and experience or to formulate a common policy. Thus the Red Cross, the National Society for the Prevention of Cruelty to Children, the National Association of Boys' Clubs, the Royal National Institute for the Blind all show different organizational patterns. Many of the voluntary societies existing today are direct descendants of the pioneer philanthropic organizations of the nineteenth century. A striking development in recent years, however, has been the emergence of a new kind of 'mutual aid' organization often composed of those people who have some particular handicap or problem in common. Examples are the British Polio Fellowship (registered as the Infantile Paralysis Fellowship), the Multiple Sclerosis Society and the National Society for Mentally Handicapped Children (started by the parents of such children). A unique organization of quite a different kind is the Women's Voluntary Service. This was created by the Home Secretary under the Air Raid Precautions Act, 1937, mobilizing women volunteers to assist local authorities in carrying out their war-time responsibilities, and thus it performed a national service acting under Government instructions. In peacetime it has remained as an essential part of government machinery to meet any emergency—whether from enemy action, fire, flood or any other disaster; but it has extended its activities to many welfare tasks co-operating with both statutory and voluntary social services.[12] Another valuable voluntary service which was begun in war-time with government encouragement and which has increased in usefulness with the growth in number and complexity of statutory and voluntary provisions, is the Citizens Advice Bureaux.[13] Staffed by some professional and many voluntary workers, the Bureaux provide a unique information and advice service helping the ordinary citizen to avail himself of the many private and public resources available for his assistance. A few local authorities provide their own information and advice service, but most subsidize independently run bureaux.

A distinction was made earlier between voluntary organization and voluntary or unpaid service. There are many men and women who give much time and energy in helping to run both statutory and voluntary bodies. They serve on the committees of voluntary organizations, local authorities, or hospital management committees, etc., they serve as voluntary helpers in youth clubs, in old people's clubs and homes, as uncles and aunts to children in care, as visitors of the sick, the handicapped and the lonely. The report on Charitable Trusts has much to say that is of interest in this connection.

> The democratic state as we know it could hardly function effectively or teach the exercise of democracy to its members without such channels for and demands upon voluntary service. Not only does voluntary service act as a nursery school of democracy, but also as the field in which good neighbourliness may be exercised. Many tributes have been paid to the voluntary worker but fewer to the good neighbour. Yet in an urban society like ours, too prone to become 'a disordered dust of individuals' it is the informal unorganised actions of the good neighbour which makes satisfactory social relationships possible. . . . More leisure and a better standard of living have provided opportunities of voluntary service to the many which were before only available to the comparatively few. It is therefore essential that such voluntary action in the form of good neighbourliness, voluntary service and financial support should come to be regarded as a normal part of citizenship in the modern democratic state.[14]

A highly organized industrial society as ours is today cannot rely only on good neighbourliness to meet the personal needs of the destitute, the lonely and the sick. Even friendly visiting requires some organization by a voluntary society or a statutory authority to ensure that those who most need such help receive it and receive it regularly.

CO-ORDINATION AND CO-OPERATION

The welter of public and private bodies all impinging in some way on the welfare of the individual citizen makes the problem of co-operating a vital one if the needs of the citizen are to be met efficiently and humanely. Co-operation is a matter of human relationships, involving a willingness on the part of each person to work with others to achieve some end, to provide a service, to meet need. Yet co-operation can be helped by organizational means, by providing conditions of employment which encourage people to work together. The clarification of the function of the various departments or organizations involved, the definition of the roles of the workers, good lines of communication to assist the exchange of information and the development of mutual understanding are all important. One could say that it is necessary to know the shape and colour of all the different pieces of the jigsaw puzzle in order to fit them together to make the whole picture, but this illustration implies something static, whereas, as we have seen, the picture is a moving one constantly changing to meet new pressures and new needs. Thus any devices which are developed in order to facilitate co-operation have to be flexible and under constant reappraisal.

At top policy level, of course, the co-ordinating machinery of the social services is that of the Government itself—through the cabinet, through meetings of ministers, etc., and within each department the minister and his senior administrators are responsible for co-ordinating the various branches of that department. Thus the Minister of Health has an overall responsibility for the co-ordination of the work of the regional hospital boards, the executive councils and the local authorities. The recent creation of a department for Education and Science has been an attempt to bring together education at all levels with the promotion of science. At local level, the Councils of the Counties and County Boroughs and their clerks are responsible for the overall co-ordination of the work of the various committees and their departments responsible for the specialized work of the Councils. There are many other devices which promote co-ordination at all levels—interdepartmental committees, cross-representation, special liaison committees, standing or *ad hoc* conferences, etc. The health service, for instance, provides a number of examples both of cross-representation and liaison committee.

Some of the changes which have been taking place recently in voluntary organizations have already been noted. A number of these organizations aim at bringing together locally and regionally, as well as nationally, all those statutory and voluntary bodies and individuals interested in one particular problem or field of activity. Examples of these co-ordinating bodies are the Old People's Welfare Committees, the National Association of Mental Health, and the Central Council for the Disabled. The Councils of Social Service are unique in that they endeavour to co-ordinate the whole range of welfare activities in a locality in the same way as the National Council of Social Service does for the country as a whole.

It is possible to distinguish at least two kinds of co-ordinating machinery that which is 'service' centred and that which is primarily 'client' or 'consumer' centred. The former endeavours to bring together organizations or departments and is concerned with the development of an agreed policy and the overlap of services, and examples have just been given. There are also co-ordinating committees or case conferences which endeavour to ensure that the resources of the community are used most effectively to meet the needs of individuals or families. Sometimes these operate in a specialized field, such as child guidance, or rehabilitation, sometimes more generally as in the co-ordinating machinery set up to deal with children neglected in their own homes. A measure of the far-sightedness of the founders of the Charity Organization Society in 1869 is to be found in the fact that they attempted to do these two things—to try to get charities organized to prevent overlapping and waste of resources, and at the same time by offering to investigate applications for help to the various charities to ensure that the needs of the individual or family were adequately and efficiently met.[15] That their attempts at co-ordination were not very successful was due in part to the same reasons that much of our present-day machinery does not always work very smoothly—for effective co-ordination the will to co-operate must be there or the co-ordinating body must have the authority to ensure that an agreed common policy is carried out.

PERSONNEL

The development of social policy has inevitably meant a large increase in the number of those employed in its implementation. A considerable number of the 529,000 civil servants and the 781,000 local government officers are involved with the working of the social services and with ensuring that other social welfare measures are effective in addition to those providing professional services such as the 812,000 persons employed in the medical and dental services and the 975,000 in education (1963 figures).

The quantitative problem is one that is of obvious importance. As soon as the State accepts responsibility for providing certain services it has to concern itself with the recruitment of sufficient workers to man the services. This concern increases as the concept of 'social rights' emerges. If there is the implication that every child has the right to receive education suited to his age, aptitude and ability, and every citizen the right to appropriate medical care, then some person or organization has the duty of ensuring that there are enough doctors, nurses, teachers and other medical and educational personnel to meet the demand or these rights are ineffective. It is not easy to ensure an adequate supply of workers, for it is the potential and future need that has to be estimated and many factors have to be taken into consideration. Thus in planning the recruitment of the requisite personnel consideration must be given to the total supply of man-power at any given time, the availability of financial resources to pay for the expected number of workers—financial resources upon which there will be many competing claims—and the length of time it may take to train the workers needed.

The second major problem that must be considered concerns the different *kinds* of personnel required, what training they should have, whether persons with particular qualifications should be recruited or whether there is need for new forms of professional or technical education to be introduced. Thirdly, there arise problems concerning the deployment of these various kinds of workers, their relationship to each other and their role in the total complex of services, services which are themselves always changing. These problems have to be considered in any discussion of the growth and development of the staff involved in effecting the implementation of social policy.

One of the outstanding achievements of the nineteenth century was the development of an efficient and impartial Civil Service to carry on the increasing activity of the State. Within this service was to be found a growing number of professional and technically qualified people who from the knowledge and experience they gained from their work exercised a considerable influence on social policy. Particularly was this true of the inspectorate. The device of inspection through which the Victorians sought to preserve some local autonomy and yet ensure some uniformity of service over the country as a whole was extremely useful to social reformers. From 1833 onwards when the first provision was made for independent factory inspectors to be appointed, government inspectors have been used in a variety of fields to ensure that reforms were carried out and social policy implemented. Doctors, lawyers, educationalists, scientists and technical experts of all kinds brought a new element into both central and local government administration and it was largely they who were responsible for seeing that policy laid down by Parliament was implemented and adequate standards attained by factory owners, voluntary school societies, local public health authorities, prison governors and lunatic asylum superintendents. Their reports served many purposes.

> They told of the willingness of industry and local authorities to adhere to governmental regulations; they explained new policies and proceedings; they described the social and moral condition of the country; they gave statistics on crime, education and pauperism; and they espoused ideas for further reform, urging it on both local authorities and Parliament.[16]

Thus the creation of new inspectorates was an important contribution of the Victorian era to the implementation of social policy and in many instances their reports were the beginning for further social reforms and of administrative developments which were to make possible the evolution of the Welfare State.

Another nineteenth-century development which must be noted was the organization of the medical profession and the establishment of nursing as a qualified and skilled occupation. Reform in medical organization was initiated by an Act of 1815 sponsored by the Society of Apothecaries which attempted to set up a licensing and examining authority for England and Wales. Following this, numerous voluntary associations of practitioners, including the Provincial Medical and Surgical Association (later the British Medical Association), were formed to promote further improvements and this campaign finally resulted in the passing of the Medical Act, 1858. The Act created the General Council of Medical Education and Registration of the United Kingdom, usually called the General Medical Council, to regulate the conditions under which persons entered the medical profession and a register was instituted to contain the names of qualified individuals. The amending Act of 1886 defined the general scope of the qualifying examination and gave the Council some measure of control over the corporate bodies licensed to grant diplomas.[17]

Although nursing has a long and honoured history it was only after the Crimean War that it evolved into a highly skilled profession chiefly owing to the genius of Florence Nightingale. It was many years before more than a handful of qualified nurses were employed by public authorities yet the standard of care, not only in private practice but also in the growing number of voluntary hospitals and dispensaries reached a high level and made a vital contribution to the improvement of medical treatment.[18]

The State made increasing use of doctors, nurses, dentists and other medical personnel as administrators, advisers, inspectors and practitioners in the latter part of the nineteenth century and indeed the first half of the twentieth century, but its chief concern at this time was with the standard of practice and the protection of the public from 'quacks'. The Medical Acts already mentioned, the Dentists Acts of 1878, 1921 and 1952, the Nurses Registration Act, 1919, and the Nurses Acts, 1943 and 1949, the Midwives Acts, 1902, 1918 and 1936, all sought to ensure at least a minimum standard of training and practice through the setting up of professional councils to approve courses and maintain registers. However, much of the actual training and education was left to independent bodies, such as University Medical Schools, although nursing and midwifery training schools became an integral part of the National Health Service in 1946–8.

The history of the teaching profession and of its relations with the Government has been somewhat different. The first government subsidies in the field of education were given towards the training of teachers and though the inspectorate endeavoured to improve the standard of teaching, the whole question of mass education was bedevilled by finance and the religious issue. After the Board of Education Act, 1899, the training of teachers was regulated by the Teachers' Registration Council of the Royal Society of Teachers, established in 1907 and constituted by Orders in Council in 1912 and 1926. This Council, however, was never very effective and was finally abolished in 1949.

L. A. Selby-Bigge, writing in 1927, said:

> In the ninety years during which the State has interested itself in training colleges its association with the arrangements for the admission of students, their instruction and examination and the award of their final qualification to teach, has been very intimate. Its concern for them has been more conspicuously paternal than for any other educational institutions, and through its regulations and inspectors it has exercised control and supervision of them in a high degree.[19]

This close connection was partly due to the high rate at which the State contributed towards the cost of teacher training, but even more perhaps because from 1870 onwards the State was forced to be concerned not only with the quality but also the quantity of teachers due to the introduction of universal elementary education. Moreover, this interest took place before teaching had really established itself as an organized profession, and indeed at a time when teachers in elementary schools were still struggling to establish any kind of status in the community. One writer in 1879 considered that 'This ignorance on the part of teachers as to their position, and as to their relations to the country, is a point about which no reticence need be shown. They must distinctly understand that their office is not one which calls for any special abilities. Pretensions such as the certificated teacher sometimes puts forth . . . must be crushed and checked without mercy.'[20] There were in the past many associations catering for sectional interests inside the ranks of the elementary school teachers in spite of the work of the National Union of Elementary Teachers founded in 1870 (since 1889 the National Union of Teachers). Moreover, there has been very little apparent feeling of identity between teachers in local authority primary and secondary schools, the older grammar schools, private preparatory and the great public schools, to say nothing of those teaching in technical colleges and universities.

A committee appointed in 1942 by the President of the Board of Education to consider the supply, recruitment and training of teachers and youth leaders anticipated the passing of the Education Act, 1944.[21] As a result of its report, much of the responsibility for the maintenance and improvement of teacher training has been given to University Institutes of Education, and thus the central government has withdrawn from the very close association with teacher training characteristic of the previous period. Further changes in organization may come about as a result of the recommendations of the Robbins Committee on Higher Education which reported in 1963.[22] There have been signs in recent years that teachers are moving towards the establishment of a more unified profession based on an educational qualification, and agitation appears to be growing for the setting up of a registering body comparable to the General Medical Council. The efforts towards a more united front, particularly on the part of the National Union of Teachers, by far the largest professional body in the educational field, may be stimulated in part by the apparent necessity to develop a strong negotiating body now that more and more teachers are affected in some measure by government policy.

The difficulties that may arise for the members of a profession when the State becomes the largest employer of their services is something about which medical practitioners have been acutely aware since the inauguration of a national health insurance scheme under the National Insurance Act, 1911. The medical profession has been increasingly incorporated into the statutory system since the development of the Emergency Medical Service in the 1939–45 war and the inception of the National Health Service, and a long series of negotiations, of committees of inquiry as well as a Royal Commission have been concerned with two major issues, the equitable remuneration of doctors in public employ and the provision of conditions of work which ensure professional freedom.

> The professional is in a position of trust, in which he is his own master, exercising his own judgment according to his professional conscience, and in which his character is quite as important as his brain or hands. This professional freedom is never easily kept alive in large organisations, and it has no chance whatever of survival if those who pay the professional man his salary come to regard him as their servant to whom they can issue orders. Equally it is doomed if he comes to regard them as his masters.[23]

Hence the compromise device of Executive Councils and *per capita* payments to general practitioners in the National Health Service. Some doctors have suggested that all doctors should be employed by a medical guild which would contract for their services with the Ministry of Health, an arrangement analagous to that under which lawyers providing legal aid are paid by their own professional association. Other important problems which have been the concern of the Government and the medical profession relate to the number of doctors required for the operation of the National Health Service—a particularly tricky problem when the length of training of a qualified medical practitioner is considered—and the need to ensure that medical education keeps abreast of the ever-increasing field of medical science and of the demands of modern society. Some of the issues involved were discussed by the Inter-departmental Committee on Medical Schools in its report in 1944, as well as by many official and un-official bodies since.

An effect of the great advances in medical science which have taken place particularly in the past few decades has been not only the increased growth of many specialisms within the medical profession itself, but also the development of a number of ancil-lary workers, radiographers, physiotherapists and occupational therapists, for example. The establishment of the National Health Service inevitably meant that the Government had to concern itself with their recruitment and training. Although the Cope Committee, set up by the Minister of Health to review the recruit-ment, training, and qualifications of medical auxiliary workers in the National Health Service, reported in 1951, it was not until 1960 that the Professions Supplementary to Medicine Act was passed providing for a Council with specialist boards for the registration of chiropodists, dietitians, medical laboratory tech-nicians, occupational therapists, physiotherapists, radiographers and remedial gymnasts.

Thus the growth of the social services has had profound effects upon a number of groups of professional people—doctors, den-tists, teachers, civil servants, local government officers, hospital administrators and, to some extent, lawyers. It has, moreover, been directly responsible for the growth of various kinds of social workers and welfare officers. The social provisions which have been briefly outlined in earlier chapters have tended to grow up in a piecemeal fashion, so that it is not surprising that workers have tended to be employed on a somewhat *ad hoc* basis to under-take jobs which have themselves been evolving rapidly.[24] The growth of 'almost a new concept of the relationship between public agencies and the public served . . . of consciously regarding the individual as the focal point of social administration', has had a profound effect on the kind of personnel employed in the public services.[25] There has been a growing emphasis on the importance of the person who is the point of contact between the service and the citizen. In some services such as social insurance and the pro-vision of family allowances this contact is not of prime impor-tance and indeed in most cases is impersonal because eligibility is determined by detailed regulations. In other services such as National Assistance, personal contact is of greater importance because there is a discretionary element in the service based on the judgment of the officer concerned. Sometimes indeed the personal relationship of the worker and the citizen is an essential part of the help given. But there is a third group of services which depend almost entirely for their effectiveness upon the professional knowledge and skill of the clinical and field workers employed in these services. One can go further and say that access to that specialized knowledge and skill *is* the service offered. It is in making available this professional help to all who may need it whether it be in medicine, in education, or some other area of professional competence that some of the most dramatic advances in social provision have been made recently. It is in this context that the development of professional social work must be seen. The help of some professional social workers, for instance, is moving from the second to the third category of service.

As each new service has developed it has tended to create its own specialized workers to mediate the service, to establish eligibility and to ensure the welfare of the recipient. But there has also been an acknowledgment of the help that can be given to individuals and groups by a skilled worker through the creation and utilization of a professional relationship. Social workers are primarily concerned with helping people to live fuller and more worthwhile lives. In the past this mostly took the form of providing for the more obvious wants of the underprivileged. As these wants have begun to be met either by the rise in the general standard of living or by more general community provision, social workers have moved on to the realization that many people still have problems which are not solved by better material standards or the availability of social resources. Thus new methods of help have 'evolved from the gradually accumulated experience of social work teachers and practitioners in this (probation) and other fields as they have learnt to apply and test a growing body of psychological and sociological theory'.[26] These new methods were pioneered by some of the older-established professional social work groups, family caseworkers, psychiatric social workers, almoners and probation officers, but are gradually permeating a variety of services and affecting the practice of many field workers. Although social casework as a method of social work has gone further in developing a more coherent body of theory and practice in recent years, group work and community organization are also beginning to be accepted as methods of professional social work.[27]

Thus present-day social workers of all kinds have evolved partly from the nineteenth-century 'do gooders', from charity organization workers, police court missionaries, rescue and preventive workers, school managers, settlement workers and a host of other voluntary workers concerned with giving personal service to aid their fellows, and partly from the relieving officers and other local government officials concerned with providing material help to those eligible for it. The marriage of the two traditions, the one which may be called 'client centred' and the other 'service centred' is still going through a difficult phase of adjustment. Moreover, there is still perhaps insufficient recognition that administrative procedures inherited from the past, which were valid for the conduct of impersonal community services, are not always suitable when dealing with the needs of individuals. The situation is not helped by the lack of adequate organization of the social work profession.

However, in recent years social workers, like teachers, have been attempting to develop a more unified profession. The British Federation of Social Workers, started in 1936, had among its objectives the greater unity of the profession. The Association of Social Workers which succeeded it keeps alive the idea of one social work profession instead of separate specialist groups limited to workers in the different services, and the formation in 1962 of a Standing Conference of Organizations of Social Workers gives some hope for the future.

One of the difficulties always encountered is the definition of a social worker.[28] Almoners, child-care workers, mental health officers, moral welfare workers, probation officers, psychiatric social workers, welfare officers for the elderly and the handicapped are all recognized as social workers. But what of home teachers for the blind, education welfare officers, as well as youth leaders, youth employment officers, community centre organizers, secretaries of councils of social service and many others? A definition by qualification has been attempted from time to time, but training itself is in a confused state. The Charity Organization Society and the Residential Settlements pioneered courses of training at the turn of the century and, as discussed in the first chapter of this book, a number of universities developed social study courses primarily as a preparation for social work. For some professional groups, notably the almoners and the psychiatric social workers, specialized training courses for those with a basic qualification in social studies were established comparatively early by the Institute of Almoners (now the Institute of Medical Social Workers) and the London School of Economics respectively.[29] Gradually other training courses developed independently, but in recent years, especially after the Report on the Employment and Training of Social Workers (published 1947) by E. L. Young-husband and its supplement, Social Work in Britain (published 1951) both sponsored by the Carnegie U.K. Trust, and after the subsequent establishment of a course in Applied Social Studies at the London School of Economics, there has been a growth of common professional training courses for caseworkers in a number of fields.

The interest which the State has begun to take in the supply and qualifications of social workers and allied professions is seen in the number of committees set up to inquire into recruitment and training. The Curtis Committee, which reviewed the provision for children deprived of a normal home life and which advocated the establishment of local authority children's departments, also made specific recommendations about the calibre and qualifications of Children's Officers and their staff. As a result, the Central Training Council in Child Care was formed in 1947 and has been active in promoting courses at universities and institutions of further education to prepare students for the child care field. The Mackintosh Committee on Social Workers in the Mental Health Services, 1951, the Jameson Committee on Health Visiting, 1956, the Younghusband Committee on Social Workers in the Health and Welfare Services of Local Authorities, 1959, the Albemarle Committee on the Youth Service, 1960, the Morison Committee on the Probation Service, 1962, are examples of government concern. In order to train as many people as possible, courses have proliferated in recent years, in universities, in colleges of commerce, in technical colleges, in teacher training colleges as well as in separate institutions such as the National College for Youth Leaders. These courses have been initiated by different government departments, and there appears to have been little attempt to develop a co-ordinated training policy or to ensure common levels of competence. The Health Visiting and Social Work

(Training) Act, 1962, passed as a result of the Jameson and Young-husband reports, made provision for the setting up of two Councils with the duty of promoting training in health visiting and in social work. However, at present, the Council for Training in Social Work is responsible for awarding a National Certificate in Social Work and approving courses in social work only for those intending to enter the health and wefare services. The Act makes provision for the possible future extension of the Council's responsibility for training for other fields, and this may ultimately bring greater uniformity into the training and standards of practice of qualified social workers. Nevertheless there is considerable concern, especially among the older established groups of professional social workers lest the high level of training and competence which they have attained after much hard work may be debased. At this stage in the development of professional social work, is it better to have a variety of training courses preparing students for the same kind of job or to develop groups of auxiliary or assistant workers as in medicine and nursing, and as indeed has begun in the creation of welfare assistant posts in local authority health and welfare departments?

The question of dilution, of the danger of lowering standards of competence in order to achieve comprehensive coverage, is seen by many to be at the heart of the problem of staffing in all the public social services. The overall shortage of man-power in modern society may be solved in part by the increased use of automation and the release of a greater proportion of the population for employment in the service industries. This will still leave further questions to be answered. Will it be possible to recruit enough workers of a sufficiently high calibre for the social services, as doctors, teachers, nurses, social workers, administrators, managers in industry and other professional people are all drawn from the same pool of workers? Will it be possible to train sufficient numbers quickly enough to meet the rising demand?

Two points emerge from any discussion of the future recruitment of appropriate personnel in the social services. The first is the need for a constant reappraisal of training to be undertaken in relation to the needs of the citizen consumer and not only to the apparent requirements of the service. For instance, it may seem more efficient for each service, department or sub-department to employ its own staff of specialized workers, yet from the citizens' point of view it may be more acceptable and, in the long run more efficient, for one worker to deal with several problems and if this is accepted, training must help the worker to meet these demands. Moreover, training for all kinds of personnel and particularly for senior administrators and field staff must be sufficiently broad in scope to enable them to see their role and that of their particular service in relation to wider aspects of social policy and the changing needs of society. At present there is mounting criticism of the methods of recruitment and training of the higher levels of the Civil Service, of those men and women who although not officially policy makers, nevertheless in practice influence policy, both through their formal role as advisers to the Government and because their grasp of many subjects inevitably outweighs that of their ministers.[30] In a world where there is increasing specialization and greater social mobility are they drawn from too narrow a social and educational group and expected to be able to administer departments which may provide services of a highly technical and expert kind?

Secondly, there needs to be a continuous reappraisal both of the organization of the services and the deployment of staff. The proliferation of field workers all of whom may be concerned with the welfare of one family can cause overlapping and waste of time and effort on the part of both the officers concerned and of the members of the family. Co-ordination of services and co-operation among workers may help the situation to some extent, but does not always seem to be the answer. The kind of administrative problem which one family can set is seen in the case study of the Fardell family.[31] Over a period of years every conceivable type of social worker and statutory officer seemed to be in touch with the family, all apparently to no purpose. While it is true that such families are not numerous and would pose problems for the most efficiently organized welfare state, yet it is legitimate to ask whether some of the overlapping, administrative confusion and waste of time and money could have been avoided by better planned services. Is the specialization within our present social services based on any clear and coherent principle or has it just grown up without adequate thought being given to function and role?[32] There are broad divisions of function between the various central and local government departments so that, as described earlier, the Ministry of Pensions and National Insurance, together with the National Assistance Board, is responsible for meeting financial need arising from many causes; the Ministry of Health is responsible for seeing that a vast array of medical services are provided and the Ministry of Education and the local authority education departments provide many different kinds of educational institutions. Yet it is also the responsibility of the education authorities to provide financial help in the form of free, or partly free, school meals where necessary and maintenance grants for a wide variety of students; of the Housing authorities to administer rent-rebate schemes or other forms of subsidized housing, and now local authorities under the Children and Young Persons Act, 1963, have power to assist families in cash or kind. At the same time Health departments are responsible for health education, Welfare departments for home teaching of the blind, Children's departments for approved schools, while residential accommodation, both short-term and permanent in homes and hostels can be provided by a vast array of statutory bodies, Regional Hospital Boards, local health and mental health departments, welfare departments, education departments, children's departments, the Home Office, and even the National Assistance Board is responsible for reception centres and re-establishment centres. No doubt good reasons can be found to account for all these divisions, but is the present allocation of functions the most rational and useful? Does it help or hinder the co-ordination of services and the efficient use of scarce personnel, and does it provide the most effective way of meeting the needs of the citizen?

NOTES

[1] *Report of the Committee on the Law and Practice relating to Charitable Trusts*, 1952, H.M.S.O., Cmd. 8710.

[2] Central Statistical Office, *Abstract of Statistics*, 1962–3.

[3] David Roberts, *Victorian Origins of the British Welfare State*.

[4] See J. S. Ross, *The National Health Service*.

[5] H. Eckstein, *The English Health Service*.

[6] F. Newsam, *The Home Office*.

[7] Godfrey Ince, *The Ministry of Labour and National Service*; Geoffrey King, *The Ministry of Pensions and National Insurance*.

[8] The Voluntary Mental Health Service, the *Report of the Feversham Committee*, 1939.

[9] Joint Circular from the Home Office, Ministry of Health and Ministry of Education, 1950, *Children Neglected or Ill-treated in their Own Homes*.

[10] For further discussion, see A. F. C. Bourdillon, *Voluntary Social Services*; H. Mess, *Voluntary Social Services since 1918*; M. Rooff, *Voluntary Societies and Social Policy*; Lord Beveridge, *Voluntary Action*.

[11] *Report on Charitable Trusts,* loc. cit.

[12] *Report on 25 Years' Work of the Women's Voluntary Service for Civil Defence*, published by H.M.S.O.

[13] M. Brasnett, *The Story of the Citizens Advice Bureaux*.

[14] *Report on Charitable Trusts*, loc. cit.

[15] For an account of the Charity Organization Society, see Helen Bosanquet, *Social Work in London 1869–1912*; C. L. Mowat, *The Charity Organisation Society*.

[16] David Roberts, op. cit.

[17] R. H. Shrylock, *The Development of Modern Medicine*. See also A. Carr-Saunders and P. A. Wilson, *The Professions*; R. Lewis and A. Maude, *Professional People*.

[18] B. Abel-Smith, *A History of the Nursing Profession*.

[19] L. A. Selby-Bigge, *The Board of Education*.

[20] Asher Tropp, *The School Teachers*.

[21] See the *Report of the Committee on the Supply, Recruitment and Training of Teachers and Youth Leaders*, 1944.

[22] *Report of the Committee on Higher Education*, 1963, H.M.S.O., Cmd. 2154.

[23] From a paper given by T. F. Fox on 'Professionalism and Socialisation' to the Conference of the British Sociological Association, 1953.

[24] For a study of the social services in a northern town, see Barbara N. Rodgers and Julia Dixon, *Portrait of Social Work*.

[25] R. M. Titmuss, *Problems of Social Policy*.

[26] *Report of the Departmental Committee on the Probation Service*, H.M.S.O., 1962, Cmd. 1650.

[27] See Cherry Morris, *Social Casework in Great Britain*; Peter Kenstler, *Social Group Work in Great Britain*; Peter Kuenstler, *Community Organisation*.

[28] For one discussion of a definition of a social worker, see the *Report on Social Workers in the Health and Welfare Services*.

[29] See, for instance, M. Ashdown and S. C. Brown, *Social Service and Mental Health*.

[30] For further discussion of this problem, see D. C. Marsh, *The Welfare State*.

[31] F. M. G. Willson, *Administrators in Action*, Volume I; 'Case Study V, The Administrative Consequences of Jim and Vera Fardell'.

[32] D. C. Marsh; op. cit.

APPENDIX A: Courses in Social Administration

Some universities provide full degree courses in Social Administration, others a degree course in one of the other social sciences with Social Administration as an optional subject. For older students there are Certificate or Diploma courses in Social Administration, Social Science or Social Studies which normally take two years to complete. It is not practicable to summarize the varieties of courses available in Britain, but the intending student is now in the fortunate position of having all the courses listed in the handbook *How to Apply for Admission to a University*, which is published annually by the Universities Central Council on Admissions. The varied patterns of courses and the different titles used to describe them may at first seem bewildering. For example, in the handbook showing the courses available for October 1965 there are nineteen universities (including colleges of advanced technology which are to be given university status) shown to be offering Social Administration as one of the subjects for a degree; four universities offering a Certificate or Diploma course in Social Administration; and seven universities offering a Certificate or Diploma course in Social Science or Social Studies. But one cannot be certain from the titles used in the handbook which of these degree courses are specifically and predominantly concerned with Social Administration. The only safe and sure method of finding out the contents of these courses is to examine the prospectuses published by each university.

In only a few of the universities listed in the handbook is there a clear reference to the difference between Social Administration and, say, Sociology, Social Science or Social Study. For example, at the University of Liverpool one may read for a degree in Social Science and in Social Studies, but the handbook expressly states that candidates whose major interest is in Sociology, Social Work, Industrial Management or Social Administration should apply for the course in Social Science; for the University of Manchester there is clearly shown a degree in Social Administration; and for the University of Nottingham a clear distinction is made between the degree in Social Administration and in Sociology. However, other universities in which Social Administration is certainly studied do not make it clear in the information which they provide for the handbook. For example, at the University of Birmingham one may read for a degree of Bachelor of Social Science in which Social Administration is one of the specialisms which may be followed, but the degree course is called Social Study; at the University of Hull the degree course of which Social Administration forms a significant part is called Social Studies; and at the University of Southampton, where a student may read for a Bachelor of Science (Social Sciences), the appropriate course of which Social Administration forms a part is Sociology. All these different titles must seem confusing and the Central Council on Admissions has attempted to show whether a course in, say, Sociology, Social Science, Social Study or Social Studies does include Social Administration by giving it a separate code number. The only certain way of making sure, however, is to look at the prospectus of each university.

All the Certificate or Diploma courses, irrespective of their titles, have an emphasis on Social Administration. Even though there are different titles for the degree courses all the universities in this country which provide in one way or another education in Social Administration are members of the Joint University Council for Social and Public Administration which publishes a useful pamphlet on *Education for Social Work in the Universities*. This is regularly revised and brought up to date and may be obtained from the Secretary of the Council at 218 Sussex Gardens, London, W.2.

Other information leaflets are also available which provide useful information on courses of these kinds. For example, the British Sociological Association publishes a leaflet on university courses in Sociology and Anthropology which may be obtained from the Secretary at Skepper House, 13 Endsleigh Street, London, W.C.1; and there is a very useful booklet published by the National Council of Social Service, in conjunction with the Women's Employment Federation, on *Training and Employment in Social Work*, which may be bought from the National Council of Social Service at 26 Bedford Square, London, W.C.1. In the series of Guides to Careers published by the Ministry of Labour there is one on careers in Social Work which is published by the Stationery Office and gives details of various courses of training in the field of social work.

II. OTHER COURSES AND FURTHER TRAINING

The best available guide to the varieties of initial courses and professional training courses is that published by the National Council of Social Service and noted above. It contains information about all the careers in social work, for which a basic education in Social Administration is essential; the training required in order to qualify, for example, as an almoner, child care, mental health and probation officer, case-worker or group worker, personnel manager and the like, and the facilities for training.

APPENDIX B: Careers in Social Administration, Social Work and Allied Professions

The first chapter of this book discussed the way in which the development of social administration as an academic study was stimulated in the universities by the demand from those preparing to enter social work. Today, the greater number of those who read social administration at universities or other institutions of further education still do so because they are interested in a career in the social services. Many of them become professional social workers such as almoners, psychiatric social workers, child care officers, probation officers. Indeed, for some professional training courses, as for example university courses in Applied Social Studies or in Mental Health, or the course in Medical Social Work organized by the Institute of Medical Social Workers, a university degree, diploma or certificate in Social Studies or Social Science which includes Social Administration is normally an essential prior requirement (see Appendix A). The demand for professionally qualified social workers has been increasing rapidly since the Second World War, and career prospects are good; salaries, although improving still tend to be low for the responsibilities involved.

Since 1948 there have been increasing opportunities for students of social administration to enter the field of youth employment and vocational guidance and recently more training courses for prospective recruits have been developed. Interesting posts demanding considerable organizing ability and initiative are often to be found in community work in settlements and community centres with councils of social service and in connection with new towns. For those who prefer to work with groups of people there is also a great demand for full-time youth leaders and other social group workers. Residential work in children's homes, remand homes, approved schools, old people's homes, hostels for the mentally disordered as well as in the prison and borstal service is another field where a basic education in social administration is useful. Such work can be most challenging; conditions of work and salary scales vary according to the kind of work undertaken.

In recent years, with the growing interest in social studies in schools and technical colleges there has been a steady increase in the number of social administration graduates who have entered the teaching profession and this increase is likely to continue. Moreover, a small but steady number of students who intend to take up full-time Church work, either as ordained ministers or lay workers, have found the study of social administration a useful part of the preparation for their intended career.

For those students who prefer an administrative job rather than one which brings them more directly into touch with clients or consumers, there are a number of openings in both local authority and voluntary services. However, there is a growing tendency for senior administrators to be chosen from those with specialist qualifications as well as administrative experience. For many years teaching experience has been considered necessary for those entering educational administration, and now chief administrators in the children's departments of local authorities are being increasingly recruited from those with professional social work qualifications. Courses in social administration are appropriate for those wishing to enter certain branches of hospital administration. Training posts for graduates and others with suitable educational qualifications and/or experience are available. Although some central government departments recruit professional social workers and others with allied specialist qualifications as inspectors and advisers, most of those involved centrally in the administration of the social services are recruited to the Civil Service in the ordinary way by competitive examination.

During recent years there has been a mounting demand for those with qualifications in social science (including social administration) as research workers. The greater acceptance of the importance of social research by the government, by industry, by the great trusts as well as by the general public has led to the rapid development of many kinds of research projects and the consequent need for research workers. Market research is one of the activities for which commerce and industry have made use of social administration graduates. Personnel management is another career which many such students take up and a number of universities offer special courses of preparation.

Because all these fields of work are changing rapidly and information about qualifications and training soon become obsolescent, it is important that any student interested in a particular career should obtain up-to-date advice. A number of pamphlets giving details of some of these careers and some addresses from which further information can be obtained are listed below. These are correct at the time of going to press.

Pamphlets issued by the Central Youth Employment Executive, and published by Her Majesty's Stationery Office, in the 'Choice of Careers' series, such as *Social Workers* (102), *The Prison Service* (76), *Local Government Service* (28), are most helpful. Also useful are *Training and Employment in Social Work*, issued jointly by the National Council of Social Service and the Women's Employment Federation, and *Careers in the Hospital Service*, issued by the Ministry of Health and also published by Her Majesty's Stationery Office.

FURTHER INFORMATION CAN BE OBTAINED FROM:

The Council for Training in Social Work, Clifton House, Euston Road, N.W.1.

The Central Training Council in Child Care, Thames House South, Millbank, S.W.1.

The Probation Advisory and Training Board, Home Office, Whitehall, S.W.1.

The Further Education Branch of the Ministry of Education, Curzon Street, W.1.

The Institute of Medical Social Workers, 42 Bedford Square, W.C.1.

The Youth Employment Service Training Board, 41 Belgrave Square, S.W.1.

The Ministry of Health (Division R.S.A.), Alexander Fleming House, Elephant and Castle, S.E.1 (for Hospital Administration).

The Institute of Personnel Management, Management House, Fetter Lane, E.C.4.

INDEX

Index

Emergency Hospital services, 221
— Medical services, 94
Employment Exchanges, 73, 74, 76ff., 82
— and Training Act, 1948, 79, 167
Executive Councils, 93, 98, 214, 231

Factories Acts, 32, 74, 75, 83ff
Factory Inspectorate, 83
Family allowances, 57, 58, 59, 202, 203
— Discussion Bureaux, 205
— Failure, 203
— Services Units, 203
— Welfare Association, 204
Feversham Committee, 218
Foundling Hospital, 192
Friendly societies, 30, 53, 221

General Board of Health, 90
— Practitioners, 99
Government Inspectors, 34, 227, 228
— Training centres, 83, 167
Gowers Committee, 84
Graduated pensions, 63–4

Haddow Committee, 125
Health; The National Health Service;
Act, 1946, 94, 169, 173, 178, 179, 182,
188, 210, 213, 217; availability of, 95;
cost of, 101; financing of, 96; principles of, 94; structure of, 97
— Ministry of, 97, 163, 171, 173,
215, 217, 238
— Visiting, committee on, 235–6
— Visiting, and Social Work (Training) Act, 1962, 236
— and Welfare, the development of
Community care, 173, 189
Hospitals, Regional Boards, 98, 213,
214, 238
Housing Associations, 112
— and Local Government, Ministry
of, 112
— and Town planning Acts, 107

Idiots Act, 1886, 177
Ince Committee, 78, 81
Industrial Rehabilitation units, 83, 166
— Revolution, 25 et seq
Ingleby Committee, 199
Insurance, see National; Local Com-
mittees, 93

Joint Universities Council for Social
and Public Administration, 8
Jones, Kathleen, 176
Jordan, W. K., 21–3

Kirkman Gray, B., 34, 36

Labour Exchanges, see Employment Ex-
changes; Act, 1909, 9
Labour, Ministry of, 77, 80, 166, 169,
216
Laissez-faire, 75
Law Society, 221
Legal Aid, 158–9; and Advice Acts,
1949, 1960, 221
Local Authorities, 107, 113; as landlords,
114; houses built by, 111
Local Government; Act, 1958, 172, 217;
Board, 213
Lunacy; Act, 1890, 176, 178, 180, 213;
Commission, 178

McGregor, O. R., 35
Malthus, Rev. T. R., 27
Market forces, 7, 12, 13
Marriage Guidance, 204, 205
Marshall, T. H., 39
Maternity and Child Welfare Act, 1918,
91, 100, 193
Medical; Act, 1858, 228; Profession, 25,
228, 231
Mental Deficiency Act, 1913, 177, 178,
180, 218
— Health Act, 1959, 179–83, 210,
213–14, 219
— Health officers, 234
— Health Review Tribunals, 182,
214
— Treatment Act, 1930, 178, 218
Midwives Acts, 229
Moral Welfare workers, 234
More, Hannah, 27
Morrison Committee (on the Probation
Service), 146, 148
Multi-purpose authorities, 214
Mutual Aid movements, 30, 223

National Assistance, 49, 50–2, 58, 60,
186; Act, 1948, 50, 170, 172, 187, 217;
Board, 50, 238
National Children's Homes and Orphan-
ages, 192, 193
— Conference on the Prevention of
Destitution, 177
— Council of Social Service, 225
— Institute for the Deaf, 164
— Insurance; Act, 1911, 9, 53, 92,
221, 231; 1946, 60–4; Ministry of and
Pensions, 59; Industrial Injuries Act,
1946, 60, 64–6
National Old People's Welfare Council,
189, 190
— Society for the Prevention of
Cruelty to Children, 193, 223
Newman, Sir George, 20